"It is hard to overstate the ti[?] ful book, which gathers an [?] what a genuinely biblical and Christian approach to our national life entails. It will speak to those American Christians, whether evangelical, mainline, or Catholic, who are deeply concerned about the racial divide in our country and want to be active in furthering the justice and reconciliation for which we all hunger. In too many cases those very individuals have been too willing to embrace entirely secular ideas and movements in seeking these worthy goals, setting aside their biblical Christian commitments in the process. This book reminds us repeatedly of the overriding nature of those commitments, all which require of us—to resurrect the still-potent term of a previous reconciliation effort—the keeping of promises, both national and individual. May it have the widest possible readership."

—WILFRED M. MCCLAY
G.T. and Libby Blankenship Chair
in the History of Liberty
University of Oklahoma

"The idea that God deals with nations, and not just with individuals, has had a long and powerful history among American ideas. In these essays, from theologians and from lay people, preachers and academics, we see the particular ways in which race has been a bright thread through our claims to have a national covenant with God. This has not always been a story of affirmation; but as these essays show, it has not always been a story of despair, either. Frederick Douglass, with his implicit faith in jubilee, looked to a pan-racial American future. One hundred and fifty years later, these essays give us hope that our steps do turn ineluctably in his direction, and to the fulfillment of Lincoln's 'last, best hope of earth.'"

—ALLEN CARL GUELZO
Senior Research Scholar in the Council of the Humanities
and Director of the Initiative on Politics and Statesmanship
in the James Madison Program
Princeton University

"Gerald R. McDermott has edited a must-read primer on what is probably the most important problem of our time: national reconciliation in the face of racial antagonism. We find ourselves drowning in an expansive and yet shallow sea of color. There is a thirst in our midst for solutions to the daunting problems informing the concept of race but confusion reigns as the question affects and divide individuals, churches, and communities while ideologues vie for controlling the narrative. This anthology is a remarkable endeavor to bring us back to first principles and to God's sovereign providence for our nation."

— ISMAEL HERNANDEZ
Author of *Not Tragically Colored*
and founder of the Freedom & Virtue Institute

"Narrowmindedness is an intellectual plague. Fortunately, the essayists in this volume introduce a necessary counternarrative for what we are witnessing: the rise of consciousness concerning racial justice. This national conversation—to be genuinely American—must represent a panorama of perspectives regarding race. Too often that truth gets trampled by uncritical and uncreative minds which reduce the discussion to one-sided noise. The research you encounter here will broaden your worldview, open your eyes, deepen your historical knowledge, and diversify our dialogue. Those who care particularly about a Christian framework will find this refreshing. After digesting this volume, I walked away more convinced than ever of this: To presume a lack of pluralism among any ethnic group constitutes its own form of racism."

— REV. JOHN ARTHUR NUNES, PHD
President
Concordia College New York

RACE
and
Covenant

RACE
and
Covenant

Recovering the Religious Roots
for American Reconciliation

Edited by **Gerald R. McDermott**

ACTONINSTITUTE

Race and Covenant: Recovering the Religious Roots for American Reconciliation

© 2020 by Acton Institute

All rights reserved. No part of this publication may be reproduced, stored in a retrieval system, or transmitted in any form or by any means, including electronic, mechanical, photocopying, recording, or otherwise without the prior permission of the publisher.

Scripture quotations marked (CSB) are taken from The Christian Standard Bible. Copyright © 2017 by Holman Bible Publishers. Used by permission. Christian Standard Bible®, and CSB® are federally registered trademarks of Holman Bible Publishers, all rights reserved.

Scripture quotations marked (ESV) are taken from The ESV® Bible (The Holy Bible, English Standard Version®), copyright © 2001 by Crossway, a publishing ministry of Good News Publishers. Used by permission. All rights reserved.

Scripture quotations marked (KJV) are taken from the King James Version. Public domain.

Scripture quotations marked (NASB) are taken from the New American Standard Bible® (NASB), Copyright © 1960, 1962, 1963, 1968, 1971, 1972, 1973, 1975, 1977, 1995 by The Lockman Foundation. Used by permission.

Scripture quotations marked (NIV) are taken from The Holy Bible, New International Version® NIV® Copyright © 1973 1978 1984 2011 by Biblica, Inc. TM Used by permission. All rights reserved worldwide.

Scripture quotations marked (NKJV) are taken from the New King James Version®. Copyright © 1982 by Thomas Nelson. Used by permission. All rights reserved.

Scripture quotations marked (NLT) are taken from the Holy Bible, New Living Translation, copyright ©1996, 2004, 2015 by Tyndale House Foundation. Used by permission of Tyndale House Publishers, a Division of Tyndale House Ministries, Carol Stream, Illinois 60188. All rights reserved.

Scripture quotations marked (NRSV) are taken from the New Revised Standard Version Bible, copyright © 1989 National Council of the Churches of Christ in the United States of America. Used by permission. All rights reserved worldwide.

Scripture quotations not otherwise noted are the author's translation.

ISBN (paperback) 978-1-880595-22-0
ISBN (ebook) 978-1-880595-23-7

Cover image is a derivative of an untitled image sourced from AdobeStock, ©AdobeStock.

ActonInstitute

for the Study of Religion & Liberty

98 E. Fulton
Grand Rapids, Michigan 49503
616.454.3080
www.acton.org

Interior composition: Judy Schafer
Cover: Tobias Design

This book is dedicated to Florence, Dot, and Mavis

Contents

List of Contributors   *ix*

Acknowledgments   *xiii*

Introduction: Our National Dilemma   *xv*
    Gerald R. McDermott

Part 1
THE NATIONAL COVENANT IN SCRIPTURE AND HISTORY

1. Covenant, Race, and the Nations in the Hebrew Bible   3
    Joshua Berman

2. Exile and Return in Israel and America   19
    R. Mitchell Rocklin

3. National Covenant in American Churches   39
    Mark Tooley

4. Martin Luther King, Jr. and the American Covenant   51
    James M. Patterson

Part 2
RACE, COVENANT, AND CONTEMPORARY AMERICAN SOCIETY

5. The Identity Politics Critique of the American Republic   79
    Joshua Mitchell

6. Race and Economics: The Question of Human Agency   99
    W. B. Allen

7. Exile and Return from Slavery 121
   Glenn C. Loury

8. Undermining the Covenant of Marriage: Racial Injustice
   and the Black Family 141
   Jacqueline C. Rivers

9. Little Black Lives Matter: The National Covenant
   and the Right to Be Born 161
   Alveda C. King with Evan Musgraves

Part 3
THE THEOLOGY AND PRACTICES OF THE COVENANT COMMUNITY

10. Racial Supremacy and Covenantal Reconciliation 177
    Carol M. Swain

11. Black Churches and the National Covenant 199
    Derryck Green

12. The Hispanic Church and the National Covenant 221
    Osvaldo Padilla

13. Race and School Choice 235
    Robert L. Woodson, Sr.

14. Geography, History, and Eternity:
    A Theological Stewardship 249
    Timothy George

Epilogue: I Don't Want No Trouble at the River 259
    Robert Smith, Jr.

Name and Subject Index 273

List of Contributors

W. B. Allen is emeritus dean and professor at Michigan State University and is currently senior scholar in residence at the University of Colorado Boulder.

Joshua Berman is a professor of Hebrew Bible at Bar-Ilan University, Israel, and an author, most recently of *Inconsistency in the Torah: Ancient Literary Convention and the Limits of Source Criticism* (Oxford University Press, 2017).

Timothy George is the founding dean of Beeson Divinity School. The author of more than twenty books, George is the general editor of the Reformation Commentary on Scripture, a twenty-eight volume series of sixteenth-century exegetical comment.

Derryck Green is a political commentator, writer, and member of Project 21, a network of black thinkers. His work has been featured and cited in a number of media outlets including *Townhall*, *The American Spectator*, NBC, *The Daily Caller*, The American Conservative, *CQ Researcher*, and many newspapers across the United States.

List of Contributors

ALVEDA C. KING is director of African American Outreach for the Gospel of Life. Both her father, Rev. A. D. King, and uncle, Martin Luther King, Jr., were slain in the civil rights movement of the 1960s. Her house was bombed and she was jailed.

GLENN C. LOURY is Merton P. Stoltz Professor of the Social Sciences, professor of economics, and professor of international and public affairs at Brown University. His books include *Race, Incarceration and American Values* (MIT Press, 2008), *The Anatomy of Racial Inequality* (Harvard University Press, 2002), and *One by One from the Inside Out: Race and Responsibility in America* (Free Press, 1996).

GERALD R. MCDERMOTT is retired from the Anglican Chair of Divinity at Beeson Divinity School. The author, co-author, or editor of more than twenty books, his co-authored *Theology of Jonathan Edwards* (Oxford University Press) was *Christianity Today*'s Book of the Year in Theology and Ethics for 2013.

JOSHUA MITCHELL is professor of political theory at Georgetown University. He has published many books including *Not by Reason Alone: Religion, History, and Identity in Early Modern Political Thought* (University of Chicago Press, 1993), *The Fragility of Freedom: Tocqueville on Religion, Democracy, and American Future* (University of Chicago Press, 1999), *Plato's Fable: On the Mortal Condition in Shadowy Times* (Princeton University Press, 2006), and *Tocqueville in Arabia: Dilemmas in the Democratic Age* (University of Chicago Press, 2013).

EVAN MUSGRAVES is a graduate of Samford University and Beeson Divinity School, where he now serves on staff as a research associate. He lives in Birmingham with his wife, Anna, and two sons.

OSVALDO PADILLA teaches New Testament at Beeson Divinity School. He is the author of *The Acts of the Apostles: Interpretation, History and Theology* (IVP Academic, 2016) and *The Speeches of Outsiders in Acts: Poetics, Theology and Historiography* (Cambridge University Press, 2008).

List of Contributors

James M. Patterson is associate professor of politics at Ave Maria University, where he teaches courses in American politics, media, religion, and political philosophy. He is the author of *Religion in the Public Square: Sheen, King, Falwell* (University of Pennsylvania Press, 2019).

Jacqueline C. Rivers is the executive director and senior fellow for social science and policy of the Seymour Institute for Black Church and Policy Studies. Her latest publications include chapters in *Not Just Good but Beautiful* (Plough, 2015) and *The Cultural Matrix* (Harvard University Press, 2015).

R. Mitchell Rocklin is research fellow at the Tikvah Fund and president of the Jewish Coalition for Religious Liberty. His writing has appeared in a number of publications including *National Review Online*, *The Forward*, and *Mosaic*.

Robert Smith, Jr. holds the Charles T. Carter Baptist Chair of Divinity at Beeson Divinity School, where he teaches Christian preaching. His book *Doctrine That Dances: Bringing Doctrinal Preaching and Teaching to Life* (B&H Publishing, 2008) won the 2008 Preaching Book of the Year Award by *Preaching* magazine and 2009 Preaching Book of the Year Award by *Christianity Today*'s preaching.com.

Carol M. Swain is an award-winning political scientist and media commentator and a former tenured faculty member at Vanderbilt and Princeton Universities. She is the author or editor of nine books.

Mark Tooley is president of the Institute on Religion and Democracy (IRD) and editor of IRD's foreign policy and national security journal, *Providence*. He is the author of *Taking Back The United Methodist Church* (Bristol House, 2010), *Methodism and Politics in the Twentieth Century* (Bristol House, 2012), and *The Peace That Almost Was: The Forgotten Story of the 1861 Washington Peace Conference and the Final Attempt to Avert the Civil War* (Thomas Nelson, 2015).

List of Contributors

ROBERT L. WOODSON, SR. is the founder and president of the Woodson Center and is a frequent advisor to local, state, and federal government officials as well as business and philanthropic organizations. He is the author or editor of several books including *On the Road to Economic Freedom: An Agenda for Black Progress* (Gateway Books, 1987) and *The Triumphs of Joseph: How Today's Community Healers Are Reviving Our Streets and Neighborhood* (Free Press, 2007).

Acknowledgments

I am deeply grateful to Val Merrill and Chelsen Vicari for administrating the conference from which this book came. Kristen Padilla and Rob Willis were also essential to its success. Timothy George and Mark Tooley contributed their abundant wisdom through the entire process of planning, conference, and book preparation. Drew McGinnis was a superb editor, making crucial suggestions at critical points along the way. I am also grateful to Dan Hugger for carefully shepherding this project in its final stages. As always, I am grateful to my beloved wife, Jean, for her suggestions and *oikonomia*, apart from which none of this would have been possible.

Introduction

Our National Dilemma

Gerald R. McDermott

In January 1862, Frederick Douglass, a former slave who became America's greatest sociopolitical prophet of the nineteenth century, declared that America was facing Armageddon. "The fate of the greatest of all Modern Republics trembles in the balance." God was in control of the nations, and America was particularly a subject of his providence. "We are taught as with the emphasis of an earthquake," Douglass told his listeners at Philadelphia's National Hall, "that nations, not less than individuals, are subjects of the moral government of the universe, and that ... persistent transgressions of the laws of this Divine government will certainly bring national sorrow, shame, suffering and death."[1] Douglass was describing America during the Civil War. In his mind the war was God's way of providing atonement for America's great sin—slavery. If white Americans repented of this great sin, the nation could experience a rebirth. "You and I know that the mission of this war is National regeneration," he told

---

1. Frederick Douglass, "The Reasons for Our Troubles," speech delivered in National Hall, Philadelphia, January 14, 1862; quoted in David W. Blight, *Frederick Douglass' Civil War: Keeping Faith in Jubilee* (Baton Rouge and London: Louisiana State University Press, 1989), 112.

audiences from city to city across the North in 1864.[2] But the nation had to pass through "fire" for the new birth to begin.[3]

The fire came of course with the death of six hundred thousand Americans and the destruction of much of the South. But the national regeneration which Douglass sought came, if at all, only in its beginning stages. The war brought a forcible end to slavery. But Douglass continued to use his legendary oratorical skills for the next forty years to remind Americans that they were in covenant with God, and that God would hold them accountable for the ways they treated their ex-slaves and their descendants.

According to Douglass' biographer David Blight, this idea of national covenant was central to Douglass' long career as America's principal prophet. "For the story in which to embed the experience of American slaves, [Douglass] reached for the Old Testament Hebrew prophets of the sixth to eighth centuries B.C.... Their awesome narratives of destruction and apocalyptic renewal, exile and return, provided scriptural basis for his mission to convince Americans they must undergo the same."[4] In innumerable speeches and extensive writings, Douglass exhorted Americans to recognize that God was treating them as he had treated ancient Israel. Just as Israel was exiled when it broke the covenant by egregious sin, so America was exiled because of her "national sin" of slavery.[5] Exile took the form of war and continued conflict. Return from exile would come in the form of peace and reconciliation between the races, but only if America truly repented and performed works befitting repentance.

* * *

Even if national repentance was barely beginning when Douglass died in 1895, the national covenant tradition helped him make sense of America's tortured history with slavery and its aftermath. National covenant is a trope with a long history stretching back to

---

2. Douglass speech quoted in Blight, *Frederick Douglass' Civil War*, 120.

3. Douglass, "Antislavery Progress," *Douglass Monthly*, September 1862; quoted in Blight, *Frederick Douglass' Civil War*, 115.

4. David W. Blight, *Frederick Douglass: Prophet of Freedom* (New York: Simon and Schuster, 2018), 228.

5. Blight, *Frederick Douglass' Civil War*, 118.

early Christianity. It is not too much to say that for most of the last two thousand years, most Christians have believed in the national covenant. This is the idea that (a) God deals with whole nations *as* nations, and (b) he enters into more intimate relationships with societies that claim him as Lord. In other words, God not only deals with individuals during their lives and at the final judgment but also deals providentially with every corporate people and enters into special relationship with certain whole societies. Those who are familiar with the Bible know that God dealt with biblical Israel as a whole society. But most moderns are probably unaware that the God of Israel also suggested that he entered into relationship with other nations: "'Are you not like the Cushites to me, O people of Israel?' declares the LORD. 'Did I not bring up Israel from the land of Egypt, and the Philistines from Caphtor and the Syrians from Kir?'" (Amos 9:7 ESV).

Because many of the authors of this book use the national covenant to analyze our race dilemma, bear with me as I take the next few pages to sketch its history. Most moderns have lost sight of the national covenant, but most premoderns were familiar with it. They would have acknowledged the first part of the tradition, that God blesses and punishes whole nations according to the ways they have responded to "the work of the law ... written on their hearts" (Rom. 2:15 ESV).[6] Nations that uphold the general principles of justice revealed in that "work of the law"—often called "natural law"—are

---

6. In his *Abolition of Man*, C. S. Lewis showed that there is historical evidence for this claim by the apostle Paul that God's law is somehow available to all human beings. In his tabulation of "The Tao," Lewis demonstrated that societies throughout history and across the world have recognized the general principles of justice even while they disagreed on the application and interpretation of those principles. For example, all taught that taking innocent human life is wrong but disagreed on what makes for innocence. Every society has held marriage to be sacred even if some have defined it differently. Nations universally have condemned theft and lying, and most civilizations have held that their notions of law have come from a transcendent source, claiming that their laws were inspired by God or the gods. Even atheistic communist regimes have pointed to an inevitable historical process or the "good of the people," both of which function as their own kinds of transcendence. C. S. Lewis, "Appendix: Illustrations of the Tao," *The Abolition of Man* (New York: Collier, 1962), 97–121.

blessed over the long run, and those that flout those principles are eventually punished. These principles roughly correspond to what the Bible calls the Ten Commandments (Exod. 20; Deut. 5).

The national covenant tradition evolved in Europe where nations typically called themselves Christian and looked to biblical Israel as a model for God's ways with their own nations. Most therefore believed that God entered into a special relationship with them—a covenantal relationship modelled on Israel's—that displayed not simply part (a) but also part (b)—a special relationship between the Christian God and the nation that called on that God. For these nations and their national covenant traditions, blessings and punishments were always administered in this world and not the next, and it often took a long time for the blessings or punishments to appear. For God is long-suffering, they believed on biblical grounds, and might wait for several generations until a society's sin had "reached full measure" (Gen. 15:16). They also believed that nations that acknowledge the God of Israel would be rewarded. For God showers special blessings on "the nation whose God is YHWH" (Ps. 33:12).[7]

Jews and Christians before modernity believed in part (a)—that no nation is free from God's administration. As Augustine put it after the fall of Rome in 410, "God can never be believed to have left the kingdoms of men, their dominations and servitudes, outside of the laws of His providence."[8] But after Constantine, Christians started to think about special blessings for those peoples and nations that called on the God of Israel and his Messiah. So when empires such as Constantine's prospered, Christians believed it was because they followed divinely revealed principles. According to the fourth-century Christian historian Eusebius, God raised up Constantine "as the due reward of his devotion" and gave him "the trophies of victory over the wicked" Galerius and other Roman persecutors.[9] For a modern example of this thinking, the nineteenth-century British historian Henry Hart Milman wrote that it was only after England started

---

7. Translations in this chapter are my own, unless otherwise noted.

8. Augustine, *The City of God*, trans. Marcus Dods (Peabody: Hendrickson, 2014), bk. 5, chap. 11.

9. Eusebius, *The History of the Church*, trans. G. A. Williamson (Harmondsworth, UK: Dorset Press, 1983), 412.

to shelter Jews under Cromwell and Charles II—thus honoring the God of Israel—that "she started forward in a commercial career of unrivalled and uninterrupted prosperity."[10]

Conversely, Christians have believed for millennia that empires have fallen not simply because of military or political failure but ultimately because God has brought them down, and typically for their sins. As the God of Israel told the prophet Amos, "The eyes of YHWH are upon the sinful kingdom, and I will destroy it from the surface of the ground" (Amos 9:8). Eusebius declared that God punished emperor Galerius (305–11) for his persecution of Christians by sending "a mass of worms, and a sickening smell" into the middle of his genitals, which contributed to his fall and Constantine's rise.[11] It was a commonplace among Christian thinkers in the medieval and early modern periods that "righteousness exalts a nation, but sin condemns any people" (Prov. 14:34). Pope Gregory I wrote that God gives to bad societies bad kings because of his anger against those societies: "[T]he wrath of God assigns us rulers to fit our deserts.... indicating clearly that he judges the conduct of the people through the agency of their masters (*magistros*)."[12] The French Huguenot author of *Vindiciae Contra Tyrannos* (1579) was addressing wholly different political circumstances but retained the presumption of both (a) God's administration of whole societies and (b) Israel-like covenants with the "commonwealths" that acknowledge him:

> [In ancient Israel] the articles of this covenant were, in sum, as follows: the king and the entire people would worship God according to the prescription of His Law as individuals and would act collectively to protect that worship; that if they did

---

10. Milman quoted in Donald M. Lewis, *The Origins of Christian Zionism: Lord Shaftesbury and English Support for a Jewish Homeland* (Cambridge: Cambridge University Press, 2010), 169.

11. Eusebius, *History of the Church*, 352–53.

12. Gregory I, *Moralia*, Book 25:34, 36, excerpted in *From Irenaeus to Grotius: A Sourcebook in Christian Political Thought*, ed. Oliver O'Donovan and Joan Lockwood O'Donovan (Grand Rapids: Eerdmans, 1999), 201–2.

so, God would be with them and preserve their commonwealth. If not, he would despise and abandon them.[13]

The author of *Vindiciae* thought that things were little different in sixteenth-century Europe: "Just as the Gospels succeeded to the Law, Christian rulers have replaced the Jewish kings. The covenant remains the same; the stipulations are unaltered; and there are the same penalties if these are not fulfilled, as well as the same God, omnipotent, avenging perfidy."[14]

This way of thinking continued into the modern period and even the first half of the twentieth century, as we shall see in the thinking of Abraham Lincoln and the German theologian Wolfhart Pannenberg. Abraham Lincoln blamed the suffering of the Civil War on divine retribution for American slavery, and the eminent German theologian attributed the destruction of Germany in World War II to her treatment of the Jews.[15] Both thought of their nations as having called at some point on the God of Israel and his Christ, and were therefore in a special relationship with him.

But since the mid-twentieth century this idea of national covenant—that God deals with whole societies and especially with those calling themselves Christian—has become the minority view in Christian theology and perhaps the church as well. Theologians have rejected the idea largely because they think it leads to idolatry—treating the society or nation as something to be revered in place of God.[16] Theologians especially took this view after the Vietnam War, which most American intellectuals regarded as a massive blunder.

---

13. *Vindiciae Contra Tyrannos* (1579), in Julian H. Franklin, ed., *Constitutionalism and Resistance in the Sixteenth Century: Three Treatises by Hotman, Beza, and Mornay* (New York: Pegasus, 1969), 144.

14. *Vindiciae Contra Tyrannos*, in Franklin, *Constitutionalism and Resistance*, 144.

15. Abraham Lincoln, "Proclamation of a National Fast, March 30, 1863," in Mark A. Noll and Roger Lundin, *Voices from the Heart: Four Centuries of American Piety* (Grand Rapids: Eerdmans, 1987), 172; Wolfhart Pannenberg, *Human Nature, Election, and History* (Philadelphia: Westminster, 1977), 79, 104.

16. This idolatry is illustrated by the title of Robert Jewett's book, *The Captain America Complex: The Dilemma of Zealous Nationalism* (Philadelphia: Westminster, 1973).

They regarded the war as immoral and concluded that America had prosecuted it precisely because of something like the national covenant idea. Worse, they believed, Americans had come to think of America as a "redeemer nation" that was called to bring salvation to the nations.[17] But where, they wondered, had this idea come from?

Many concluded that the idea had come from the Puritans and found this explanation in Harvard intellectual historian Perry Miller's famous essay, "Errand into the Wilderness."[18] Miller argued that the seventeenth-century English Puritans gave up on trying to purify (hence *Puritan*) the Church of England and thought they were called by God to start over in the New World. Here they would set up church and state as they ought to be, and their new commonwealth in Massachusetts would be a city on the hill whose light would reflect back to old England and all Europe. New England would be a redeemer nation.

According to Miller, the Puritans believed that God was dealing with England as a whole society and was raising up the Puritans to challenge the nation. The Puritans thought they were new prophets, just as Old Testament Israel was challenged repeatedly by her prophets. For the Puritans, it was obvious from the Bible that God deals with whole societies and not just individuals. Just as God told Israel that he would reward Israel when she was faithful to the covenant, he also told her that he would chastise her, and sometimes with exile, when she disobeyed the terms of the covenant (Deut. 28).

Like most Christians in the centuries before them, Puritan preachers saw the biblical God dealing with whole nations in ways that were similar to the ways he dealt with his chosen people Jewish Israel. Look, they said, how God took the society of Noah's time to task when it ignored his basic commandments (which the rabbis would later call the Noahic commandments) in the early stages of humanity. The result was destruction by the great flood. God did something similar, but on a smaller scale, to Sodom and Gomorrah. The plagues God sent through Moses are also an example of God dealing with a whole

---

17. Ernest Tuveson, *Redeemer Nation: The Idea of America's Millennial Role* (Chicago: University of Chicago Press, 1968).

18. Perry Miller, "Errand into the Wilderness," in Perry Miller, ed., *Errand into the Wilderness* (New York: Harper and Row, 1956), 1–15.

nation, in this case Egypt. The conquest of the Canaanite tribes is another example, because the conquest was divine retaliation for the egregious sins of those tribes.[19]

Puritan preachers routinely observed that God told the prophet Amos that he treated the Cushites (the Ethiopians) and Philistines and Syrians as whole peoples in his sovereign control of ancient near eastern history (Amos 9:7). Occasionally these preachers pointed out that a repeated criterion in the prophets for divine judgment was the way the nations treated God's people Israel. As the prophet Joel put it, "I will gather all the nations and bring them down to the Valley of Jehoshaphat. And I will enter into judgment with them there, on behalf of my people and my heritage Israel, because they have scattered them among the nations and have divided up my land, and have cast lots for my people, and have traded a boy for a prostitute, and have sold a girl for wine and have drunk it" (Joel 3:2–3 ESV).[20]

When after the Vietnam War scholars said that it was the Puritans who fed the idea of a redeemer nation into America's consciousness, they also pinned blame on Jonathan Edwards (1703–58). It was he who allegedly transmitted that concept to the early American Republic. Edwards was schooled in Puritan theology but was not a Puritan.[21] And while he believed in national covenant, he did not promote it in a chauvinistic or proto-nationalist way. He wrote in fact that New England (there was no United States then) was the most sinful nation ever because it had received the greatest degree

---

19. These are common themes in Alan Heimert and Andrew Delbanco, eds., *The Puritans in America: A Narrative Anthology* (Cambridge: Harvard University Press, 1985).

20. For example, Jonathan Edwards notes that God punished the nations that "came against Judah" and will do the same to the church's enemies in the future. Jonathan Edwards, *The "Blank Bible,"* ed. Stephen J. Stein, vol. 24, *The Works of Jonathan Edwards* (New Haven: Yale University Press, 2006), 792.

21. Edwards's emphasis on revival was not typical of Puritanism, and his epistemology and aestheticism were new developments that eclipsed Puritan limits. See Michael McClymond and Gerald McDermott, *The Theology of Jonathan Edwards* (New York: Oxford University Press, 2012), especially chapter 3 on intellectual context.

of revelation but had spurned it. He also preached that the Puritan colonists had treated Native Americans shamefully.[22]

Edwards wrote at considerable length about God's covenant with the colonies of the New World, led by New England. He interpreted New England's eighteenth-century droughts, plagues, and earthquakes as judgments on the people and churches of New England for their sins. And Edwards clearly stipulated the differences between the national covenant and the covenant of grace. For him, as for most of the tradition, a national covenant is with a whole people, but the covenant of grace is with an individual. The long-term progress of peoples and nations is governed by God's sovereign purposes, using among other devices the national covenant. It pertains to this life only. While the covenant of grace pertains primarily to the next life, the national covenant pertains to sublunar affairs. In fact, God is stricter in punishing a society in this world—in the long run, that is—than punishing individuals in this world. After all, the wicked often prosper in this world. Of course, so do wicked regimes, but eventually, Edwards and the Puritans argued, every wicked nation or empire falls in this world because of God's judgment.[23]

Edwards found it to be a biblical pattern that one can know, so to speak, when the hammer of judgment is bound to fall. When wickedness is pervasive and a nation's leaders defend that wickedness, that nation is close to destruction. Warnings of that imminent fall come in a variety of forms. The nation can be threatened with attack, as Jerusalem was in the years before AD 70. Or lesser judgments come, as they did in Egypt's nine plagues before the last decimating one. Or there is a judgment on a neighbor, as there was on the northern ten tribes of Israel roughly one century before the two southern tribes were conquered. Often God sends messengers to warn of the coming debacle, as God sent Noah and Jonah to warn of judgment, and other Hebrew prophets when Israel or Judah were straying from the covenant.[24]

---

22. Gerald McDermott, *One Holy and Happy Society: The Public Theology of Jonathan Edwards* (University Park: Penn State Press, 1992), 11–36, 164–65.

23. McDermott, *One Holy and Happy Society*, 12–20.

24. Jonathan Edwards, "Sermon on 2 Chronicles 36:15–17," in *Works of Jonathan Edwards Online*, vol. 55, http://edwards.yale.edu/archive?path=aHR-

Sometimes, Edwards insisted, even religious revival can be a warning of imminent destruction. Revival came to Nineveh after Jonah's visit but before the later judgment that Nahum wrote about. Revival came to Jerusalem in the time of the early church, but judgment followed within just a few decades. If revival does not produce reformation, Edwards argued, then revival is a sign not of God's approval but the opposite. In other words, if religious revival does not change the moral life of a people in a deep way, the revival was leading to destruction. Revival was a sign not that God approved but that he was about to judge.[25]

If Edwards was a principal exponent of the national covenant in the eighteenth century, Abraham Lincoln was its chief theologian in the nineteenth—even if he did not teach the tradition with Douglass' passion for it. In an 1863 proclamation of a national fast, Lincoln asked, "[I]nsomuch as we know that, by His divine law, nations like individuals are subjected to punishments and chastisements in this world, may we not justly fear that the awful calamity of civil war, which now desolates the land, may be but a punishment, inflicted upon us, for our presumptuous sins, to the needful end of our national reformation as a whole People?"[26] In this same proclamation, Lincoln showed he believed that the United States was in a special covenantal relationship with God: "[I]t is the duty of all nations as well as of men ... to recognize the sublime truth, announced in the Holy Scriptures and proven by all history, that those nations only are blessed whose God is the Lord."[27] Lincoln clearly believed that his nation had acknowledged the Judeo-Christian God as the Lord.

In his "Second Inaugural Address," Lincoln was more specific about his nation's covenantal relation with its God, charging that the Civil

---

0cDovL2Vkd2FyZHMueWFsZS5lZHUvY2dpLWJpbi9uZXdwaGlsby9nZXRvYmplY3QucGw/Yy41Mzo4LndqZW8=.

25. Edwards, "Sermon on 2 Chronicles 36:15–17."

26. Lincoln, "Proclamation of a National Fast," in Noll and Lundin, *Voices from the Heart*, 172.

27. Lincoln, "Proclamation of a National Fast," in Noll and Lundin, *Voices from the Heart*, 172.

War was judgment on the nation's slavery. Lincoln made clear that the war was a judgment on both the South and the North.[28]

> If we shall suppose that American Slavery is one of those offences which, in the providence of God, must needs come, but which, having continued through His appointed time, He now wills to remove, and that He gives to both North and South, this terrible war, as the woe due to those by whom the offence came, shall we discern therein any departure from those divine attributes which the believers in a Living God always ascribe to Him?[29]

In the twentieth-century German Lutheran theologian Wolfhart Pannenberg concluded that the destruction of Germany in World War II was divine judgment on that nation for its treatment of Jews.[30] Toward the end of the 1960s, after scholars had dismissed the idea of national covenant, sociologist of religion Robert Bellah raised it again: If the Bible suggested that ancient nations were dealt with by God as whole societies, he asked, why should America not be considered a nation in God's providence, understood theologically in terms of the national covenant?[31]

* * *

Political theorists will be frustrated with this brief recounting of a theological concept. They will ask about implementation (How does a nation or society enter into the national covenant?), participants (Who are members of the covenant? What about immigrants and non-citizens?), and obligations (What is required: natural principles of justice or religious principles and laws?). Precise answers to these questions cannot be teased out of what Augustine, Edwards, Douglass,

---

28. Lincoln, "Second Inaugural Address" (1865), quoted in Mark Noll, *One Nation Under God? Political Faith and Political Action in America* (San Francisco: Harper & Row, 1988), 101.

29. Lincoln, "Second Inaugural Address" (1865), in Noll and Lundin, *Voices from the Heart*, 175.

30. Pannenberg, *Human Nature, Election, and History*, 79, 104.

31. Robert Bellah in Donald R. Cutler, ed., *The Religious Situation in 1968* (Boston: Beacon, 1968), 391.

Lincoln, and Pannenberg wrote on the covenant idea. Arguably, however, they would agree on the following. A nation enters into the national covenant when its founders or leaders formally acknowledge that it recognizes the God of Israel and his Messiah as its Lord, and declares that the nation falls under that God's laws. Lincoln believed that in the Declaration of Independence, the founders had done just that. So did Douglass. These theologians of the national covenant would say that citizens of the nation are implicitly included in the covenant if they accept the notion that their nation is "under God," but that even those unwilling to accept that thesis will share nonetheless in the blessings and punishments that will fall on the whole nation.

Finally, all of these theologians agreed that every nation has the obligation to follow natural law, which is revealed to all human beings, and that they will prosper or suffer accordingly. So although they would have disagreed on what shape justice should take, all would have agreed that social justice ought to be a goal for every polity. Those nations that acknowledge the Christian God are further obliged to protect Christian worship. Twentieth-century advocates like Pannenberg would say this protection simply means ensuring religious freedom for all.

Douglass went further, spending most of his career spelling out the precise implications of the covenant for the United States. For him it meant providing equal justice for blacks—including freedom from racial discrimination in voting and hiring as well as protection from white violence against them.

Racial relations in America have come a long way since Douglass's time when lynching was a regular occurrence. The civil rights movement of the 1960s put an end to legal segregation. Affirmative action programs in government, corporations, higher education, and the media have opened access to women and minorities in unprecedented ways. Twice recently our nation has elected a black president.

Yet recently it has seemed that we are going backward as a nation. As Gerald Seib has put it, race remains "the great unresolved issue" in our country.

> The country may have thought it had moved beyond its racial problems when the slaves were freed, when blacks were allowed to vote, when the army was integrated, when drugstore counters

were desegregated, when civil rights legislation was passed or when an African-American man was elected president. But racial tensions keep recurring, like a virus that runs through the bloodstream long after you thought the disease was gone.[32]

Seib concludes on a pessimistic note: "If slavery was America's original sin, our society's penance for it may never fully end."[33] His pessimism is not completely unwarranted. Racial separatism has become the norm at elite universities such as Yale, Brown, and Wesleyan, and at a wide range of other schools. Peter Wood and Dion Pierre reported in 2019 that 46 percent of colleges and universities were segregating student orientation programs, 43 percent were segregating residential arrangements, and 72 percent were segregating graduation ceremonies. Racial organizations on campus were composed of students "primed to see themselves not as individuals but as members of persecuted racial groups."[34]

David Brooks observed recently that among progressive whites in America, more and more political issues are seen through the lens of race. While at the end of the last century only 10 percent of white liberals wanted higher immigration levels, in 2019 that figure had jumped to 50 percent. "Many want to dismantle the border enforcement agencies and eliminate criminal sanctions against undocumented crossings precisely because they are seen as structures of oppression that white people impose on brown people."[35] Foreign policy is viewed similarly. Whereas, for example, the Israeli-Palestinian conflict during most the twentieth century was seen as "an intractable regional conflict between a democracy and a series of authoritarian regimes trying to destroy it, it is now [in 2019] seen as a conflict between a white colonialist power and the brown people it oppresses."[36]

---

32. Gerald F. Seib, "Race Remains the Great Unresolved Issue," *Wall Street Journal*, July 20–21, 2019, C3.

33. Seib, "Race Remains," C3.

34. Peter W. Wood and Dion J. Pierre, "Segregation by Design on Campus," *Wall Street Journal*, April 30, 2019, A17.

35. David Brooks, "How White Democrats Moved Left," *New York Times*, July 25, 2019, A23.

36. Brooks, "How White Democrats Moved Left," A23.

Oddly, Harvard University is still using race to discriminate in admissions. Jason Riley writes that a century ago, Harvard "argued that Jews were excellent students with deficient personalities."[37] So in the 1920s and later, Jewish enrollment was capped at 15 percent despite the fact that many more Jews qualified for admission. As Riley and others have shown recently, Harvard is now using a similar approach to Asian applicants. They are disproportionately strong in academics, but because Harvard has decided that Asians do not possess "the personal qualities that Harvard is looking for," they need SAT scores 140 points higher than their white peers to be accepted.[38] More than a half century after the Civil Rights Act forbade discrimination based on race, in 2019 Harvard was still "us[ing] the racial makeup of admitted students to help determine how many students it should admit overall."[39]

Ironically, at the same time when many voices cry that America is systemically racist, two heroes for black liberationists of the 1960s now believe blacks can succeed if they work within the American system. Tom Jones, the "rhetorical leader" of the black students at Cornell University who brandished guns when taking over its student union in 1969, now calls on blacks in America to embrace hard work, education, and self-improvement. After his time at Cornell, Jones went on to become president of TIAA and is now founder and senior partner of TWJ Capital. Ed Whitfield, his partner in the Cornell take-over and now a director of the Fund for Democratic Communities, rejects the new calls for busing to majority white schools and says black majority schools can be their own powerful learning environments.[40]

Another irony is that in 2019, when many on the Left were saying that the system is stacked against blacks, economic prospects for blacks were looking better than they had in a long time. In 2018,

---

37. Jason L. Riley, "Harvard's Asian Quotas Repeat an Ugly History," *Wall Street Journal*, October 9, 2019, A17.

38. Riley, "Harvard's Asian Quotas," A17.

39. Riley, "Harvard's Asian Quotas," A17. The last quote contains the words of Judge Allison Burroughs, who ruled in favor of Harvard's admissions policies.

40. Glenn C. Altschuler and Isaac Kramnick, "Ivy Leaguers with Guns, Then and Now," *Wall Street Journal*, April 19, 2019.

the labor-force participation gap between whites and blacks virtually vanished. Demographer John Iceland found that "differences in family structure are the most significant variable in explaining the black-white affluence gap."[41] In other words, the gap is attributable to the difference between families headed by a married couple and those led by a single parent. Black columnist Jason Riley notes, "Blaming bad outcomes among blacks on the malevolence of others is not only wrong but insulting to Americans of every race. This isn't 1950."[42] Riley concludes that racism has "never been less significant in America," and blacks have never had "more opportunities to seize."[43]

So we were left in 2019 with a strange mix. On the one hand, economic and social prospects for blacks had rarely been better. Racism was denounced in every institution of American society—government, business, the universities, and the media. Black and other racial minority representation was notable in all of those institutions. Yet at the same time it was widely reported that American society and its institutions were still permeated with racism.[44] If one were to believe that report, things looked depressing indeed. Despite all the gains of the last sixty years for America's racial minorities, one hears a continual refrain that our racial conflict is worse than ever.

This book rejects both this pessimism and its two underlying presumptions. The first presumption is that the only racial problem in America is white racism. The second is that more government money and legislation are the best solutions to the problem. Instead, I would suggest that our racial dilemma cannot be understood properly without spiritual and religious analysis. Racism is sin, and one of our national sins—perhaps our greatest—has been slavery. Slavery did not begin here, and our nation's history is filled with the quest

---

41. John Iceland, quoted in Jason L. Riley, "The Race Card Has Gone Bust," *Wall Street Journal*, July 17, 2019, A21.

42. Riley, "The Race Card," A21.

43. Riley, "The Race Card," A21.

44. Even Ben and Jerry's ice cream corporation tells this to its fans: "7 Ways We Know Systemic Racism is Real," n.d., https://www.benjerry.com/home/whats-new/2016/systemic-racism-is-real.

xxix

for human rights.⁴⁵ But Frederick Douglass was right. America has been sent into a kind of exile because of this massive iniquity against God's covenant with this nation. Our continuing racial conflicts show that this exile continues. What must we do to come out of exile?

Perhaps our first step is to recognize that white racism, while pernicious, is not the only problem. It is not the only racism that prevents reconciliation in this country. Second, more government programming is not the answer and in fact is often counter-productive. The problems are far deeper, and the solutions therefore must also be deep if they are to be practical. The essays that follow spring from a February 2019 conference at Samford University in Birmingham, Alabama. They suggest a variety of ways to deeper and more practical solutions than most of what is currently on offer.

In part 1 on the national covenant, Rabbi Joshua Berman uses the biblical stories of Rahab and Ruth to show how America can use its own story of covenant to "overcome ethnic disparity" by considering our own relationship to God and recalibrating our relationships with one another. Rabbi Mitchell Rocklin tells a poignant story of his grandparents who survived the Holocaust and his own visit to Germany to discuss how to reject old hatreds while keeping a proper self-respect. Historian Mark Tooley suggests that if American churches revisit the national covenant tradition, those on the Left might realize the possibility of national redemption, and those on the Right might focus more on the justice and love that are necessary for racial healing. James Patterson traces Martin Luther King, Jr.'s vision of God's covenant with America, in which the Christian church was at the heart of what he called the Beloved Community.

Part 2 probes race and covenant in contemporary society. Historian Joshua Mitchell argues that our nation is at an impasse between the liberal politics of competence and the identity politics of innocence, but he thinks a realistic way forward is a radical asymmetry between God and humanity founded in covenant. William B. Allen

---

45. Katherine Kersten, "The New York Times '1619 Project' revisited: The newspaper's slavery-at-the-fore reframing of American history distorts this country's progress and the exceptional ideals that drive it," *Minneapolis Star-Tribune*, December 8, 2019, http://www.startribune.com/the-new-york-times-1619-project-revisited/565907662/.

proposes that the proper connection between race and economics was misunderstood by Presidents Franklin Delano Roosevelt and Lyndon Baines Johnson and civil rights leader Martin Luther King, Jr., and he points toward the connection suggested by Booker T. Washington. Economist Glenn Loury recommends a new ideal of "transracial humanism" that recognizes that the plight of so many descendants of slaves is more a relationship problem than a justice problem, and that the solution lies in redefining identities, not redistributing resources. Sociologist Jacqueline Rivers argues that racial injustice has undermined the practice of covenantal marriage in the black community, while activist Alveda King maintains that the greatest violence against blacks today is abortion.

Part 3 considers the theology and practices of the covenant community. Political scientists Carol Swain and Derryck Green call on blacks and their churches to return to Christian identity first and black identity second. New Testament scholar Osvaldo Padilla suggests that the Hispanic community, when gathered out of several races as a community of faith in Jesus Christ, can have a bridging vocation to help heal racial brokenness. Community leader Robert Woodson, Sr. relates how for sixty years his Woodson Center has helped inner-city parents create after-school academies, community residential schools, and community boarding schools. Beeson Divinity School's founding dean Timothy George looks at how Birmingham, seminaries, and Americans have struggled with race and racism.

In an inspiring epilogue that was a sermon at the conference, Robert Smith, Jr. tells how war was avoided among the tribes of ancient Israel, showing Americans a way to escape division based on racial identity.

* * *

The arguments in these chapters are powerful and innovative in many ways. But they will go unheeded if we don't recognize four dangers. The first is *historical perfectionism* which assumes that no repentance has taken place. The civil rights movement of the 1960s saw great political and spiritual change. The Civil Rights Act and many other laws following made illegal many racist practices that previously were legal. Today affirmative action is enforced in public education and the universities, government, corporations, and the media, so that blacks and other minorities are often preferred over whites and Asians. Whole generations of white Americans in the ensuing decades have come to regard as evil what previous generations thought unimportant or even justified—judging other human beings by the color of their skin. Americans today disagree about who is racist and what makes a racist, but the vast majority agree that racism is a deep moral wrong.

A second danger is *historical presentism* which judges past generations by the standards of this generation. The latter's standards are changing all the time. Just twenty years ago, maybe even ten, most Americans believed that gay marriage was beyond the pale. Today at least a plurality and perhaps a majority think it is *morally* acceptable and perhaps even a virtue. Most of these same Americans would not want to be judged for what they believed in good conscience twenty and even ten years ago. By the same measure, we should not condemn as morally worthless—and not worth a hearing—thinkers and leaders from past eras who did not hold our same views. Aristotle, for example, justified slavery.[46] So did Thomas Jefferson, though he was a conflicted and tortured soul over it.[47] Even Abraham Lincoln did not hold the same view of human equality that most of us do.[48] Do these views mean that we cannot learn from these eminent minds? I think not.

The same applies to Jonathan Edwards, a slave owner. He and his wife, Sarah, owned at least one slave; two were sold after his death. While Edwards condemned the slave trade and defended "the nations of Africa" against it, historians have noted the "glaring contradiction" in his defense of the institution of slavery.[49] For a while he believed

---

46. Aristotle wrote in his *Politics*, "It is clear, then, that some men are by nature free, and others slaves, and that for these latter slavery is both expedient and right" (1254b36). See Richard McKeon, ed., *Introduction to Aristotle*, trans. W. D. Ross (New York: McGraw-Hill, 1947), 561.

47. John Chester Miller, *The Wolf by the Ears: Thomas Jefferson and Slavery* (New York: Free Press, 1977).

48. Henry Louis Gates and Donald Yacovone, eds., *Lincoln on Race and Slavery* (Princeton: Princeton University Press, 2011).

49. Sherard Burns, "Trusting the Theology of a Slave-owner," in *A God Entranced Vision of All Things: The Legacy of Jonathan Edwards*, ed. John

that the Bible condoned polygamy and later condemned it. But unlike the later abolitionists, who included his chief disciple Samuel Hopkins and his own son Jonathan, Jr., Edwards did not see the same pattern in the Bible's treatment of slavery. He fought for the rights of Indians against predatory whites, including his own cousins, but not for the rights of blacks to be free. Edwards taught that blacks and whites are equal before God ("we are made of the same human race"), and his church admitted nine blacks to full membership. But he failed to see that slavery was a profound human sin.[50]

Edwards's sorry record on slavery demonstrates that every great theologian has blind spots. We have seen that in Martin Luther's last years, for example, he said terrible things about Jews, and that Karl Barth used theology to justify his own adultery for all the years that he was writing his *Church Dogmatics*.[51] But we can still learn from Luther, especially through his warnings against our human tendency to think that our merit can save us. We can also learn much from Barth's exposure of liberal Protestantism's human projects to reach the divine through human thinking and social action. So too we can learn much from Edwards, especially through his vision of God's beauty, which was more integral to his theology than to the theology of any other thinker in the history of Christian thought.[52] As I argue in this chapter, we can also learn from Edwards's understanding of how God deals with nations.

The third danger is *reverse racism*. This is the sort of racism that asserts that because a certain person is a certain color, he or she must think in a certain way. For example, a conservative black friend of mine is criticized for not being truly black because she disagrees with the dominant narrative about blacks today. The criticism assumes that blacks think—or should think—in only one way. Is this not profoundly racist? To assume that skin color determines a way

---

Piper and Justin Taylor (Wheaton: Crossway, 2004), 153.

50. This paragraph is based on McClymond and McDermott, *Theology of Jonathan Edwards*, 526–27.

51. Martin Luther, "On the Jews and Their Lies" (1543), trans. Martin H. Bertram https://www.prchiz.pl/pliki/Luther_On_Jews.pdf; Christiane Tietz, "Karl Barth and Charlotte von Kirschbaum," *Theology Today* 74, no. 2 (2017): 86–111.

52. McClymond and McDermott, *Theology of Jonathan Edwards*, 93–101.

of thinking? Is it not radically disrespectful to my friend to suggest that she must agree with black elites and cannot exercise the creativity of her own mind?

This new reverse racism takes another form. It presumes that if I am of a different color from someone with whom I am reading or hearing or conversing, I could never possibly understand what he or she is saying. This thinking appears to presume that a person of another color from mine does not share a common humanity with me, such that her mind cannot communicate with my mind. This thinking is precisely the way racists have thought for centuries, and the very presumption that the civil rights movement of the 1960s fought to destroy. Martin Luther King, Jr.'s profound declaration that we should judge people not by the color of their skin but by the content of their character presumes just the opposite of the new racism. His declaration implies that whites and blacks are united in their humanity and can share a common character, either good or bad. It presumes that blacks and whites share the capacity to think and understand each other, if they would only make the effort.

It is deeply disrespectful to a person to assume that anyone can know what he or she is thinking—or capable of—because of his or her race. That assumption refuses to acknowledge that person's dignity as a unique individual endowed by God with the freedom to think in ways that might differ with others of the same race. When Jesus praised the good Samaritan, who acted differently from the ways many thought all Samaritans must act, Jesus was affirming the truth that ethnicity does not determine character.

A final and fourth danger is the *pride* which thinks I have nothing to learn about race. Or nothing to learn from people who are of a different race. As a white person I must learn from those of different races about race, and I must listen to other whites who disagree with me. I might find in this conversation that race is relatively superficial, which seems to have been King's conviction. Of course the present divisions are deep, and wounds from racism are terribly deep. But I am reminded of what the great Russian novelist Alexander Solzhenitsyn wrote, that "[t]he line separating good and evil passes not through states, nor between classes, nor between political parties either—but right through every human heart—and through all human hearts."[53]

* * *

Here, perhaps, is where the national covenant can help. It says that God can forgive and heal not only an individual but a whole society. The Bible says that God appeared to Solomon in the night and declared to him, "If my people who are called by my name humble themselves, and pray and seek my face and turn from their wicked ways, then I will hear from heaven and will forgive their sin and heal their land" (2 Chron. 7:14 ESV). This vision in the night from God suggests that whole societies can be forgiven and healed. It also suggests that healing depends on people turning to God in freedom and humility. This is the spiritual dimension to our nation's division that can never be mandated by a government. There is no room for coercion here—only prayer and humility.

This nation is hurting. In many ways it is broken, and racial division is a big part of that brokenness. But there is hope. The source is spiritual, not political. It comes from humility and prayer and seeking God's face. The God of Israel is Lord, even of this hurting land. Our racial divisions suggest that we have experienced covenantal judgment and exile. But we can also experience covenantal forgiveness and healing.

---

53. Alexander Solzhenitsyn, *The Gulag Archipelago 1918–1956* (New York: Collins, 1974), 168.

Part 1

THE NATIONAL COVENANT IN SCRIPTURE AND HISTORY

1

Covenant, Race, and the Nations in the Hebrew Bible

Joshua Berman

Covenant is an inherently religious word. It differs from *social contract* in that it speaks not only to how citizens of a polity relate to one another and to the polity as a whole. Rather, *covenant* speaks to how those citizens relate to the Almighty, and how their commitment to him in turn reshapes how they think of each other and about the polity in which they reside. The notion of *covenant*, therefore, has an enormous role to play today as we take stock of the state of disrepair between white Americans and black Americans. Indeed, the term *covenant*, as I have defined it here, may not speak to many Americans, especially those for whom religion plays no central part in their lives. But for many other Americans, the term covenant is part of their theological and existential identity. And it is precisely these Americans who are uniquely poised to draw upon the religious category of covenant to shine a guiding light to help show the rest of the country how Americans—black and white—can build a bridge with others, in spite of the differences of race, class, and social experience. At the Second Vatican Council in 1964, the Catholic Church demonstrated the potential of this kind of approach in *Nostra Aetate*. In that document the church searched the reservoir of its own theological terms to redefine its relationship with non-Christian religions, seeking resources to build bridges in an increasingly global village.

The religious concept of covenant has its origins in the Hebrew Bible, with the covenant between God and Israel in Sinai, as told in the book of Exodus. Today, after two thousand years of exile and dispersal, the Jewish people are a racially diverse people; to walk the streets of modern day Israel is to walk between people of nearly every imaginable complexion. But in the times of biblical Israel, the covenant established Israel as a bounded community of the ethnic descendants of Abraham, Isaac, and Jacob. The genealogies listed in Ezra 2 and in the first eleven chapters of the book of Chronicles underscore just how central this ethnic element was, especially following the return from exile. Ezra speaks of intermarriage as the debasement of "holy seed" (Ezra 9:2). And yet at several junctures throughout Israel's biblical history, the question of boundary is challenged: what happens when an outsider wishes to join the community? Can such a person do so, and if so, how is that achieved? And how can the covenantal community's natural sense of boundedness be overcome so as to make welcoming room for such an outsider? In a primary sense, "outsider" means an ethnic outsider. But since early Israel valued its genealogical connection to the patriarchs, "outsider" includes a racial component as well. Nowhere, though, does the Hebrew Bible underscore how the Israelites differed physiologically from their neighbors, so in this study I will speak of the "outsider" as an ethnic outsider.

I pursue these questions through the study of two narratives. The first is the account of Rahab in Joshua 2. Here we see an account which negotiates what an ethnic outsider must do and demonstrate in order to be admitted into the community. The second text that I will examine is the book of Ruth, or an aspect of it that I shall call here the "book of Boaz." Ruth the Moabite seeks entry into the covenantal community of Bethlehem. This study will probe how Boaz seeks to change prevailing prejudicial attitudes toward ethnic outsiders such as Ruth. These paired studies will in turn shed light on our own predicament of ethnic and racial tension in the United States. The Rahab account will provide us with a model for how to look at someone from a different ethnicity and to consider them as "belonging" to us and with us, using the conceptual resources of our religious commitment through sacred Scripture. The "book of Boaz" narrative will likewise draw from these resources to help us better understand the dynamics through which prejudice may be overcome.

Through these two studies we will see how the biblical characters address the issue of ethnicity and the covenantal community. But no less important, we will see how the authors of these texts address the issue. Time after time, we will see that the authors deftly and deliberately allude to other scriptural passages in their accounts, often incorporating those passages into the speech of the characters, as if, as it were, the characters themselves were quoting Scripture. In fact, we must assume the characters themselves spoke plain language. Any resemblance to other scriptural passages is the artful construction of the author; it is his way of signaling to us, his readers, that he is invoking and often reinterpreting Scripture in order to convey his message to us about his views of ethnicity and covenant.

Welcoming the Ethnic Outsider: The Account of Rahab in Joshua 2

While the Bible places a premium upon the notion of Israel as a nation that is the ethnic descendants of Abraham, Isaac, and Jacob, the story of Rahab and the spies in Joshua 2 may be mined for principles that determine when ethnic outsiders can and should be brought into the community. Let us briefly recall the parameters of that story. Poised to enter the land of Israel, Joshua sends two spies to scout out Jericho. Upon arrival they steal themselves into the brothel of a Canaanite woman named Rahab. They apparently, however, had been spotted entering the city, and sentries immediately make their way to Rahab's house to apprehend the spies. Rahab manages to conceal the spies, and sends the sentries on a diversion. Rahab explains to the stunned spies that, in fact, the whole town is stricken with fear due to the impending invasion of the Israelites. She proposes a deal: that in return for having harbored them, she would be spared when the Israelites conquer the city.

Although the book of Deuteronomy envisioned Israel as an almost hermetically bounded ethnic culture, the account of Rahab in Joshua 2 adduces a mechanism to allow for the entry of an ethnic outsider into the camp of Israel. Put differently, the narrative puts forward a series of criteria through which ethnicity is set aside and the outsider becomes deemed full kin.

The primary criterion for determining Rahab's worthiness is the cultural and ideological compatibility that she exhibits. The author of the narrative achieves this by crafting her speech to the spies to resonate closely with a range of verses from the Five Books of Moses, the Torah. In verses 9–10, Rahab reflects upon Israelite history as an Israelite should. In fact, her speech in these verses bears a striking affinity with verses in the Song of the Sea in Exodus 15. This is seen in Joshua 2:9: "The fear of you has fallen upon us, and all of the inhabitants of the land have melted away from before you," a clear echo of Exodus 15:15–16: "All of the inhabitants of Canaan have melted away. Let fear and awe fall upon them."[1]

Later in the narrative, Rahab strikes a deal with the spies. She will shelter them and release them when it is safe. They will descend from her window out of the city via a red cord that she must then tie to her window. When the Israelites invade, the red cord will be a sign to the Israelite troops that they are to spare the residents of that domicile. The imagery here is highly resonant with the account of the blood placed by the Israelites on their doorposts in anticipation of the coming of the plague of the firstborn (Exod. 12:7–28). In each story, those to be saved must be indoors, and anyone outside of the protected enclosure is subject to death (Exod. 12:13, 22–23; Josh. 2:18–21). In each story, a red sign on the portal of the guarded enclosure signals to the destroying force that those inside are to be spared. The Lord sees the blood and passes over the house. Likewise, the red cord serves to alert the invading Israelites that Rahab and her family inside are to be spared annihilation. As one expositor explains, "Rahab and her family participate in one of the constitutive events in Israel's history. Rahab's family will experience its own Passover.... the incorporation of Rahab into Israel is now complete."[2] We may add that this event will allow Rahab to identify with Israel and Israel with her. They will see in her their own narrative, and thus

---

1. All Bible quotations in this article are my own translations.

2. L. Daniel Hawk, *Joshua*, Berit Olam (Collegeville: Liturgical Press, 2000), 50.

ethnic difference is overcome through an empathetic understanding of the other's history.

Let me add to this line of interpretation. Within Rahab's soliloquy (Josh. 2:9–13) there are carefully weaved references and allusions to the first stipulations of the Decalogue (Exod. 20:1–14 = Deut. 5:6–18). I propose that her speech communicates on two separate narratological levels. On one level, the character Rahab communicates her knowledge and desires to the Israelite spies. She is ignorant of the Decalogue as such, and knows only that the Lord of Israel has performed mightily for Israel and that she wishes to be saved. On a second level, however, the author of the account communicates with his audience. Here, in the hands of the author, Rahab's words resonate with the language and imagery of the Decalogue. The author alludes to some of the stipulations, or "commandments," so that his audience will perceive Rahab as a paragon of covenantal behavior. These allusions function much as does the allusion in Joshua 2:9 to the Song of the Sea. By highlighting Rahab's exemplary "covenantal" behavior, the narrator explains why she should she spared, in spite of the call of Deuteronomy 20 to kill all Canaanites. In essence, the poetic strategy seeks to eliminate the identity tag of foreign race. Rahab's ethnic identity as Canaanite becomes of no consequence once her behavior and belief system are revealed to be in consonance with that of the covenantal people of Israel.

Let's examine how the author of Joshua 2 achieves this consonance. In her soliloquy of vv. 9–13, Rahab professes her belief in the potency of the God of Israel, seen through his salvific acts on Israel's behalf in Egypt and against the Transjordanian kings Sichon and Og. She concludes that the townsfolk of Jericho are dispirited, "because the Lord your God ... is God in the heaven above and on the land below" (2:11). Our author has reached for language found twice in Deuteronomy, at 4:39 and at 5:8. The former proclaims that the Lord reigns "in the heavens above and on the earth below," while the same language is used in Deuteronomy 5:8, proscribing the fashioning of graven images of anything "in the heavens above and on the earth below" (Exod. 20:4 = Deut. 5:8). I would suggest that the author of Joshua 2 reached for this phrase in a call to the reader to engage one of those texts—the Decalogue—as an intertext to animate the reading of Rahab's soliloquy. The immediate impression is that Rahab affirms God's sovereignty over the heavens and earth, as Israelites are instructed in Exodus 20:4 (cf. Deut. 5:8).

Other elements of Decalogue terminology and motif are tightly woven into Rahab's soliloquy. She affirms what the talmudic tradition (b. *makkot* 24a) understood as the first commandment, and what other traditions refer to as the prologue to the commandments (Exod. 20:2; cf. Deut 5:6): "I am the Lord your God who has taken you out of Egypt the house of bondage." Rahab affirms God's role in the Exodus in similar terms (Josh. 2:10): "For we have heard that the Lord dried up the waters of the Red Sea before you, as you came out of Egypt."

Rahab's request to the spies for shelter in Joshua 2:13 expressly mentions both her father and her mother. Rahab is seen here fulfilling what the Decalogue would consider a fulfillment of one's duties to father and mother. Indeed, the reward to one who honors father and mother, "so that you lengthen your days in the land" (Exod. 20:12; cf. Deut. 5:16), is Rahab's reward (Josh. 6:25): "And Joshua delivered Rahab the harlot, her father's house, and all that was hers, and she dwelled in the midst of Israel to this very day." Further, it is Rahab who reminds the spies of the promise of the land alluded to in the reward for honoring one's parents. Rahab opens her soliloquy with the declaration (2:9), "I know that God will give you the land," language that echoes the reward proffered in that commandment (Exod. 20:12; cf. Deut. 5:16): "so that you lengthen your days in the land which the Lord, your God has given you."

Rahab's behavior also implicitly affirms the injunction against taking the Lord's name in vain (Exod. 20:7; cf. Deut. 5:11). She enjoins the spies (Josh. 2:12) to swear in the name of the Lord that they will protect her and her family, putting all of her stock in the belief that the name of the Lord is so sacrosanct that they would not dare take his name in vain and fail to abide by their oath. The language of that commandment is echoed further on in the Rahab narrative. The Decalogue states that one who does not uphold his vow and takes the Lord's name in vain, shall not be "cleared" or "exonerated." The spies express their understanding that they will be "clear" of the oath only if they uphold it (2:20): "And if you divulge our plan with you, we shall be clear of your oath" (cf. 2:17).

Finally, Rahab demonstrates her fidelity to the spirit of the Sabbath commandment. To be sure, Rahab is not "Sabbath observant." But the Sabbath commandment is the only one that offered a rationale for its observance, an explanation of its commemorative function. While Rahab may not refrain from work on the Sabbath, she does display a keen appreciation of the events that the Sabbath is meant to commemorate. For the Decalogue in Exodus 20:8–11, the Sabbath is enjoined because in six days the Lord your God created the heaven and the earth. Rahab, as we already saw, affirmed God's sovereignty over the heaven and the earth in Joshua 2:11: "because the Lord your God is God in the heaven above and on the land below." Rahab also appreciates Deuteronomy's rationale (5:15) for the Sabbath—that the God of Israel is the God who took them out of Egypt (Josh. 2:10).

To summarize, the author of Joshua 2 invokes not only the Song of the Sea and the narrative of the paschal sacrifice of Exodus 12, but also the Decalogue, creatively adapting those texts to portray the ethnic outsider Rahab as one who is nearly "Israelite" in her comport and outlook, and thus worthy of being spared. His exercise in appropriating the language of the Pentateuch and repurposing it in his characterization of Rahab sends a powerful message to us about race and culture. There are times when a group's ethnic identity is intricately bound up with its cultural identity. When such a group stands in opposition to a group of a different ethnicity, the difference will then be deeper than skin deep. It can potentially be part of a profound cultural difference as well, a difference that leaves the two groups in tension and incompatible. But the author of Joshua 2 teaches us that there are times when members of another ethnicity actually seek to realize the same ideals that we hold dear. And when that is the case, we are to embrace one another in covenant, even as the Israelites could embrace and welcome Rahab the Canaanite into their own covenantal community.

Uprooting Ethnic Prejudice: The "Book of Boaz"

We know from our own American society that getting rid of prejudicial laws is one thing, but getting rid of prejudice itself is quite another. We know that in order for a culture to begin the process of reforming itself, of healing itself of racial prejudice, it often takes a bold mover and shaker to step up and make a principled—if unpopular—stand. And if that person carries enough weight, their own personal example begins to sway the hearts and minds of others, and the process of communal reform and penance can begin. Think here of the white celebrities who spoke at the march on Washington in 1963 such as Bob Dylan, Charlton Heston, and Marlin Brando.

We find such a hero in what is nominally referred to as the book of Ruth, but which I would like to call the "book of Boaz." When we call this short story the book of "Ruth," we focus on the merits and courage of a young Moabite woman as she seeks her place within the community of Bethlehem. The book of "Boaz" is comprised of the same words and the same verses. But it is a different book.

This is the story of the book of Boaz—a man of power and influence, whose understanding of God's covenant with Israel leads him to the conviction that Ruth, an ethnic outsider, must have a place within the covenantal community. But that community—the community of Bethlehem—treats Ruth with hostility and alienation. Boaz realizes that to welcome Ruth with open arms is insufficient. Instead, he must take steps—at times confrontational—to reform his people, to rid them of their prejudice. Here I engage the book of Boaz through a strategy of close reading of the text to lay bare the tactics of leadership that Boaz takes to spur this reform.

Scripture tells us that the young widow, Ruth, cut ties with her Moabite heritage and accompanied her mother-in-law, the widow Naomi, on a trek across the desert to return to Naomi's homeland in Bethlehem. Along the way, Ruth declares the words that to this day are the archetype within the Jewish tradition of joining the fold of the covenantal community (Ruth 1:16): "Your people are my people; your God is my God." But while the Lord may have accepted Ruth into the covenantal community, the community itself does not. We can see this very vividly when Ruth sets out to the field to gather with the poor so that she and Naomi can eat. Boaz arrives on the scene and asks the foreman about her identity (Ruth 2:4–6). The foreman might have said, "That's Ruth." He might have said, "That's Naomi's daughter-in-law." But the foreman cannot see past Ruth's ethnicity. Instead he says, "She is a Moabite girl, who came from Moab with Naomi" (Ruth 2:6). In the context of the historical tensions between Israel and Moab, that opening identifier, "She is a Moabite girl," can only be construed as a derogatory ethnic and xenophobic slur.

Enter Boaz. Scripture details Boaz's addresses to Ruth, but for our purposes what is important is that he does so in a public setting: in front of all the other field hands present that morning. His address to her is designed, of course, to make her feel welcomed. But we may also mine it for the messages it sends challenging communal norms concerning ethnicity and membership in the covenant.

Let's look closely at what Boaz says. Boaz offers Ruth assistance in a number of ways, each generous in its own right. But each form of assistance implicitly draws the spotlight to a particular aspect of ethnic prejudice and the ways in which it needs to be called out, and therefore combated. Boaz's words take up all of two verses, but they contain within them a five-point plan for combating ingrained prejudice:

I will parse his words (2:8–9), one phrase at a time, and lay bare Boaz's five-point plan:

1. Boaz opens: *"Listen carefully my daughter."* With a single word, Boaz changes the discourse. The foreman had referred to her dismissively, "She is a Moabite girl." Boaz does not address her by name, but still redefines Ruth's identity, her essence. He addresses her not as "a Moabite girl"—an ethnic outsider—but as "my daughter"—a family insider.

2. Boaz continues, *"Don't go to glean in another field, nor leave this place."* Note that Boaz does not extend to Ruth a one-time handout. He realizes that for this ethnic outsider to feel a part of the community, she will need economic stability and a sense of rootedness in place. But we should also note how Boaz deftly manipulates Torah law here. The fields are his fields. However, the Torah states that designated portions of the field and of the produce are to be given to the poor of Israel (Deut. 24:19–22). Here Boaz grants Ruth the right to glean with the Judahite poor of Bethlehem. Every sheath that this Moabite girl gleans is a sheath that will not be available for a member of the local poor. These resources are a win-lose proposition. Therefore, it is not with his own resources that Boaz makes the statement that Ruth is a member of the community, but with God's.

3. Boaz goes further: *"Stick right here with my maidens; see where they are gleaning, and go with them."* Boaz realizes that Ruth is an ethnic outsider with no kindred ties in the community. His instruction to Ruth—and by extension to the maidens—ensures that she will now join a community of field hands. Field work is team work. She will work alongside the team and will naturally develop a sense of social connectedness. Boaz's plan of integration ensures that the maidens will become accustomed to her presence in their ranks and work in sync with her.

4. Boaz adds, *"Behold I have warned the boys not to lay a hand on you."* Boaz realizes that Ruth's needs are not only material and social, but that her personal safety must be safeguarded as well. Ethnic outsiders are always vulnerable. Add gender to the mix, and that woman is doubly vulnerable. In patriarchal clan-based societies such as biblical Bethlehem, a woman walks freely not because of police protection but because would-be attackers know they would face the fury of her extended clan of male relatives. Absent those safeguards, Ruth is protected by Boaz who stands in as that phalanx of next of kin.

5. And finally, Boaz gives assurance: *"And when you thirst, you shall go to the trough and drink from the water drawn by the boys."* Here he ensures much more than a steady supply of water during the hot harvest season of early summer. Boaz declares that in his fields, there will be no separate water fountains for Israelites and for Moabites. What Boaz seeks here is more than just a statement of equality. Rather, he seeks to address a social imbalance. The water that Ruth will drink will be drawn for her by none other than the very boys who may have had thoughts of laying hands on her. Precisely because the boys would contemplate denigrating her, Boaz determines that they must serve her with the water they draw on her behalf.

Ruth asked for none of this, and it is a tribute to Boaz's sensitivity and moral courage, indeed to his sense of covenantal responsibility, that he so quickly implemented this five-step plan to overcome ethnic prejudice. His actions paved the way for Ruth's entry into the community.

But before we leave Boaz's soliloquy, let us return to his opening words, "Listen well, *my daughter.*" When we stand back and appraise the situation before us, a familiar pattern emerges: an older, powerful man—here Boaz—creates for a vulnerable young woman—here Ruth—a situation of utter dependency on him. Today, we are acutely aware of how such situations can be manipulated. What the powerful, older man offers seemingly in largesse winds up coming with a price tag—and a hashtag as well. When Boaz says to Ruth, "Listen carefully, *my daughter,*" those words at once signal both intimacy and distance. In Boaz's eyes, she is not a Moabite, but a person to be drawn in—she is a daughter. Yet the phrase "my daughter" also signals to Ruth appropriate distance, for a man does not start up with his own daughter.

Even still, Scripture records that Ruth is wary (2:10). So Boaz turns to a different set of arguments to assuage her and to signal to those around that Ruth is worthy of entrance into the covenantal community. Here too, a close reading of the text reveals layers of meaning. Boaz replies to her, "I have been told of all that you did for your mother-in-law after the death of your husband and how you left your father and mother and the land of your birth and came to a people you had not known before" (2:11). On the surface of these words, we see Boaz publicly acknowledge Ruth's sacrifice on behalf of her mother-in-law, Naomi. Implicit here is the message that when an ethnic outsider sacrifices for the sake of the covenantal community, the community must take note and reciprocate. We are reminded here that during World War II, when blacks and Jews fought and died alongside their fellow American servicemen, many Americans began the long process of shedding racist and anti-Semitic attitudes.

But notice what is under the surface of Boaz's words: they contain a pregnant allusion to another well-known biblical scene. When Boaz heralds Ruth, "For you left your father and mother and the place of your birth" to come to a foreign unknown land, he echoes the command to Abraham in the book of Genesis (12:1): "Go forth from the place of your birth, from the house of your father—to the land that I shall show you." Now Ruth—a recent arrival in Bethlehem—would not have caught the allusion. But all those present would have, and no less important, so do sensitive readers of the text. By invoking God's first command to Abraham, Boaz offers Ruth the highest praise he can, equating this seemingly ethnic outsider with no less than the father of the covenantal people. But on a deeper level, Boaz instructs us in a key move necessary to overcome ethnic prejudice. Here he makes the move from sympathy to empathy: I see in your narrative our narrative. When we can see in the other a mirror of ourselves, when we can see in others the commitment to covenant that we recognize in ourselves, the bridges overcoming ethnic prejudice are built.

Boaz concludes by offering Ruth a blessing (Ruth 2:12): "May the Lord reward you for your efforts, and may you receive full recompense from the Lord, the God of Israel, under whose wings you have come to seek shelter." But this is more than a blessing. These are the very terms in which Boaz would describe his own relationship with the Almighty: he is under the watchful eye of the God of Israel, and his deeds are measured and rewarded accordingly. Boaz seeks out for himself that God's protective grace. In addressing her in these terms, Boaz grants Ruth not only material assistance, as earlier, but existential legitimation: your essence, your inner world as a spiritual being, is no different than our own.

A leader can implement a plan, as Boaz does here. But when the plan fails to produce results, the plan must be adjusted. Scripture relates that the field hands return to their work, and presumably Ruth joins the maidens and drinks from the water drawn by the boys. Scripture says that at the lunchtime siesta (2:14), Boaz calls to Ruth to join the community in its repast. The text says that Ruth sat herself at the periphery of the reapers. Apparently no one made room for her in the middle. Ruth was still being treated as an alien. Nowhere is social status established and noticed as at a collective meal. Scripture says that Boaz personally served her the meal, thereby not only equating her with the others, but offering her preferential treatment. The story concludes by saying that for the remainder of the harvest season, Ruth works daily in the fields providing for her mother-in-law. The text is reticent; it seems that Ruth is quietly accepted, but never truly embraced.

Until this point in the narrative, all the steps that Boaz takes are within his domain. All answer to him, and he need answer to no one. But the mark of a true leader is when he is prepared to challenge those of status equal to his in the name of the ideals he believes.

The climax of Boaz's actions is in chapter 4, where Boaz presses his case to overcome the ethnic prejudice against Ruth. Now it is no longer with his underlings in the field, but with kin of equal status, and with the elders of the town. Here's the background: Scripture tells us that by local custom, a next of kin was required to marry Ruth, as widow of a fellow tribesman. The Bible places great value on this form of marriage, called the levirate marriage, since progeny of such a union are considered to be the descendants of the deceased first husband. Although Boaz was a clansman of Ruth's deceased husband, another member of the clan was a closer relation. Boaz desired to marry Ruth, but by custom he could do so only if the closer kinsman abdicated his right to do so. Boaz summons the kinsman to a court of elders to determine the kinsman's intentions vis-à-vis Ruth. Scripture relates that the man demurs, stating that to marry a Moabite woman would be tantamount to destroying his heritage. Boaz promptly announces his desire to perform the levirate marriage and that he has no qualms about Ruth's race. Their union will be bi-ethnic, and his progeny from her will have Moabite blood. Boaz admires her willingness to consummate the levirate marriage even though, as Scripture relates, he was significantly older than she was. She was prepared to sacrifice marriage with a younger man for the sake of perpetuating the name of her deceased husband.

Boaz's marriage to Ruth was a bold personal statement of his own. When a person of high standing makes such a statement, his actions begin to create waves within society. Following Boaz's marriage to Ruth we see a dramatic change in the attitudes of the townsfolk to both Ruth and Naomi. The community adopts the posture to Ruth that Boaz had from the outset. We saw earlier that Boaz's address to Ruth was laced with allusions to the patriarch Abraham. At the wedding ceremony, we see the town elders following suit: now they bless Ruth by saying that she should be as Rachel and Leah, the matriarchs of Israel (4:11). Until this point in the book, no other member of the community had uttered a word to Ruth, with the exception of her mother-in-law, Naomi. But once Boaz marries Ruth, who bears him a son, we see a dramatic shift in the attitudes of the townswomen toward her. The women celebrate with Naomi over the birth of the child. They exclaim, "He will renew your life and sustain your old age; for he is born of your daughter-in-law, who loves you and is better to you than seven sons.... And the women gave him a name, saying, 'A son is born to Naomi!' They named him Obed (which means servant of the Lord); he was the father of Jesse, father of David" (4:15, 17).

The book ends with a genealogy connecting Boaz and Ruth to King David. The genealogy is often interpreted as a sign of divine reward. When righteous individuals, such as Ruth and Boaz, marry they merit progeny who rise to greatness. But perhaps we may read the concluding genealogy otherwise. The book of Ruth—the book of Boaz—is a story of communal penance. It is a book that demonstrates how a community took account of its xenophobic past, and through bold and inspired leadership overcame those prejudices. They learned to see the ethnic outsider as truly one of their own. The entire community, the book concludes, merits the rise of David, its greatest king.

The account of the "book of Boaz" amplifies the lessons of the story of Rahab. When a person such as Rahab or Ruth demonstrates that she is worthy of admission into the covenantal community of Israel, she effectively becomes embraced as a full-fledged member, and her ethnicity fades away as a marker of otherness. But the reality is that ideal and reality must be made to match; prejudicial dispositions will need to be overcome. The book of Boaz demonstrates that integration of the ethnic outsider must be translated into actions—resources are shared, integration is promoted, equal status is constantly affirmed. This integration also mandates attitudinal shifts in which we look at each other empathically and see in each other mirrors of ourselves. We see in one another persons who share in the same high ideals we do because we see their narrative as reminiscent of our own.

Religious communities in the United States are the historical bearers of the concept of covenant, a concept whose origins are in the covenant between God and Israel in the Torah. This study has shown how the authors of the biblical books of Joshua and Ruth mined their spiritual heritage to uncover resources that allowed for an expanded notion of covenant, one that could overcome ethnic disparity. It is incumbent upon religious communities to mine this heritage in our time and lead the way to demonstrating how our relationship with the Almighty can serve as a resource to recalibrate our relationships with one another.

2

Exile and Return in Israel and America

R. Mitchell Rocklin

I was on my way to Iraq, and I was worried. My main source of stress, however, was not the destination but the journey. I serve as a chaplain in the Army National Guard, and I was sent on a short deployment to perform Hanukkah services for Jewish service members in theater in December 2018. After leaving my family, my main fixation was on the transportation. I was worried not about Iraq itself, or about walking in Kuwait's airport where a soldier told me it was not safe for me to wear a yarmulke on my head, but about what was supposed to be the most comfortable part of my trip: the commercial flight to Kuwait that the military had generously purchased for me. When I checked my flight itinerary from United Airlines, I saw that most of my trip would be on its codeshare partner Lufthansa, transferring through Frankfurt, Germany.

I am the grandson of Holocaust survivors, and like many grandchildren of survivors whom I know, memories of the Holocaust still linger with us, having percolated down the generations in the form of stories that became part of our characters. To many of us, the Holocaust is no distant historical event but a recent development that is still experienced in the traumatic memories of its survivors and their descendants. I grew up with nightmares of being pursued by the Germans and their collaborators, recreating in my mind the stories my grandparents told me at a very young age.

This experience was enough to make me palpably uncomfortable with most things German and with many things Eastern European as well; sitting on an airplane with German announcements from the cockpit was certainly enough to make me uneasy. This flight marked the only time during my trip to Iraq when I felt uncomfortable for any significant length of time. This despite my ability to wear my yarmulke with no issue whatsoever, both on the airplane to Frankfurt and in the Frankfurt airport, while I could not do so in Kuwait (at least if I did not want to be detained and hassled by hostile Arab security guards, as a Jewish chaplain had been that year).

Just as the bitterness of the Holocaust pushed me and many of my friends to live a proud and uncompromising Jewish life, it also instilled in me a desire for separation from most things central and eastern European. I know many people who, like me, avoid purchasing anything made in Germany or even in Eastern Europe. We personally cannot bring ourselves to contribute anything financial, however indirectly, to perpetrators or collaborators who might benefit even indirectly from our purchases. We are well aware of the massive efforts in Germany to address the Holocaust, and we harbor no ill will toward the German population, which has rejected the terrible crimes of the past. Nevertheless, these memories are still painful for us.

While my love for European culture grew over the course of my classical education, and while I am perfectly aware of the ways in which Germany has defined its modern existence largely in opposition to the Holocaust, I was still not prepared to reconcile with a nation that still contained some of the perpetrators.

Orthodox Jews pray three times daily, and the time for one of my prayers coincided with my layover in Germany. Another Jewish chaplain, who was traveling with me, suggested that we pray in the airport synagogue. I was surprised that there was such a thing, as I was only familiar with one US airport that has a dedicated synagogue, as opposed to a neutral chapel. But there it was, a German-sponsored synagogue less than seventy-five years after the Holocaust. As I prayed, I thought of Rabbi Samson Raphael Hirsch, the most prominent Orthodox rabbi in Frankfurt of the late nineteenth century, whose writings informed my intellectual development. I wondered what he might think of it all. Yet I was still uneasy, wondering what I was doing there. I felt as if I was praying in a cemetery, haunted by visions of the dead who once frequented this city and its country.

The problem of Germany would soon follow me to Iraq. One day, on the Jewish holiday of Hanukkah, I was praying in Camp Taji, a base just northwest of Baghdad. I was in a tent waiting for a flight, wearing traditional Jewish prayer garments over my uniform. There were many people circulating around, including US forces, coalition forces, and contractors. As I was praying, a couple of German soldiers happened to walk into the crowded tent. They stood in the empty space before me, chatting quietly as I prayed. An American soldier, somewhat amused while also impressed, later told me that he wanted to snap a picture of that moment, to capture what he saw as something at the same time both awkward and moving. And, I added, historic—a Jew praying next to two German soldiers, all fighting the same war together.

Several days later, I found myself at Erbil Air Base in northern Iraq, when I bumped into one of those two German soldiers, who warmly greeted me in the dining hall. We struck up a conversation, and he recalled how he admired my prayers from the day before. I could not help but think about how, in historical terms, the Holocaust just happened. I am a historian as well as a rabbi, so for me the word *history* does not do the Holocaust justice. It is more like a current event. When that German soldier reached out in friendship to this rabbi, I could not help thinking that something truly wondrous has happened in the last decades. We have moved to a time and place where we have the freedom to consider the problem of reconciliation between the victims and perpetrators of the Holocaust.

But how is reconciliation possible? Many of my Christian friends talk about the need for forgiveness as the basis of reconciliation, arguing that we must forgive wrongdoings out of a sense of love rather than hold on to the desire for justice or revenge. Yet many Jews, including myself, strongly believe that forgiveness for something like the Holocaust is not only impossible, but unconscionable. If that is true, how can there be reconciliation? How can the Jewish nation reconcile with the German nation? How can any two peoples achieve reconciliation when one has victimized the other with unspeakable horrors?

The answer may lie in the biblical understanding of exile and return, a process that stems from the idea that God creates covenants with nations. The notion of a "covenant" derived from human treaties signed between peoples. These were alliances made between ancient near eastern kings and lesser vassal kings, outlining the obligations between the superior and his inferiors. The Bible continues to use the term *covenant* in the context of human agreements, but it uniquely carried over the concept to man's relationship with God.[1] Beginning with Noah, the Bible depicts a series of covenants, first with mankind and then with Abraham's descendants, as integral to the maintenance of the world itself. The Bible also shows that if Israel violates its special covenant by sinning against God or men, the nation must go into exile for the purpose of renewing its commitment toward its responsibilities.

But it is not only Israel that has a covenantal relationship with God. Scripture suggests that every people is under God and has some relationship with him, even if it is not as pronounced and special as that of Israel. For example, God gave responsibilities to all the world's peoples in the generations after Adam (Gen. 5). But when these peoples failed to live up to those responsibilities, God brought a flood to start the world anew. After that flood, he formed an explicit covenant with Noah, demanding a new and better creation. God took man's evil into account and promised not to send another great flood upon the earth. Rabbinic Jewish writers explained that this Noahide covenant involved seven commandments (or categories of commandments) that form the basis for civilized life for all nations.[2]

God's care for all nations extended long after the rise of Israel, as the Book of Jonah demonstrates. God went out of his way to make an offer to save even the wicked Assyrian Empire, if it would merely repent. Without repentance, God would eventually send punishment. To the ancient biblical empires, God sent conquerors and defeat, and in Assyria's case an offer to save; to Israel he sent not only defeat but exile and a chance to repent. For the "remnant of Israel," which

---

1. For examples of covenants made between people, see Gen. 21:22–34; 26:26–31; 31:43–54.

2. Aaron Lichtenstein, *The Seven Laws of Noah* (New York: Z. Berman Books, 1981).

would always survive, repentance would bring redemption, just as Assyria had the chance to repent at the time of Jonah.[3] As Americans, this model of exile and redemption may provide a way for us to deal with our history of slavery and racial oppression, during which we did not live up to our principles of liberty and equality before the law.

Exile and Return in the Bible: A Way to Renew a Covenantal Mission

The process of exile and return makes true reconciliation possible, whether between a nation and God or between nations, even when a nation has committed terrible crimes. But reconciliation is by no means the same thing as forgiveness—it is decidedly different. Forgiveness of the perpetrators of the worst evils is impossible. Yet perhaps there can be reconciliation between the descendants of victims and the descendants of perpetrators.

For reconciliation to be possible, a nation that perpetrated a great crime must enter a state of exile. In this condition it can renew itself by recommitting to the responsibilities it once shirked. But almost invariably it takes a new generation to do this, one that is removed from and rejects the evil behavior of the prior generation. Typically it is only this later generation that can recommit to goodness.

In 1952, Menachem Begin, then the right-leaning opposition leader in the Israeli Knesset (parliament), delivered what many still consider to be the most passionate speech of his career. In a fiery oration he lambasted the Israeli government's acceptance of German reparations after the Holocaust. Begin argued that it would be undignified for the Jewish nation to accept reparations. While he did not say this explicitly, he implied that reparations would make Jewish reconciliation with Germany more difficult, since they would create the illusion that forgiveness is possible—that the wrongs of the Holocaust could somehow be compensated. In fact, he said, reconciliation is possible only when a perpetrator nation has given up its sense of stability, has gone into exile by removing itself from its sinful past, and has

---

3. Jews continue to link their prospects for repentance and redemption with those of other nations by reading the story of Jonah in synagogues on the annual Day of Atonement.

renewed itself for the future. Israel, Begin implied, might be able to reconcile with different Germans, but only if they were truly different. It could never reconcile itself with the perpetrators themselves, or with their descendants offering reparations.

The Bible addresses the pattern of exile and redemption in many places, but perhaps the most helpful for Americans seeking racial reconciliation can be found in Jeremiah chapter 34. In the sixth century BCE, the inhabitants of Jerusalem were suffering under a Babylonian siege. They made a desperate gamble to avoid conquest, exile, and death by abolishing slavery. This had existed as a biblically regulated institution that allowed impoverished people to sell their labor for sustenance. At the same time that the Bible regulated slavery, it implicitly condemned Israelite slavery by proclaiming that the children of Israel are God's slaves. They could never be the slaves of other people.[4] At this point, therefore, they were eager to live up to their biblical principles to an even higher degree. They crafted a new covenant in which they committed to completely abolishing slavery for their own people.

But the abolition was not to last. Economic pressures soon lowered labor costs, freed people felt compelled to resell themselves into slavery, and former masters purchased them again.[5] Jeremiah rebuked the Jewish people for their behavior, telling them that because they had not been more generous, preferring instead to violate the spirit of the covenantal promise they had made to free the slaves, this was the last straw that would lead to exile. This re-enslavement of freed people, who were given their dignity by being freed only to have it stolen again, necessitated a new birth of the Jewish people. But the new birth would come only after exile.

What Is a Covenantal Nation?

If exile is a punishment for the failure to live up to human responsibilities toward God and other people, then we must understand the biblical covenant and its stipulation of a people's responsibilities

---

4. Lev. 25:55.

5. I am indebted to Prof. Joshua Berman of Bar-Ilan University for this economic explanation of the phenomenon.

under God. Several chapters in this book analyze this concept, but for our purpose it is important to understand that this unbreakable bond between God and man is the result of God's sacrifice for us, to the point where it is as if his very being depends on us.

Trying to understand the Bible's many mentions of God's intense love for his people, the rabbis argued that it is impossible to understand God in any meaningful way without relating to him in a covenantal manner, that is, without appreciating human responsibilities toward him and his creation. This was true of the entire human race from the beginning, and then became especially true for God's chosen people, Israel, who were supposed to serve as a source of blessing for all men. As the Sifre put it, Isaiah charges us with the task of being God's witnesses. "When you are my witnesses," God says, "I am God. And if you are not my witnesses, then I am not God."[6] The thirteenth-century *Holy Letter*, an important Jewish mystical work, explains that God loves us so much that he needs us to help create with him, even to the point of needing us to help create our own natures as human beings.[7] Our task as human beings, therefore, is to sacrifice our entire lives to the divine-human project of constantly recreating the world.

This understanding lies at the roots of Judaism (and in some Christian mystical writings as well).[8] Abraham's binding of Isaac on the altar was the archetypal sacrifice for all of Jewish history, displaying the fundamental difference between Jewish and pagan sacrifice. While Agamemnon, for example, sacrificed Iphigenia for the sake of an extant nation, Abraham was willing to sacrifice an entire nation before it came into being. Isaac's descendants did not even

---

6. *Sifre* on Deuteronomy, 343.6. This *Sifre* ("books" in both Hebrew and Aramaic) was a rabbinical commentary on the Bible from the classical era that uses both literal and poetic-moralistic interpretations.

7. The authorship of this work, one of the most important in Jewish mysticism for a half-millennium, is unknown. It has been attributed to Nahmanides, one of the foremost Jewish scholars of thirteenth-century Spain, but it is not clear that he was the author.

8. For example, Meister Eckhart (c. 1260–c. 1328) wrote, "Know this, *God loves my soul so much* that *whether He* wishes it or *not, His very life* and *being depend* upon *His loving me.*" See Meister Eckhart, *Sermons and Collations* (London: John M. Watkins, 1924), 26.

exist when he was bound on the altar, and yet he was sacrificed for their sake. God's decision to spare Isaac reflected his wish to ensure that Isaac's descendants would be sacrificed—that is, dedicated—to God. As Haim Gouri, a twentieth-century Zionist poet put it, to be a Jew means to be born with a knife in one's heart—to be born with a sense of sacrifice and devotion to God in every moment of life. Every breath a Jew breathes is a living moment of life upon the altar. They never come off that altar.[9]

This sense is one of the many things that make biblical sacrifice unique. Unlike their pagan counterparts, biblical sacrifices required people to think of themselves as sacrificially dedicated to God at every moment. A pagan priest would wash his hands after ritual offerings to symbolize moving away from the altar, a place of death, and coming back to a place of life. The pagan might say, "Zeus, I gave you this cow, and now I'm going to go back to living." The Jew, on the other hand, never washed his hands after offering a sacrifice because he was obligated to live a life that was constantly unfolding in a state of sacrifice on the altar. This was why human sacrifice has always been abhorrent to Jews. They believe that their whole lives are devoted to God, so that in life they already experience death. In fact, that is how Jews understand the biblical concept of being chosen by God.[10]

On this matter of chosenness, Jews and Christians generally agree. This is why both of our communities see Isaac's binding as a precedent for the Passover sacrifice, the most important of the annual cycle of biblical offerings. No Jews are allowed to remain in their nation if they shirk their obligation to commemorate the first Passover holiday, when the Jews followed God into a barren desert,

---

9. For a discussion of Haim Gouri's poem, see Ruth Kartun-Blum, "Isaac Rebound: The Aqedah as a Paradigm in Modern Hebrew Poetry," in *The Shaping of Israeli Identity: Myth, Memory and Trauma*, ed. Robert Wistrich and David Ohana (London: Frank Cass, 1995): 188–89.

10. See H. Hubert and M. Mauss, "Essai sur la nature et la function du sacrifice," *L'Anee Sociologique* (1898): 47–48. I plan to provide a further analysis of this phenomenon in *Creative Tradition*, co-authored with Leon Chernyak and soon to be published by Kodesh Press.

risking their lives for the sake of freedom and accepting covenantal responsibilities.[11]

A Covenantal Home for a Covenantal Nation: The Origin of Exile

On account of its responsibility to God at all times, a covenantal nation can never truly feel at home. Exile is always a possible consequence for failing to live up to covenantal obligations. A covenantal nation is always on alert for the possibility that it is not living up to its potential. It does not settle down or become comfortable in a land the way other nations do. It has no fatherland or motherland per se, but a land that constantly requires awareness of God as the source of its inspiration and life.

The land of Israel, God's ultimate covenantal land, requires its chosen people to be constantly looking toward the heavens. For as Deuteronomy emphasizes, the land's unique characteristics drive its people closer to God than did Egypt: with no River Nile to water its land every year, the Israelites had to depend on God's rains for irrigation of their thirsty land. And it was here that their covenant with God took full force. Just before they entered the land of Israel, Moses told the Israelites that on "this day" they were becoming a nation before the Lord their God (Deut. 27:9). Abraham had left Mesopotamia for Canaan long before, but his descendants were now being formed into a true nation only as they entered a covenantal land. Here they were given promises of success for fulfilling the commandments and promises of exile as punishment for rejecting them.

This is why Deuteronomy emphasizes that the land of Israel has no great river, but a water supply from the heavens. The two biggest rivers in Israel, the Jordan River and the Yarkon River, are quite tiny compared to the Nile in Egypt. God wanted it that way. He said that his people would receive their moisture from the heavens. They would be constantly wondering whether there will be enough water for the crops, or whether there will be a drought. Is God with

---

11. Jewish rabbis linked Passover to the binding of Isaac in the *Mekhilta* on Exodus 12:13.

us and are we with God? A chosen nation must be ever mindful of the source of its sustenance and responsibilities.[12]

The same passage in Deuteronomy notes that the land of Israel contains hills and valleys.[13] Unlike the plains of Egypt, where the Jews were enslaved, hills allow a person to be far from others while still seeing them. Those whom the Israelites were responsible for treating properly—these they could see easily. The hills of Judea and Samaria therefore *compel* Israelites to be responsible for their neighbors. You may be very far from them on foot, but you can see them easily across the valley.

This topography dovetails with the biblical commandments to observe the sabbatical year and the Jubilee year, during which the Israelites would not work the land.[14] This is because, as God says in Leviticus, the land is his and not a mere human possession.[15] The Israelites are to remember that they labor on the land for a higher purpose.

The land of Israel does not allow its chosen people to take root fully, since rootlessness is a precondition for the covenantal nation's particularly high level of self-responsibility. Israelites are, as the Bible puts it, roaming shepherds and not sedentary farmers. Abel was favored over Cain. The most beloved leaders of the Jews were mostly shepherds, not farmers—from Moses to David. This tradition was understood by the Jews who became the first Christians. Their apostle John said that Jesus called himself the good shepherd (John 10:1–18).[16]

At least partially because so many of Israel's greatest leaders have been shepherds, and because that is a peculiar characteristic

---

12. Deut. 11:10–12.

13. I am indebted to my wife, Rachel, for this observation, which she made as we gazed at the hills of Samaria in the distance.

14. The sabbatical year required a cessation of agricultural work once every seven years, while the Jubilee required the same every fifty, as well as the freeing of all Israelite slaves. See Lev. 25.

15. Lev. 25:23.

16. For further discussion of the association between Israel and shepherds, see Yoram Hazony, *The Philosophy of Hebrew Scripture* (New York: Cambridge University Press, 2012), 103–39.

of those who have lived in the Israelites' promised land, as a covenantal people in a covenantal land, Jews must always remember that the Israelites were not only slaves but "strangers" in the land of Egypt.[17] The people of Israel became a nation upon entering the land of Israel, but the nation is always rooted in its wandering past.[18] It is constantly called to account to be responsible for its freedom at every moment, and with every commandment that it is entrusted to obey. As the rabbis put it in a homiletic reading noticing the similarity of the Hebrew words for "engraved" and "freedom," the Ten Commandments were engraved on the tablets not as mere letters, but as a statement of freedom.[19]

A nation with this special covenantal mission must not tolerate slavery. As the Bible says in Leviticus when curbing the worst elements of ancient slavery, because God took the Jewish people out of Egypt, they are to be slaves only to him and not to other men. This realization, that Jews are meant to be free, took time to develop. It would eventually help the West realize that all men and women are to be free. (As with so many realizations, the Bible does not revolutionize the entire change, but sets in motion a historical process.) But the covenant to end slavery in Jeremiah was an important step along the way. It was a failed step, and one that served as the final straw that pushed the Jewish people into exile.

Exile Helps Us Recover Our Sense of Responsibility by Remaking a Covenant

The Bible describes a unique dynamic of exile and return, one which allows a sinful nation the chance to return to its homeland in a fundamentally new and better situation. The same biblical prophets who predicted destruction were also the ones who promised return

---

17. See Gen. 43:32, where the Egyptians consider shepherds to be abominable, and Gen. 46:31–47:6, where Joseph has his brothers differentiate themselves from the Egyptians by emphasizing their vocation.

18. See Deut. 26:5; 27:9; 1 Chron. 29:15.

19. *B. Talmud Eruvin* 54a.

and redemption, articulating this promise in terms such as "new heavens," "new earth," and "new covenant."[20]

Because slavery involves the violation of the dignified freedom of others, and because this violation strikes at the heart of the national covenant between God and the Jewish people, exile is the logical response to slavery and other violations of human dignity. Only with covenantal renewal—by rediscovering why the Israelites came to the promised land and by considering what they ought to be doing—can they achieve proper reconciliation with each other.

Covenantal renewal is a vital concern not only for people, but for God himself, who is bound together with his covenantal partners as their God.[21] Unlike in pagan mythology, we know absolutely nothing of him other than what is revealed in his relationship with people. Or, as the rabbis put it in another midrashic teaching, God created the world against the advice of his angels and against considerations of strict justice, which involved the prediction that man would do evil. Nevertheless, the rabbis wrote, he created and stuck with the human race despite its sins, as Isaiah said of the God who gave birth to humanity: "Even to old age I am the same, and even to gray hairs will I carry you; I have made, and I will bear; yea, I will carry, and will deliver" (Isa. 46:4). God is stuck with humanity, and will not even bring another flood against them, even though "the imagination of man's heart is evil from his youth" (Gen. 8:21). Instead, he eventually made a higher covenant with Abraham, one which was meant to serve as a source of blessing for "all the families of the earth" (Gen. 12:3). As Hosea describes this special relationship, when the Israelites break their covenant and act against God, they cause him pain. As Isaiah puts it, God suffers with them when they are afflicted

---

20. See Isa. 65:17; 66:22; Jer. 31:31–34.

21. There are many biblical examples demonstrating this point. In Lev. 26:41–45, God promises that he will never break his covenant with the Israelites, no matter how much they sin against him, because of his covenant with them and because he is their God. Similarly, in 1 Sam. 12:22, the prophet Samuel tells the Israelites that God will "not forsake his people, for his great name's sake, because it hath pleased the Lord to make you a people unto Himself." (All Bible quotations in this chapter are from the Jewish Publication Society's 1917 translation.) And Hosea insists that God's love triumphs over his desire to destroy his people for their sins (Hos. 11:8–9).

in turn.[22] And as Jeremiah notes in verses that Jews ritually connect with the prophet's admonition to abolish slavery, God will abandon his covenant with Jacob's descendants only when he also eliminates the laws of heaven and earth, which were produced for the fulfillment of the covenant (Jer. 33:25–26). In short, he is faithfully and irreversibly committed to mankind in general and to the Jewish people specifically, and he wants all people to take responsibility for the weight that this places on their shoulders.

The Bible repeatedly emphasizes in Genesis, Exodus, Ezekiel, and Daniel that to renew the Israelites' covenant and get them back on track, God goes with them into exile. He exits the promised land with Jacob, escorting him down to Egypt (Gen. 46:4). Upon leaving Egypt, Jacob's descendants had a chance in the desert to renew their covenantal mission in an everlasting national covenant that was stronger and fundamentally new in relationship to the old.[23]

It is instructive to contrast the biblical view of exile with its closest pagan counterpart. In the *Aeneid*, the Trojans must bring their family gods with them. The Bible, by contrast, describes God as deliberately sending—and accompanying—the Jewish people into exile for the purpose of covenantal renewal. God tells the Jews through the prophet Jeremiah to leave. They must do so because of their sins, but they will return with a renewed covenant, just as they did when they left Egypt for the promised land (Jer. 29; 31:31–40). The people had sinned; they needed exile to reconstitute themselves, and only then would they return.

Similarly, when the prophet Ezekiel found himself in the midst of the Jewish exile in Babylon, the heavens opened up, and God appeared to him far from the promised land (Ezek. 1:1–3). Daniel also had visions from God in Babylon (Dan. 10:3–21). As God said to Jacob long before in Genesis 46:4, "I will go down with you to Egypt, and I will go up with you." Throughout the experience of exile, God

---

22. See especially Hos. 11:8 and Isa. 63:9: "In all their affliction he was afflicted, and the angel of his presence saved them; in his love and in his pity he redeemed them; and he bore them, and carried them all the days of old."

23. The covenant was renewed twice in the desert, at Sinai and in the land of Moab. Only after these renewals did the Israelites enter the promised land as a true nation (Deut. chaps. 10 and 11; 28:69 [in the JPS translation] and 29:1–29).

pursued the Jewish people wherever they were, remaining their God and calling them in exile to repentance and return.

No other god of the ancient world was thought to be permanently attached to a people and committed to going with them wherever they went. Athena was the goddess of Athens but not the goddess of the Athenian people. Both Greeks and Trojans worshipped her, but she was committed to neither. The prophet Jonah thought that he could run away from the God of Israel by fleeing to the faraway land of Tarshish (Jonah 1:3). But he found that he could not escape his God. Part of the reason for this was God's national covenant with his people. It served his people well when they renewed it after exile.

Of course, the Jewish covenant is not entirely new, but is based on the old. As Isaiah put it, the Jews are to rebuild new cities upon the old in the very same places (Isa. 58:12). There was to be renewal in a way that no pagan society thought possible. It was not merely replanting in a different place, as many other nations experienced. No, the Jewish people were to remain in the same place, but with profoundly new possibilities. Theodore Herzl, the founder of Zionism, said about the land of Israel that it is an *altneuland*, an "old-new land."[24] This term captures both the covenantal land and the covenants that the Jews keep forming.

History has taught the Jewish people that they cannot always rely on God alone without their cooperation and obedience. They have also learned that they must tend to their covenantal obligations to their neighbors. The Roman exile motivated the Jews to appreciate their common dignity. The rabbis noted that King Ahab won wars despite his people's idol worship, since they behaved respectfully toward each other.[25] The rabbis blamed the Roman exile on *sin'at chinam*, "baseless hatred" among Jews toward one another.[26] To return from exile, the Jewish people would eventually need to engage in the opposite sort of behavior, uniting behind a common cause and establishing bonds of love among fellow members of the national covenant.

---

24. See for instance Shlomo Avineri, "Rereading Herzl's Old-New Land," *Jewish Review of Books* (Summer 2012), https://jewishreviewofbooks.com/articles/213/rereading-herzls-old-new-land/.

25. *Leviticus Rabbah* 26:2.

26. *B. Talmud Yoma* 9b.

Modern Zionism effectively mixed secular vision and religious obligation with this goal in mind. It sought to unite Jews of different ethnic backgrounds and religious beliefs behind the goal of national revival. In 1977, Menachem Begin gave another rousing speech that propelled him to the office of prime minister. He told the story of a nation that came together regardless of racial or ethnic barriers—European and eastern Jews alike—to redeem the land of Israel through sacrifice in war. "Ashkenazi? Iraqi?" Begin asked. "No. Jews! Brothers! Fighters!" The long exile from the land had clarified the need for Jewish unity.

As Begin implied in his speech against accepting reparations from Germany, only a strong and independent Jewish nation could reconcile with those who wish to reconcile with it. Forgiveness plays no role here. Just as the exiled Jews had to wander in the desert for forty years so that only a new generation could enter the promised land, so too other nations could produce new and better generations who dissociate from sins of the past and reconcile with their ancestors' victims. New generations allow us to overcome the sins of the past, just as new personalities provide new possibilities in ordinary human relations.

The same is true for reconciliation between nations. Even the Egyptians, who enslaved the Jews and drowned their baby boys in the Nile, were permitted to marry into the Jewish people after three generations.[27] The future does not have to be like the past. This is especially true for a nation that is aware of the biblical tradition. When it finds itself defeated and goes into exile, its later generations may become an old-new state, renewed in their respect for human dignity and thereby making reconciliation possible. Forgiveness is not the relevant issue at hand, for forgiveness is not the business of the descendants of victims, as Menachem Begin insisted decades ago.

But reconciliation is nevertheless possible. When descendants turn from the wicked ways of their ancestors, as rabbinic *midrash* and the medieval commentator Rashi emphasized, they do not deserve to be

---

27. *Yevamot* 78a. The same is not true for three nations—Amalek, Ammon, and Moab—due to their historic enmity for the Jewish people (Deut. 23:3–5; 25:17–19). In general, however, with new generations, reconciliation is possible.

punished for the sins of prior generations. Only when they persist in sin are prior sins counted against them.[28]

Ontological Suffering, Existential Evil, and the Hypocrisy of Identity Politics

We might wonder, however, whether modernity has made reconciliation between peoples far more difficult. After all, we moderns do not approach evil in quite the same manner as the ancients. If it was not clear enough before the Holocaust, it should be clear now that there are existential evils that are simply unforgivable. If we believe that modern Western slavery was particularly brutal and took place in societies that violated their own enlightened principles and ought to have known better, then racial reconciliation will be much more difficult. After all, we appreciate ontological suffering (suffering associated with being itself—a particularly individualistic form of suffering) much more than our ancestors. We are troubled by the problem of the unique and infinite nature of every individual's suffering, asking the question that Ivan posed to Alyosha in Dostoevsky's *Brothers Karamazov*: How could God allow the suffering of *one* innocent child, even for the sake of the creation of the world? Our greater appreciation for the individual personality means that it may no longer be possible for *nations* to choose to reconcile with one another, since the suffering of every *individual* is infinitely meaningful and demands an accounting on its own terms. If each individual counts, how can there be a communal decision to bury the hatchet?

The answer to this problem lies in its source. We moderns possess a greater appreciation for the significance of evil because of our greater appreciation for the importance of individual personalities. This new individualism, however, also allows us to separate the personalities of the perpetrators from those descendants who reject them. The Bible pointed the way toward the possibility of reconciliation with the descendants of perpetrators of even modern ontological suffering, since it ultimately pointed to the uniqueness of every human being and the separability of our individual personalities from the evils of

---

28. *B. Talmud Sanhedrin* 27b and Rashi on Exod. 20:5.

the past and sins of our fathers. The concept of the old-new covenant allows us to renew a national covenant on the basis of human dignity.

Reconciliation can only happen, however, when both sides conduct themselves with dignity. Reparations are an easy way out that can prevent giving and receiving that dignity. There are two reasons for this. First, reparations allow the descendants of perpetrators the false comfort of believing that the existential evils of the past are somehow forgivable. Second, they encourage the descendants of victims to see themselves as perpetual victims who would do better to blame the righteous descendants of evil perpetrators than to forge new bonds of friendship with a new people constituted in a new national covenant. If we treat each other as equals—as covenantal creatures with divinely granted dignity—we can reconcile on the basis of our distance from crimes of the past.

Modern identity politics rejects this possibility, seeking to base our significance on our belonging to particular groups, usually racial and ethnic. Some groups are seen as underprivileged and others as privileged. A debt is said to be established across history, created by the mistreatment that (some of) the ancestors of privileged groups meted out on (some of) the ancestors of the underprivileged. This debt is only to be made good when a state of equality is achieved. The arrangement sounds a great deal like tribalism, but without a mechanism for communal reconciliation.

Identity politics involves both internal contradiction and hypocrisy. On the one hand, it requires us to see people in tribal terms, as responsible for the sins of those related by blood, past or present. But while they adopt a premodern tribalism, identity politics on the other hand adopts a modern approach to ontological suffering and existential evil by arguing that tribes cannot reconcile because suffering at the hands of the irresponsible is not forgivable.

In identity politics, therefore, there are no options for reconciliation—neither premodern national forgiveness nor modern individualistic reconciliation is possible. Neither is there hope for covenantal renewal, since identity politics assumes that race—not national covenant—forms the basis of group identity. This approach is actually religious in nature, even if it has no room for the vital elements that Judaism and Christianity take for granted. As in the tribal world, there is room for holding the sins of past generations against future ones, as in Exodus 20:5. But there is no mechanism for expiating those sins, since moderns do not believe that individuals can forgive sins committed against others.

It is precisely because Jews did not succumb to identity politics, precisely because they did not fall into the typical narrative of victimhood that afflicted much of the colonized world, that they have been able to move forward in life. It is also why we witnessed a resurgence of anti-Semitism in Europe and the developing world.

The perpetrators of a permanent victim mentality in the United States tend to hate Israel. Their anti-Semitism is bound together with the refusal of the Jew—including both liberals and conservatives—to become victims. For we are not victims but dignified human beings. To insist on remaining victims is not only to hinder our own development, but to crush all hope of reconciliation through changes in our national covenants. Because we can see the repentant descendants of perpetrators as individual human personalities and not as simply members of a transgenerational tribe, we can find it easier to reconcile with those who reject the evils of their predecessors.

This is how Israel reconciled with Germany and other nations that perpetrated the Holocaust. It never did and never can forgive the perpetrators, but reconciliation with their descendants is possible. Many, like Menachem Begin, argued that forgiveness was impossible immediately after the war. I agree with him. But the birth of new generations who rejected their parents' crimes created new possibilities for covenantal renewal and national reconciliation.

While we cannot forgive those who took innocent human lives, we can appreciate and celebrate later generations as our fellow human beings. Together with them we can look toward a better future in which we all judge each other, in the words of Martin Luther King, Jr., by the content of our character rather than the crimes of our fathers. The Jewish example shows that this is the only way to achieve true redemption.

America, which John Winthrop described long ago as a "New Israel," can surely learn from the nation of Israel in this respect.[29] We are sorely in need of a national covenantal renewal when it comes

---

29. Edmund S. Morgan, "John Winthrop's 'Modell of Christian Charity' in a Wider Context," *Huntington Library Quarterly* 50, no. 2 (1987): 145–51.

to race, particularly because we are haunted by our repeated failed attempts to renew our national covenant in a manner that fulfills our own highest principles. The American Revolution, despite its appreciation of freedom, failed to abolish slavery—although it did take steps against the institution. Instead of reaching understandings with Native Americans, a growing nation pushed even Westernized tribes out of their ancestral lands. Instead of a covenantal renewal, in the aftermath of the Civil War whites resisted equal rights for blacks in practices that consigned millions of freed people to continued oppression and poverty.

The civil rights movement served as an essential corrective for our past failures, but it did not fully succeed. It eventually gave rise to an identity politics that makes reconciliation impossible. Our challenge is to make good on our nation's promises through a renewed commitment to live out our principles. Only a new national covenant, one in which we acknowledge past sins and reaffirm our commitment to ensuring that we apply the true realization that "all men are created equal," will provide an alternative to the divisive politics that have become all too familiar.

3

NATIONAL COVENANT IN AMERICAN CHURCHES

Mark Tooley

To speak of or imply a national covenant with God, as Abraham Lincoln or Martin Luther King, Jr. assumed, is today so unfashionable in much of elite American Christianity as to be almost unrecognizable to many in the church—except perhaps as a gross caricature. For many Christian thought leaders today, the concept is automatically associated with idolatrous forms of civil religion, with Religious Right activism, with at least semi-Reconstructionist or Dominionist forms of ultra-Calvinism,[1] with thoughtless folk religion, or with hyper-nationalism. To these leaders, national covenant seems to equate America with Israel, which is bad enough. But even worse, and indeed blasphemous for them, is to think of the *American* church as a specially chosen people.

Some of this dismissive attitude comes from what might be called the Left side of American Christianity, especially that influenced by neo-Anabaptist thought originating with the late Mennonite theologian

---

1. These forms of Calvinism advocate a form of Protestant theocracy under biblical law including many Old Testament civil punishments. See Glenn A. Moots, "Deconstructing Christian Reconstructionism," *The Gospel Coalition*, February 13, 2018, https://www.thegospelcoalition.org/reviews/christian-reconstructionism/.

John Howard Yoder (author of the popular *The Politics of Jesus*, originally published in 1972). This attitude was popularized by Yoder's faithful disciple Stanley Hauerwas of Duke University and expanded by high-profile preachers such as Greg Boyd, Brian Zahnd, and many others today who are focused on what they call "empire."[2]

For these critics, to presume America has a relationship or covenant with God is to subordinate the gospel and church to this "empire," which they commonly equate with the United States. By their lights, God may *condemn* Babylon, but he has no interest in *redeeming* Babylon. Nor should the church, these neo-Anabaptists largely insist. God relates only to humanity writ large, and maybe peculiarly the church, along with perhaps a special covenant with the most downtrodden. But nation-states do not factor in God's economy.

Others who dismiss the idea of national covenant would be within right-of-center Christianity. They are typically Reformed but reject any hint of Reconstructionism. For many of them, covenant occurs only between God and his chosen, Israel and/or the church. Nations are under God's sovereignty, but they are not central players in God's purposes.

This discomfort with nation-states as central players in God's economy often entails critiques of nationalism, civil religion, and American exceptionalism. John Wilsey's 2015 book *American Exceptionalism and Civil Religion* is one recent thoughtful critique of American exceptionalism by a Southern Baptist academic with a Reformed perspective.[3] Other critics understandably are reacting to patriotic hoopla in non-liturgical evangelical churches and by the frequent primacy of conservative politics in white evangelicalism.

These Reformed thinkers stress ecclesiology and often have little interest in public theology that considers the nation as a corporate entity. They tend to be disturbed by conservative evangelical calls to

---

2. Mark Tooley, "Christians and American Empire," *Providence Magazine*, 24 May 2017, https://providencemag.com/2017/05/christians-and-american-empire/.

3. John Wilsey, *American Exceptionalism and Civil Religion: Reassessing the History of an Idea* (Downers Grove, IL: IVP Academic, 2015); Nathan Finn, "The False Gospel of American Exceptionalism," *The Gospel Coalition*, March 20, 2018, https://www.thegospelcoalition.org/reviews/american-exceptionalism-and-civil-religion/.

national piety that imply covenant between God and America, such as the National Day of Prayer, a tradition dominated by conservative Christians in recent decades. According to these Reformed, the oft-cited reference to 2 Chronicles 7:14 is misused: "If my people who are called by my name humble themselves, and pray and seek my face and turn from their wicked ways, then I will hear from heaven and will forgive their sin and heal their land" (ESV). These Reformed think that, whatever the intent of organizers, participants are wrongly conflating Americans with "my people."

When I have described the purpose of this book about national covenant to friends, often the response has been, "Oh, you don't intend to compare America to Israel, do you?" Or, "You don't mean to echo white Christian nationalism, do you?" They seem to imagine the flamboyant fireworks-studded July 4 patriotic worship at Pastor Robert Jeffress's First Baptist Church in Dallas. That Rev. Jeffress is a prominent supporter of President Trump and frequently appears on Fox News only exacerbates the fear of what national covenant might be about.

So today's political climate is not conducive to careful consideration of national covenant. But for just this reason, reflecting on national covenant in a thoughtful and rigorous fashion is more important than ever. The social justice and racial reconciliation that critics of national covenant (who usually don't understand it) advocate are arguably unattainable without some version of national covenant.

Critics of national covenant usually do not appreciate the history of national covenant in the American project. Or they are aware of only a negative caricature of it. Yes, the Puritan divines spoke of it, they admit. But their theocracy is not relevant for today. Yes, the founding fathers spoke of it, sometimes supported by clergy of their time. But the founders were, from the Left's perspective, self-servingly sanctifying their racist patriarchal republic. Or, from the conservative purist view, they were corrupting American religion with their deism and presumptuous identification with the ancient Hebrews.

Yes, Lincoln relied on national covenant, the national covenant skeptics concede, but he was a founding theologian of American civil religion, which perfectionists of Left and Right reject as a dilution or usurpation of authentic Christianity. There are very few defenders of civil religion in today's polarized American Christianity, where

Mainline Protestantism, civil religion's main architect, is increasingly diminished.

Critics or skeptics of national covenant usually don't realize that Martin Luther King, Jr., with much of the civil rights movement, relied on it (see chapter 6). But those who do realize this often dismiss it by saying that King and his allies employed it cynically—only when they had to appeal to white audiences. Others would say King was relying on outdated rhetorical tools from a now-discredited Christendom. Those tools are no longer effective or even relevant in an ostensibly post-Christian age.

These same critics are typically unaware that the national covenant has been a theme for Christian political witness throughout America's history and has suffused nearly all of America's great reform movements, from abolitionism through the preachers of the Social Gospel and liberal Protestant political activists in the twentieth century. Methodist Bishop Matthew Simpson as an early herald of the Social Gospel pronounced during the Civil War that as America was the "great emigrant depot of the world," amid Europe's strife, "God could not do without America," and hence the Confederacy was doomed to defeat because, "This country could not be divided."[4]

That God "could not do without America" and was in continual relationship with it motivated women suffragists, labor reformers, League of Nation supporters, Prohibitionists, New Dealers, anti-Fascists, anti-Communists, advocates for the United Nations, and civil rights activists. All struggled to get America right with God so that America could be a lamp to the nations. Woodrow Wilson, the progressive Presbyterian, spoke of America as the suffering servant to the world. In his 1919 Pueblo, Colorado speech for the League of Nations, he recalled that mothers who had lost boys in World War I tearfully called divine blessing upon him. They did so because "their sons saved the liberty of the world" and were "crusaders" whose "transcendent achievement has made all the world believe in America as it believes in no other nation organized in the modern world."[5]

---

4. Matthew Simpson, "The National Conflict: Eloquent Address by Bishop Simpson at the Academy of Music," *New York Times*, November 4, 1864, 8.

5. Woodrow Wilson, "President Woodrow Wilson's Address in Favour of the League of Nations, 25 September 1919," https://www.firstworldwar.com, https://www.firstworldwar.com/source/wilsonspeech_league.htm.

God's purpose for America undergirded the Great Society, as Lyndon Johnson, under the Social Gospel's influence, spoke in biblical terms about proper use of America's wealth, with the implied threat of divine judgment if America was selfish and uncaring toward the needy. "So the ultimate test of our beloved America is the larger purpose to which we turn our prosperity," he warned. "We must first turn it toward relief of the oppressed, the underprivileged, and the helpless. We must, in the words of the Bible, 'Learn to do well, seek judgment, relieve the oppressed, judge the fatherless, plead for the widow'" (Isa. 1:17).[6]

Johnson was brought down politically by anti-Vietnam War protesters, many of them clergy and religious activists, who themselves operated from premises of national covenant in their war opposition. In a 1968 *Christian Century* column, Edward Fiske spoke for a growing number of increasingly radicalized Mainline Protestant clergy when he pronounced, "A growing consensus among mature, morally sensitive people is that the spiritual integrity of the United States, rooted as it is in the Judeo-Christian tradition, cannot be secured by our present policy in Vietnam."[7] Clergy and church activists later cited similar arguments when calling for President Richard Nixon's resignation during Watergate.

Use of the national covenant so relatively recently is hard for most Christians today to imagine because our era's liberal activists routinely denounce the idea. But the original Social Gospelers saw their exertions as getting America right with God and brightening America's calling to be a light unto the nations. Even if the loftier version of national covenant was later obscured by the much less America-friendly Religious Left of the late twentieth century, it was still unconsciously operating from at least the vapors of the premise.

Ironically, today's religious and evangelical Left firmly rejects national covenant, but its leaders speak and act as though America

---

6. Lyndon B. Johnson, "Remarks at a Fundraising Dinner in Detroit," June 26, 1964, The American Presidency Project, https://www.presidency.ucsb.edu/node/239191.

7. Edward B. Fiske, "Religion; The Clergy on Vietnam," *New York Times*, January 7, 1968, E9, https://timesmachine.nytimes.com/timesmachine/1968/01/07/110088825.html?pageNumber=190.

is under divine judgment. When they adopt this posture, they are buying into the vision of national covenant without knowing it. They imagine a national judgment but seem unable to conceive of national redemption.

Today's more conservative skeptics of national covenant are more consistent in their minimization of America in God's focus. But their witness for social righteousness is shackled to the extent that they cite only the utility of the church's proclamation of, and model for, God's perfect kingdom. The church's proclamation is incomplete if it doesn't seek to reshape all society toward divine justice and love, which by necessity entails identifying providential purpose in polities outside the church.

There is another source of resistance in American Christianity toward national covenant. Covenant is associated most especially with Calvinism. Non-Calvinists are often deeply suspicious of it or at least not entirely comfortable with it. Calvin of course constructed a systematic system of lay governance in Geneva, in which church-approved saints ruled.[8] Knox sought the same in Scotland, as did the Puritans in New England. Lincoln was not theocratic but was deeply shaped by the Calvinism of his youth and of the Presbyterian clergy who preached to him in later life.[9]

Calvinist political theology was insightful about national covenant partly because of its belief that even in a Calvinist society, only a minority are truly redeemed. So language aimed at wider society needed to be rooted in widely accessible common grace, often more tied to the Hebrews Scriptures than to the Gospels. American national covenant rhetoric, though often Calvinist-birthed, has been remarkably ecumenical and ultimately even interfaith, adaptable to a religiously diversifying America.

Non-Calvinist Christians are often slow to understand the wide ecumenical and interfaith utility of national covenant. And they often fail to fully appreciate that all branches of traditional Christianity

---

8. W. Stanford Reid, "John Calvin: One of the Fathers of Modern Democracy," *Christian History* 12 (1986), https://christianhistoryinstitute.org/magazine/article/calvin-father-of-modern-democracy/.

9. On Lincoln's religion, see Allen Guelzo, *Redeemer President* (Grand Rapids: Eerdmans, 2002).

have also believed that nations, both biblical and postbiblical, are under divine judgment and mercy. In his sermon "National Sins and Miseries," the supremely non-Calvinist John Wesley explicitly warned of divine wrath upon Britain and counseled how Britain might escape God's judgment by national repentance.[10] Wesley did not advocate, much less construct, a Calvinist-style theocracy. But he did operate within a national state church and sought spiritually to renew it and society through the proliferation of local Methodist societies. This incremental path to societal godliness would bring the nation into a more correct relationship with God, they hoped, even if Wesley and Methodists did not typically call this national covenant.

This Methodist notion of national relationship with God was influential in America throughout the nineteenth century. It did not contradict but was a complement to the Calvinist view of social covenant. Lincoln's Presbyterian pastor during his presidency, Phineas Gurley, reinforced Lincoln's concept of national covenant. But the other side of this reinforcement was Lincoln's friend and political counselor Methodist Bishop Matthew Simpson, who was far more politically outspoken than Gurley. While Calvinists may have offered the cerebral concept of national covenant to Lincoln and his times, the more heart-focused idea of national relationship with God came from the heart-warmed Methodists like Simpson. They too saw America as a nation choosing to be reprobate or, by divine grace, repentant and holy.[11]

Simpson, like Lincoln, believed America's relationship with God required ending slavery. He also agreed that America was the "almost chosen" nation perhaps even more zealously than Lincoln. Simpson was more optimistic than Lincoln and most orthodox Calvinists about America's ability to become righteous.[12] Methodism stressed the possibility of perfection through sanctification in the individual

---

10. John Wesley, "National Sins and Miseries," 12 November 1775, ChurchAges.net, http://churchages.net/en/sermon/wesley/national-sins-and-miseries.

11. John H. Wigger, *Taking Heaven by Storm: Methodism and the Rise of Popular Christianity in America* (Champagne: University of Illinois Press, 2001).

12. W. W. Sweet, "Bishop Matthew Simpson and the Funeral of Abraham Lincoln," *Journal of the Illinois State Historical Society* (April 1, 1914), https://archive.org/stream/jstor-40193943/40193943_djvu.txt.

believer. It was not a long stretch to imagine that some form of at least approximate perfection could be achieved by whole societies thru sufficient spiritual and moral exertion. Simpson's daughters bequeathed their inheritance to Methodism's temperance board, which itself gave America Prohibition as the supreme project of making America righteous. Lincoln was himself abstinent, but his dark realism almost certainly would have disapproved of utopian schemes like Prohibition.

Prohibition was the transition from nineteenth-century Protestant revivalist moralism to the Social Gospel of the twentieth century. It is no coincidence that the social creed adopted by the Methodist Episcopal Church and the Federal Council of Churches in 1908 coincides with the creation of the Methodist Board of Temperance and Prohibition, founded that same year as the architect of Prohibition. Theological modernism was already firmly rooted in Mainline Protestant seminaries, but Prohibition united modernists and traditionalists, who both believed in national covenant.

Prohibition failed, but from it sprang countless liberal Protestant crusades to purify America through political action. Theological modernists no longer believed that a personal deity would directly vent his wrath on a sinful nation. But they did believe that injustice in America placed the nation at odds with progressive history and other cosmic forces for justice. Their version of providence was impersonal.

Martin Luther King, Jr. in his appropriation of national covenant was an heir both to the Social Gospel and of course to the black church tradition, which had its own robust version of national covenant. In his July 4, 1965 sermon at Ebenezer Baptist Church in Atlanta, King cited the Declaration of Independence's affirmation of human equality as a judgment by which God would judge America:

> But now more than ever before, America is challenged to realize its dream, for the shape of the world today does not permit our nation the luxury of an anemic democracy. And the price that America must pay for the continued oppression of the Negro and other minority groups is the price of its own destruction.

For the hour is late. And the clock of destiny is ticking out. We must act now before it is too late.[13]

Like Thomas Jefferson, whose words of human equality King quoted in his 1963 "I Have a Dream Speech" at the Lincoln Memorial, King was a theological modernist who did not necessarily believe in Christian creed but did believe in biblical justice and providence. This providential notion of history assumed that the Creator presided over the affairs of men and nations. Unitarians of early America, like Jefferson, and mid-twentieth-century theological liberals, like King, believed in a form of providence that rewards and punishes both men and nations. King would have agreed with Jefferson who, when contemplating the simmering injustice of slavery in 1791 in his *Notes on the State of Virginia*, did not sound like a deist when he warned of divine judgment.[14]

> And can the liberties of a nation be thought secure when we have removed their only firm basis, a conviction in the minds of the people that these liberties are of the gift of God? That they are not to be violated but with his wrath? Indeed I tremble for my country when I reflect that God is just: that his justice cannot sleep for ever: that considering numbers, nature and natural means only, a revolution of the wheel of fortune, an exchange of situation, is among possible events: that it may become probable by supernatural interference! The Almighty has no attribute which can take side with us in such a contest.[15]

---

13. Martin Luther King, Jr., "'The American Dream,' sermon delivered at Ebenezer Baptist Church," July 4, 1965, The Martin Luther King, Jr. Research and Education Institute, Stanford University, https://kinginstitute.stanford.edu/king-papers/documents/american-dream-sermon-delivered-ebenezer-baptist-church.

14. Yet some heterodox religious believers like Jefferson did believe in occasional providence, and most of the other founding fathers believed God intervened in history at the American founding. See Gerald McDermott, *Jonathan Edwards Confronts the Gods: Christian Theology, Enlightenment Religion, and Non-Christian Faiths* (New York: Oxford University Press, 2000), 17–33.

15. Thomas Jefferson, *Notes on the State of Virginia, Query XVIII: Manners*, 1781, https://teachingamericanhistory.org/library/document/notes-on-the-state-of-virginia-query-xviii-manners/.

Unlike Jefferson, who was an Anglican who privately identified with Unitarian rejection of the Trinity, King's theology was Trinitarian. But his use of the national covenant was similar to Jefferson's. King might have also been the last major liberal Protestant voice who confronted America's sins with the language of national covenant. The Vietnam War, reinforced by theological revolutions and the start of Mainline Protestantism's implosion, helped ensure the demise of national covenant as a widely employed national tool. Liberal Protestantism thereafter saw America deserving doom but was unsure about the desirability of redemption. National covenant was by the late 1970s fully ceded to the rising Religious Right, which saw America as almost chosen, but also wicked and in danger of divine wrath thanks to abortion, pornography, the end of organized school prayer, and the emerging embrace of gay rights.

The Religious Right, through promotions like the National Day of Prayer, frequently cited the promise of 2 Chronicles 7:14: "If my people, which are called by my name, shall humble themselves, and pray, and seek my face, and turn from their wicked ways; then will I hear from heaven, and will forgive their sin, and will heal their land" (KJV). If conservative evangelicals prayed this prayer, it was surmised, God might have mercy on all America, as he had offered to spare Sodom and Gomorrah for only a few righteous found in those wicked cities (Gen. 18:22–33).

Language of national covenant has remained embedded in American civil religion. Modern presidents and other politicians cite the happy side of it, God's blessing, while largely ignoring the uncomfortable side of divine judgment for national sin. Ronald Reagan's 1989 farewell address cheerfully spoke of America as a "tall, proud city built on rocks stronger than oceans, windswept, God-blessed, and teeming with people of all kinds living in harmony and peace."[16] Lincoln's suggestion that the Civil War was divine punishment on America for slavery would not be acceptable to many today:

> If God wills that it continue until all the wealth piled by the bondsman's two hundred and fifty years of unrequited toil shall be sunk, and until every drop of blood drawn with the lash shall

---

16. Ronald Reagan, "Farewell Address to the Nation," January 11, 1989, https://www.reaganfoundation.org/media/128652/farewell.pdf.

be paid by another drawn with the sword, as was said three thousand years ago, so still it must be said "the judgments of the Lord are true and righteous altogether."[17]

After the 9/11 terror attacks, Religious Right leaders Jerry Falwell, Sr. and Pat Robertson were widely reviled for suggesting the calamity was God's judgment on America for abortion and homosexuality.[18] Their smiles and chuckles during the televised exchange, swiftly disavowed by the White House of President George W. Bush, did not enhance their message. Today's common avoidance of national sin as a major divine concern largely echoes many contemporary evangelical churches which, though theoretically orthodox, also prefer to avoid themes of divine judgment, whether for persons or nations.

Despite the avoidance of conversation about national sin, America has unconsciously retained the guilt and judgment side of national covenant, or at least a parody of it. Violators of political correctness are routinely shamed and forced to recant. Our nation is routinely excoriated by academic and media elites for alleged racism, homophobia, and imperialism. But for these critics there is no atonement, since there is no personal deity in the new popular religion of secular culture—only impersonal forces of progressive history that judge and condemn but never forgive.

Any return to national covenant will require renewed appreciation of this biblical tradition by America's churches. Christians who believe in the American project will have to rediscover the tradition, both in American and in universal church history. This challenge is difficult because most American non-denominational Christians are untutored in church history. They need to rediscover a deity who offers both judgment and mercy. Liberal Christians tend to prefer only judgment for the nation, even as they prefer only mercy for individuals. Conservative Christians need to learn how to articulate

---

17. Abraham Lincoln, "Second Inaugural Address," March 4, 1865, https://en.wikipedia.org/wiki/Abraham_Lincoln%27s_second_inaugural_address.

18. Laurie Goodstein, "Falwell: blame abortionists, feminists and gays," *The Guardian*, September 19, 2001, https://www.theguardian.com/world/2001/sep/19/september11.usa9.

divine judgment for America more comprehensively and not just over culture war hot buttons, important though they are.

No less importantly, Christian elites both liberal and conservative will need to rediscover and embrace the nation as providential tool. This challenge too will be hard. But both conservative and liberal Christians claim to want versions of righteous societies where God's justice is sought. Yet such societies cannot be sought if the nation itself is not recognized, loved, served, prayed for, honored, and warned when necessary with tearful pleas.

As Abraham appealed to God for mercy toward the wicked cities on the plain and Jonah implored Nineveh to repent, so American Christians will need to move beyond their individualism to seek an America more conscious of a watchful providence. Christians of all places cannot fully serve God and fully appreciate His sovereignty—not to mention assurance of his love—unless they seek his purposes for their nation. This concern for society under God is traditionally described as a national covenant. It is this concept—amply demonstrated in both Scripture and the Christian tradition (as earlier chapters have shown)—that can offer grounds for hope, unity, and social reconciliation in a religiously diverse society comprised of sinners and saints.

Rediscovery of Lincoln's and King's concept of national covenant, with its focus on societal justice and love, could be a powerful solvent for America's racial pains. Contemporary America is awash in racial grievance, anguish, and guilt—whose roots are often justified by history but for which no healing solutions are typically offered. Historic black churches have been legendary in their patience and forgiveness. White churches, if late, have often been prolific with apologies. Black and white Christians often have focused on admirable intra-church racial reconciliation, which can be a model for wider society.

But if Christians care about the public good, they can achieve a broader harmony with the tools of national covenant. God forgives individuals, yes. But he also redeems nations, even when guilty of racial injustice, by his infinite mercy. Here is truly good news for all—but news that contemporary churches have been oddly reluctant to admit.

4

Martin Luther King, Jr. and the National Covenant

James M. Patterson

Dr. Martin Luther King, Jr. preached a national covenant for America, but one will search in vain through his public speeches and sermons to find any extended discussion of the word "covenant." One has to go back to 1948. That year, while a student at Crozer Theological Seminary and seven years before King would lead the Montgomery bus boycott, he wrote a paper on the relationship between the old covenant and the new covenant in the book of Jeremiah. The old covenant was written on stone and required no personal conversion but only outward obedience. Without conversion, King argued that the old covenant had become "a snare and a delusion" and filled the leaders of Israel with "foolish presumption" of their righteousness.[1] Jeremiah prophesied that God would write the new covenant "in their inward parts, and ... in their hearts" (Jer. 31:33 KJV). King concluded:

> The law written in the heart will become an inseparable part of man's moral being. Principle would take the place of external

---

1. Martin Luther King, Jr., *The Papers of Martin Luther King, Jr., Volume I: Called to Serve, January 1929—June 1951*, ed. Clayborne Carson, Ralph E. Luker, and Penny A. Russell (Berkley: University of California Press, 1992), 184.

> ordinances. Such principles as truth, and justice, and purity, love to God and love to man, would be enshrined in the hearts of men.... It is this inwardness of true religion which causes men to do the will of God spontaneously from inward inclination rather than from commands of an external law.[2]

In other words, the new covenant started with personal conversion and not with following the rules. No wonder King broke some rules to win hearts.

When King applied this thinking about covenant to his reflections on America, he started with his understanding of the new covenant of the gospel, to love God and one's neighbor.[3] One has to do both, but loving God comes first. God always returns the love one shows him with a love that infinitely exceeds one's own. God's love also furnishes persons with the ability to love their enemies, and if persons love their enemies as God commanded, then they might be open to that same conversion and become a fellow neighbor sharing in God's love.[4] This is where King's version of the national covenant began: For persons to love God and each other this way forms what King called "the Beloved Community." A Beloved Community has members who know the covenant and will write it on stone, but they first and foremost commit in their hearts to live it out in their lives. In sum, King understood the new covenant to be a spontaneous outpouring of love by God into the human heart and out of one's heart into the hearts of one's neighbors. Therefore when King referred to "love," he was referring to the covenant generally. When he called for Americans to love one another, he was calling them to keep their covenant with God.

---

2. King, *Papers*, 185.

3. Martin Luther King, Jr., "Love, Law, and Civil Disobedience," in *A Testament of Hope: The Essential Writings and Speeches of Martin Luther King, Jr.*, ed. James M. Washington (San Francisco: HarperSanFrancisco, 1991), 47. I say "his understanding" because many scholars, both Jewish and Christian have pointed out that loving God and neighbor is taught in the Old Testament, not only the New (Lev. 19:18; Deut. 6:4–9).

4. Martin Luther King, Jr., "Loving Your Enemies," in *Strength to Love* (1963; repr., Minneapolis: Fortress, 2010), 43–52.

This chapter will examine King's Christian covenant for America in the following steps: first by defining what King meant by "love," then by describing the covenant theology grounding the "Beloved Community," and finally by illustrating how King applied the covenant to voters, clergy, and elected officials.

This interpretation of King is currently under contention, as recent scholars have sought either to diminish or outright ignore the centrality of King's Christian message.[5] One such scholar has gone so far as to recommend a "counterfeit" King who lacks the Christian message but nonetheless radically opposed white supremacy and corporate capitalism.[6] Others have sought to reduce King's message to merely a Christian call for color blindness in American laws.[7] These views of King roughly align with the current American ideological map of the Left wanting King's activism but not his faith and the Right wanting King's faith but not the full force of his activism. The historical King does not fit well with either.[8] King called himself above all a "minister of the Gospel," and he preached sermons tied to the long tradition of black Baptist preachers.[9] However, just because King was a Christian does not mean that he was economically conservative. King advocated for reparations for slavery, federal redistribution programs, and the integration of trade unions to increase their power against large corporations. Rather than force King to fit ideological preconceptions, one should engage him as a minister of the gospel and a nonviolent activist against racial segregation.

---

5. George Shulman, *American Prophecy: Race and Redemption in American Political Culture* (Minneapolis: University of Minnesota Press, 2008).

6. Paul C. Taylor, "Moral Perfectionism," in *To Shape a New World: Essays on the Political Philosophy of Martin Luther King, Jr.*, ed. Tommie Shelby and Brandon M. Terry (Cambridge: Belknap, 2018), 35–57.

7. Clarence B. Jones and Joel Engel, *What Would Martin Say* (New York: HarperCollins, 2008).

8. James M. Patterson, "The Vanished World of Martin Luther King," *Law & Liberty*, January 16, 2017, https://www.lawliberty.org/2017/01/16/the-vanished-world-of-martin-luther-king/.

9. Martin Luther King, Jr., "Why Jesus Called a Man a Fool," in *A Knock at Midnight: Inspiration from the Great Sermons of Reverend Martin Luther King, Jr.* (New York: Hachette, 1998), Kindle, 1,813–2,049, quote at 1,826.

The Origins of King's "Beloved Community"

Among King's professors at Boston University (BU) during his PhD studies (1951–1955) were Edgar S. Brightman and L. Harold DeWolf, who were proponents of "personalist" theology. Personalism refers to the belief that God is "conscious personality" known to us as "both the supreme value and the supreme reality in the universe."[10] Persons come to know God from the mutual love between persons and the Supreme Personality as well as through reason, which reveals to us the supreme reality of God through his creation. These supreme values are what save human persons and enable them to live together in communities. Patrick Parr notes that this view of God deeply impressed King, but he objected that personalism seems unable to account for the problem of evil.[11]

While at BU, King also studied the liberal Protestant idealism of Walter Rauschenbusch.[12] Rauschenbusch was a central figure in the Social Gospel movement that swept through white Mainline Protestantism at the turn of the century. He argued that industrialization introduced great social ills that required the church to organize social action. Social Gospel leaders were part of the broader progressive movement that sought not merely to organize charitable relief for the poor but also to use state power to regulate and redistribute economic goods. The relative failure of these efforts, coupled with the First World War, the Great Depression, and the failure of Prohibition, had done much to discredit the Social Gospel by the late 1940s and early 1950s, when King was moving through Crozer and BU. Yet King sought to renew these efforts, even if they were chastened by the critiques of Reinhold Niebuhr.[13] Niebuhr rejected

---

10. Patrick Parr, *The Seminarian: Martin Luther King, Jr. Comes of Age* (Chicago: Lawrence Hill, 2018), 202. Parr is summarizing Brightman and secondary work in this quotation. See also Rufus Burrow, Jr., *God and Human Dignity: The Personalism, Theology, and Ethics of Martin Luther King, Jr.* (South Bend: University of Notre Dame Press, 2006), 69–87.

11. Parr, *Seminarian*, 203.

12. Martin Luther King, Jr., *Stride Toward Freedom: The Montgomery Story* (1958; repr., Boston: Beacon, 2010), 78; Burrow, *God and Human Dignity*, 34–67.

13. Parr, *Seminarian*, 200–201; Burrow, *God and Human Dignity*, 168; King wrote about the influence of Niebuhr in "Pilgrimage to Nonviolence," *The*

the idealism of the Social Gospel in favor of "Christian realism" that took seriously the problem of evil as a permanent feature of human life. In *Moral Man and Immoral Society*, Niebuhr argues that evil is more of a problem for large groups of people than for an individual, an observation King's experiences would confirm.[14] King came to admire Niebuhr's critique of the Social Gospel, affirming that it had "refuted the false optimism characteristic of a great segment of Protestant liberalism."[15] King, however, insisted that Niebuhr misunderstood the full strength of nonviolence. King explained:

> True pacifism is not unrealistic submission to evil power, as Niebuhr contends. It is rather a courageous confrontation of evil by the power of love, in the faith that it is better to be the recipient of violence than the inflicter [sic] of it, since the latter only multiplies the existence of violence and bitterness in the universe, while the former may develop a sense of shame in the opponent, and thereby bring about a transformation and a change of heart.[16]

Other black pastors including King's own father had embraced Rauschenbusch before, but King added Niebuhr's realism that urged meeting political power with other kinds of power, even if nonviolent.[17]

Christian Century, April 13, 1960, https://www.christiancentury.org/article/pilgrimage-nonviolence.

14. Reinhold Niebuhr, *Moral Man and Immoral Society: A Study in Ethics and Politics*, 2nd ed. (1932; repr., Louisville: Westminster John Knox, 2013).

15. King, *Stride Toward Freedom*, 86–87.

16. King, *Stride Toward Freedom*, 86. King studied Niebuhr in several of his Boston University courses and developed this critique of Niebuhr during his time there. See Martin Luther King, Jr., "The Theology of Reinhold Niebuhr," in *The Papers of Martin Luther King, Jr., Volume II: Rediscovering Precious Values, July 1951–November 1955*, ed. Clayborne Carson, Ralph Luker, Penny A. Russell, and Peter Holloran (Berkeley: University of California Press, 1994) 269–79.

17. Burrow, *God and Human Dignity*, 33–67; Gary J. Dorrien, *Breaking White Supremacy: Martin Luther King, Jr. and the Black Social Gospel* (New Haven: Yale University Press, 2018).

Love, the Church, and the Covenant

King spent his entire public ministry attempting to navigate between Social Gospel utopianism and Niebuhrian pessimism. At the core of that effort was King's view of love. "Love" for King had three definitions corresponding to the three classical Greek words: *eros*, *phileo*, and *agape*.[18] *Eros* refers to physical love between spouses. *Phileo* refers to love among friends. *Agape* is the sacrificial love that God has for humanity as revealed in Scripture and manifested by Christ's passion at Calvary. Of the three, *agape* is the love that serves as the foundation for America. Only the sacrificial love one must have for one's enemies can close the fissure that divides one from God and neighbors from each other. To love with *agape* means enduring insults, violence, and even death at the hands of one's enemies.[19]

No laws, customs, or even physical restraint can provoke the true conversion of an enemy to a friend. The enemy would at best be like the Israelite leaders with their "foolish presumption" that they fulfilled their obligations by merely following the law. But for America to fulfill its covenantal calling, King sought the inward conversion of an enemy to a friend. He saw legal changes and constitutional rulings not as causes for political reform but as effects. Only when enemies became friends did they change the laws to confirm in stone what already exists in their hearts. As King put it, "But be ye assured that we will wear you down by our capacity to suffer. One day we shall win freedom, but not only for ourselves. We shall so appeal to your heart and conscience that we shall win *you* in the process, and our victory will be a double victory."[20] After winning the hearts of so

---

18. Martin Luther King, Jr., "An Experiment in Love," 16–20; "Love, Law and Civil Disobedience," 46–47; and "Facing the Challenge of a New Age," in *Testament of Hope*, 140–41. For a more detailed examination of *agape* as King's political foundation for America, see James M. Patterson, *Religion in the Public Square: Sheen, King, Falwell* (Philadelphia: University of Pennsylvania Press, 2019), 64–96.

19. King drew from theologians Paul Tillich, Anders Nygren, George Davis, L. Harold DeWolf, Paul Ramsey, and Howard Thurman in his treatment of *agape*. See John J. Ansbro, *Martin Luther King Jr.: Nonviolent Strategies and Tactics for Social Change* (1892; repr., Lanham: Madison, 2000), 8–29.

20. King, "Loving Your Enemies," *Strength to Love*, 51.

many enemies, King prophesied the transformation of America into "the empire of Jesus, built solidly and majestically on the foundation of love."[21]

The laws still had to change, for King had internalized the Niebuhrian critique of the Social Gospel and so understood that those who meet hate with love could not suffer forever and would eventually succumb to "bitterness."[22] The human person is imperfect, and the toil of *agape* is too much for many to take. Besides, there are always those who refuse to give up their hate, and the law needs to protect the innocent from their depredations. King's recognition of the problem of bitterness was the result of his own experience and proved to be among his most prophetic observations.

King tied the centrality of *agape* to the broader religious consensus in the United States. In his view, *agape* as a foundation began with the Hebrew prophets and found its fullness in Christian testimony. This common bond ensured that Jews and Christians, as well as Protestants and Catholics, could agree on *agape* as the foundational principle of America. King referred to this consensus as the "Hebraic-Christian heritage" or "Hebraic-Christian tradition."[23] This shared *agape* tradition meant that the task of the civil rights movement was to *remind* Catholics, Protestants, and Jews of their own beliefs and encourage them to bring them to public life. In his 1957 speech "Give Us the Ballot," King preached, "We must meet hate with love. We must meet physical force with soul force. There is still a voice crying out through the vista of time, saying: 'Love your enemies, bless them that curse you, and pray for them that despitefully use you.'"[24] Later in the speech, King tied the loving sacrifices of his activists to the Hebraic-Christian faith in a loving God:

---

21. King, "Loving Your Enemies," in *Strength to Love*, 51.

22. King, "Suffering and Faith," 41–42; and "The Current Crisis in Race Relations," in *Testament of Hope*, 87.

23. Martin Luther King, Jr., "'Give Us the Ballot,' Address Delivered at the Prayer Pilgrimage for Freedom," in *The Papers of Martin Luther King Jr., Volume IV: Symbol of the Movement, January 1957–December 1958*, ed. Clayborne Carson et al. (Berkeley: University of California Press, 2000), 214.

24. King, "Give Us the Ballot," 213.

> Let us realize that as we struggle for justice and freedom, we have cosmic companionship. This is the long faith of the Hebraic-Christian tradition: that God is not some Aristotelian "unmoved mover" who merely contemplates upon Himself. He is not merely a self-knowing God, but an other-loving God forever working through history for the establishment of His kingdom.[25]

King reminded audiences that Thomas Jefferson, despite living in "an age amazingly adjusted to slavery[,] could cry out in words lifted to cosmic proportions, 'All men are created equal, and are endowed by their creator with certain unalienable rights, that among these are Life, Liberty and the persuit [sic] of Happiness.'"[26] He later recalled that Jefferson owned slaves and how one among them had to purchase her own emancipation, along with nineteen others, with her life savings.[27] By King's analysis, Jefferson "was a child of his culture who had been influenced by the pseudoscientific and philosophical thought that rationalized slavery." King saw Jefferson's perspective in "his *Notes on Virginia*, [where he] portrayed the Negro as inferior to the white man in his endowments of body, mind and imagination."[28] King had the same view of Abraham Lincoln whose Emancipation Proclamation confirmed the truth of Jefferson's words

---

25. King, "Give Us the Ballot," 214.

26. Martin Luther King, Jr., "'The Role of the Church in Facing the Nation's Chief Moral Dilemma,' Address Delivered on 25 April 1957 at the Conference on Christian Faith and Human Relations in Nashville," in *The Papers of Martin Luther King, Jr., Volume IV*, 190. See also King, "The Power of Nonviolence," in *Testament of Hope*, 14–15; King, "'A Look to the Future,' Address Delivered at Highlander Folk School's Twenty-Fifth Anniversary Meeting," in *The Papers of Martin Luther King Jr., Volume IV*, 276. King frequently used the "maladjusted" set piece in his speaking and writing to join Jewish and Christian figures who were maladjusted to the sins of the world and to join them to Jefferson and Lincoln as inheritors of the Hebraic-Christian tradition as evinced by their maladjustment to American slavery.

27. Martin Luther King, Jr., *Why We Can't Wait* (1963; repr., New York: Signet Classics, 2000), 141.

28. Martin Luther King, Jr., *Where Do We Go from Here: Chaos or Community?* (1967; repr. Boston: Beacon, 2010), 80–81.

in the Declaration. Like Jefferson, King, explained, Lincoln also felt the contradictions on matters of race:

> A civil war raged within Lincoln's own soul, a tension between the Dr. Jekyll of freedom and the Mr. Hyde of slavery.... Morally, Lincoln was for black emancipation, but emotionally, like most of his white contemporaries, he was for a long time unable to act in accordance with his conscience.... He saw that the nation could not survive half slave and half free; and he said, "If we could first know where we are and whither we are tending, we could better judge what to do and how to do it." Fortunately for the nation, he finally came to see "whither we were tending."[29]

King recounted how Lincoln sought to change the heart of his enemy, Edwin McMasters Stanton, who became one of the most important members of Lincoln's cabinet. In King's view, Stanton gave the most moving tribute to Lincoln after his death.[30] Jefferson and Lincoln provided examples of imperfect statesmen who nonetheless acted with sacrificial love and thereby moved America ever closer to racial justice.

Because *agape* is America's foundation, American citizens have to live with one another in a Beloved Community—which is King's rendition of what this book is calling a national covenant. The Beloved Community is a theological concept King learned from the Boston personalists during his time at BU.[31] King defined the "Beloved Community" in terms of the sacrifices activists made to usher it in:

> [Noncooperation and boycotts] are not ends themselves; they are merely means to awaken a sense of moral shame in the opponent. The end is redemption and reconciliation. The aftermath

---

29. King, *Where Do We Go from Here*, 82–83.

30. King, "Loving Your Enemies," in *Strength to Love*, 48–49.

31. Burrow, *God and Human Dignity*, 155–79. See also Kenneth L. Smith and Ira G. Zepp Jr., *Search for the Beloved Community: The Thinking of Martin Luther King, Jr.* (Valley Forge: Judson, 1974); Charles Marsh, *The Beloved Community: How Faith Shapes Social Justice, from the Civil Rights Movement to Today* (New York: Basic Books, 2005).

of nonviolence is the creation of the beloved community, while the aftermath of violence is tragic bitterness.[32]

Nonviolent direct action ushered in the Beloved Community, which in turn ushered in racial redemption and reconciliation. This held out the promise that God might grant "the salvation of our nation and the salvation of mankind."[33]

At the heart of King's Beloved Community was the Christian church.[34] King said that in each church there are worshipers who experience God's love, which they then bring to each other and to the world outside. God provides them the love they need to experience not only salvation but also to serve their community. If a woman from this church comes to work on Monday, the love she brings to her work bears witness to the gospel, and this in turn exposes those she serves to the love of God. Consequently, the daily encounters of loving persons loving each other yield a community founded in that love—the Beloved Community. Because the church is at the center of the Beloved Community, King spent much of his time criticizing the church, especially the majority white churches who wanted to keep their congregations racially segregated. Speaking as though he were St. Paul, King said, "Americans, I must remind you, as I have told so many others, that the church is the Body of Christ. When the church is true to its nature, it knows neither division nor disunity.... [So] how can segregation exist in the true Body of Christ?"[35] King continued, "I understand that there are Christians among you who try to find biblical bases to justify segregation and argue that the Negro is inferior by nature. Oh, my friends, this is blasphemy and against everything that the Christian religion stands for."[36]

For all the Social Gospel preaching and activism, King never forgot the Niebuhrian critique. The Southern Christian Leadership

---

32. King, "Nonviolence and Racial Justice," in *Testament of Hope*, 8.

33. King, *Strength to Love*, 50.

34. Patterson, *Religion in the Public Square*, 81–82. See also Lewis V. Baldwin, *The Voice of Conscience: The Church in the Mind of Martin Luther King, Jr.* (New York: Oxford University Press, 2010).

35. King, "Paul's Letter to American Christians," in *Strength to Love*, 148, 149.

36. King, "Paul's Letter to American Christians," 149.

Conference (SCLC) signs at civil rights marches read, "Freedom Now!" and King famously spoke of the "fierce urgency of now."[37] On the margins of the civil rights movement were more radical elements, both secular and Nation of Islam activists who saw racial reconciliation as impossible and even undesirable. These groups abandoned love out of frustration with the slowness of political change and instead, according to King, embraced "bitterness." King singled out Elijah Muhammad, founder of the Nation of Islam, as the ultimate future for civil rights activism if white Americans did not repent of segregation, embrace African Americans as brothers and sisters, and together demand racial integration. In his own words, King said, "[The Nation of Islam] movement is nourished by the contemporary frustration over the continued existence of racial discrimination. It is made up of people who have lost faith in America, who have absolutely repudiated Christianity, and who have concluded that the white man is an incurable 'devil.'"[38] King cautioned, "I am further convinced that if our white brothers dismiss us as 'rabble-rousers' and 'outside agitators,' those of us who are working through the channels of nonviolent direct action, and refuse to support our nonviolent efforts, millions of Negroes, out of frustration and despair, will seek solace and security in black nationalist ideologies."[39] King was right to be worried.

The Beloved Community in Action

The Beloved Community requires those within it to dedicate themselves to the spiritual work of the church as well as the need for justice in places that Beloved Community has not reached. On December 1, 1955, Rosa Parks refused to leave a "whites only" seat on a bus in Montgomery, Alabama, leading to her arrest. Upon hearing the news, local church leaders selected King to lead the Montgomery bus boycott, with King and others quickly forming the Montgomery Improvement Association (MIA). King was a young man when he assumed the

---

37. King, "I Have a Dream," in *Testament of Hope*, 218.
38. King, "Letter from Birmingham City Jail," in *Testament of Hope*, 296–97.
39. King, "Letter from Birmingham City Jail," 297.

mantle of leadership and gave the now legendary "Address to the First Montgomery Mass Meeting at Holt Street Baptist Church."[40]

Leading this organization required extraordinary skills. Often forgotten is that this coalition of rival black churches contained pastors and congregations that did not get along with each other. The Beloved Community was hard to preserve amid all the egos, class tensions, and long memories shared among the very people seeking to overthrow white supremacy in their city. In the abstract, the Beloved Community sounded idyllic, but King knew better than anyone that the Beloved Community meant discipline, prayer, and frequent wrestling with Scripture.

After Montgomery integrated its bus system, King sought to export the MIA model of nonviolent direct action to other cities, turning the MIA into the SCLC. In places such as Albany, St. Augustine, and—most famously—Birmingham, King sought out church leaders as the starting point for developing the Beloved Community. In each city, King and his SCLC associates trained activists in nonviolent direct action. These activists were told they could not run away or fight back when marching, and that they would bear witness to God's love by refusing to return violence with violence. Only after the SCLC had networked with churches, trained their congregations, and organized the nonviolent direct action did King ask activists to sign a covenant. After praying, worshiping, singing, and reading Scripture, they signed statements pledging they would live by gospel principles of nonviolent direct action for the sake of racial justice. Only then were they permitted to march into the streets to face insults, high pressure water hoses, police dogs, rocks, gun shots, and church bombings. Here is the pledge that activists took before their march on Birmingham:

> I hereby pledge myself—my person and body—to the nonviolent movement. Therefore I will keep the following ten commandments:

---

40. Martin Luther King, Jr., "Address to the First Montgomery Improvement Association Mass Meeting (December 5, 1955)," in *A Call to Conscience: The Land-mark Speeches of Dr. Martin Luther King, Jr.* (New York: Warner, 2001), 1–11.

1. **Meditate** daily on the teachings and life of Jesus.
2. **Remember** always that the nonviolent movement in Birmingham seeks justice and reconciliation, not victory.
3. **Walk and Talk** in the manner of love, for God is love.
4. **Pray** daily to be used by God in order that all men might be free.
5. **Sacrifice** personal wishes in order that all men might be free.
6. **Observe** with both friend and foe the ordinary rules of courtesy.
7. **Seek** to perform regular service for others and for the world.
8. **Refrain** from the violence of fist, tongue, or heart.
9. **Strive** to be in good spiritual and bodily health.
10. **Follow** the directions of the movement and of the captain on a demonstration.

I sign this pledge, having seriously considered what I do and with the determination and will to persevere.[41]

Why march in the first place? Sometimes lost in the accounts of King's public ministry is the rationale behind nonviolent direct action. Drawing from Mahatma Gandhi's *satyagraha* with the help of veteran activist Bayard Rustin, King sought to dramatize the racial injustice that simmered just beneath the surface of Southern life.[42] He knew that journalists would record these events, and that seeing them through TV and newspapers would provoke the conscience of middle America. Gandhi's tactic became King's. As King himself said, "People who had never heard of the little brown saint of India

---

41. King, *Why We Can't Wait*, 67–69; Ansbro, *Martin Luther King, Jr.*, vii.

42. Gandhi's *satyagraha*, Sanskrit and Hindi for "holding onto truth," was a form of "passive resistance" to British imperial control of India. He succeeded at the time in bringing together disparate Indian populations in that effort, and he was aided by international press coverage. Nonviolence as a strategy requires a large audience beyond those in the place where demonstrations occur. See King, *Stride Toward Freedom*, 84–93. See also Ansbro, *Martin Luther King, Jr.*, 3–7.

were now saying his name with an air of familiarity. Nonviolent resistance had emerged as the technique of the movement, while love stood as the regulating ideal. In other words, Christ furnished the spirit and motivation, while Gandhi furnished the method."[43] The result was that mass media broadcast both the reality of violent white supremacy and the Beloved Community that hoped to defeat it with sacrificial love.

African Americans had suffered massive violence as slaves, but the violence continued in the wake of the Civil War in 1865. The ensuing years of Reconstruction lasted until 1877, but even then there were paramilitary and terrorist acts against African Americans. Through the 1880s, the Supreme Court threw out federal protections of African American civil rights while states redrew constitutions and laws in order to reinstitute racial segregation. Jim Crow segregation reached its completion with the Supreme Court's "separate but equal" doctrine in *Plessy v. Ferguson* (1896). African Americans migrated into midwestern and northeastern cities to flee poverty and violence only to find the same laws passed upon their arrival. By the turn of the twentieth century, local and state institutions as well as informal customs sought to condition African Americans into viewing themselves as inferior to whites, and periodic race riots and lynchings served as regular reminders of white supremacy. Lynching became so common that there were efforts to pass federal legislation, the Dyer Anti-Lynching Bill in 1922 and the Costigan-Wagner Bill of 1934, but these efforts failed because of the interference of Southern senators.[44]

The years following the Second World War brought a beginning to the end of this tragic history, but progress was slow and intermittent at best. Southern Democrats were leaders in the Senate who helped lead the 1948 "Dixiecrat" revolt at the Democratic Party Convention in response to party efforts to support African American civil rights. A mere six years later, however, the Supreme Court handed down a unanimous decision against "separate but equal" racial segregation

---

43. King, *Stride Toward Freedom*, 85.

44. In the years following the failure of the Costigan-Wagner Bill, Abel Meeropol composed the poem "Strange Fruit," later performed by Billie Holiday to protest continued violence against African Americans.

in public schooling with *Brown v. Board of Education* (1954). In 1956, elected officials in the Virginia state government responded with "massive resistance" against desegregation in the schools, preferring to shut down their public schools rather than integrate them. In the 1959 federal district court decision *James v. Almond*, student Ruth Pendleton James successfully sued Governor J. Lindsay Almond, Jr. to reopen the schools to African American students. Almond directed Virginia schools to accept these decisions with deliberate unhurriedness.

National media coverage of Virginia's resistance outraged white moderates. After all, the post-war years were highlighted by religious revivals led by Billy Graham and Catholic bishop Fulton Sheen, and the recent memory of Nazi concentration camps and the racial theory that prompted them started to haunt the nation. King understood this when he wrote the Birmingham pastors that "everything Hitler did in Germany was legal."[45]

However, King had no mass media venture of his own and competed for press coverage against everything from Soviet aggression to local sports events. The Montgomery boycott had started nonviolent campaigns against segregation, but the momentum slowed when King went to Albany, Georgia. King's book *Stride Toward Freedom: The Montgomery Story* had just been published, detailing the methods he used to turn public opinion in his favor. Unfortunately for King, Albany chief of police Laurie Pritchett snatched up King's book and learned from it how to subvert the activists. The police chief avoided using violence and only arrested activists for disturbing the peace rather than violating Jim Crow laws. As a result, King and Students Nonviolent Coordinating Committee (SNCC) activists could not draw attention to their efforts and left.[46]

---

45. King, "Letter from Birmingham Jail," 96.

46. S. Jonathan Bass, *Blessed Are the Peacemakers: Martin Luther King, Jr., Eight White Religious Leaders, and the "Letter from Birmingham Jail"* (Baton Rouge: Louisiana State University Press, 2001), 97–99; Harvard Sitkoff, *King: Pilgrimage to the Mountaintop* (New York: Hill and Wang, 2008), 81–83; Steve Fayer, Sarah Flynn, and Henry Hampton, *Voices of Freedom: An Oral History of the Civil Rights Movement from the 1950s Through the 1980s* (New York: Bantam Books, 1991), 105–11.

In 1963, the situation in Birmingham was different. Because of the peculiar local politics at the time King arrived, Theophilus "Bull" Connor sought support from hardline segregationists by using brutal tactics against nonviolent marches, and these efforts produced some of the most shocking photographs of the civil rights movement. Ignoring Pritchett's example, Connor used high pressure hoses, police dogs, and other forms of police violence while white vigilantes harassed and attacked activists in between demonstrations. In response, one of King's associates "jumped for joy" and "proclaimed over and over 'We've got a movement. We've got a movement. We had some policy brutality. They brought out the dogs. We've got a movement.'"[47] At first blush, the reaction seems perverse, but civil rights activists were spiritually disciplined to suffer this very violence in order to draw press attention to racial conditions in the South. Connor had fallen for the trap. His tactics helped reveal the racial hatred of white supremacists who were willing to use violence to preserve their power. The press descended on Birmingham and covered the violence daily. White clergy called for King to stop marching, but he continued. When Connor had King thrown in jail for violating a circuit court injunction against marching, King used the opportunity to compose the now famous "Letter from Birmingham City Jail." He addressed the letter nominally to the white clergymen who had asked him to stop marching. The letter was publicized nationally, and public pressure on Birmingham exploded. Birmingham business owners felt compelled to integrate, and Connor released jailed activists. In the days following, however, members of the Ku Klux Klan came to Birmingham and bombed King's hotel and the house of A. D. King, Martin's brother. In response, African Americans began to riot, requiring A. D. King to help restore order and preserve the gains he had helped achieve.[48]

King's success in Birmingham placed pressure on President John F. Kennedy to take meaningful action against segregation. The previous President Dwight D. Eisenhower had set a precedent that Kennedy might follow. In 1957, locals tried to prevent nine black students

---

47. Bass, *Blessed Are the Peacemakers*, 104.

48. Steven Levingston, *Kennedy and King: The President, the Pastor, and the Battle Over Civil Rights* (New York: Hatchett, 2017), 374–85.

from entering Little Rock Central High School, but Eisenhower sent in the 101st Airborne Division of the US Army to protect the "Little Rock Nine." He had also signed two major civil rights laws, one in 1957 and another in 1960, but there was little enforcement. While still a candidate, Kennedy had sought King's support by using party connections to free King from an Atlanta jail. But as president, Kennedy seemed reluctant to use his own authority or to encourage Congress to consider more capacious legislation. Through all of 1962 and during the Birmingham Campaign of 1963, Kennedy was silent. King demanded that the president issue a "Second Emancipation Proclamation"[49] to end state resistance to racial integration and to prosecute violence against African American political participation.

The climax of this appeal was King's address at the August 1963 March on Washington for Jobs and Freedom, where King gave his famous "I Have a Dream" speech.[50] Bayard Rustin, one of King's long-serving SCLC associates, originally wanted the march to end at the Capitol but decided on the Lincoln Memorial both to placate a worried Kennedy administration and to take advantage of better symbolism.[51] The setting also served to remind those listening or watching at home of the promises from the century prior that were not kept. Several other important speakers preceded King, such as John Lewis and Whitney M. Young, Jr., with messages emphasizing both the restoration of civil rights for African Americans and bettering their economic opportunities. King spoke last, using the metaphor of "cashing a check" with the "bank of justice" only to

---

49. "President Urged to End Race Laws, King Wants Proclamation for a 2d 'Emancipation,'" *New York Times*, June 6, 1961; "Dr. King Asks New Laws, Urges Kennedy to Initiate Civil Rights Measure," *New York Times*, October 28, 1961; "JFK's Action on Civil Rights Lagging, Says Rev. Dr. King," *Washington Post*, April 10, 1962; "Kennedy Finds 'Good Deal Left Undone' in Field of Civil Rights but Hopes for Progress," *New York Times*, May 18, 1962. For the original text, see Martin Luther King, Jr., "Appeal to the President of the United States," May 17, 1962, https://www.crmvet.org/info/emancip2.pdf.

50. King, "I Have a Dream," in *Testament of Hope*, 217–21.

51. Clarence B. Jones and Stuart Connelly, *Behind the Dream: The Making of the Speech That Transformed a Nation* (New York: Palgrave MacMillan, 2011), 84–85.

have it returned "marked insufficient funds."[52] His rhetoric stressed economic and political liberty to underscore the African American need for both, repeating a theme he had delivered elsewhere. But this time the language did not resonate with King or the audience. As King came to the end of his written speech, Mahalia Jackson, known as the "Queen of Gospel Music," shouted to King, "Tell them about the Dream, Martin. Tell them about the Dream."[53] King heard her and delivered now legendary preaching on the American dream that became the high watermark for King and his leadership of the civil rights movement.

Kennedy was preoccupied with the Cold War and uncertain about King. He was afraid that the new push for civil rights would upset the Southern Democrats. In fact, one reason Kennedy took his fateful trip to Dallas, Texas, was to shore up Southern support for his reelection. After Kennedy's assassination there, newly inaugurated Lyndon B. Johnson embraced civil rights legislation as a way of honoring Kennedy's legacy.[54]

On February 10, 1964, the House passed its version of the Civil Rights Act—290–130—but the Senate had always proved to be the barrier to serious legislation. One reason was that the Senate retained many of its old customs such as ranking members by seniority, which enabled so many long-serving Southern senators to wield considerable influence over civil rights legislation. Another custom was the filibuster that allows for continuous debate over legislation unless two-thirds of the members present vote for "cloture" to end debate.[55]

---

52. King, "I Have a Dream," 217.

53. Emily Crockett, "The woman who inspired Martin Luther King's 'I Have a Dream' Speech," *Vox*, January 16, 2017, https://www.vox.com/2016/1/18/10785882/martin-luther-king-dream-mahalia-jackson.

54. Patterson, *Religion in the Public Square*, 96–105.

55. The filibuster still exists today. The number of senators needed to end a filibuster is now three-fifths, and the filibuster itself functions differently. During the 1960s, senators had to go to the floor and speak for as long as they could to extend the filibuster until senators either moved to end debate or to table the bill. The filibuster, in this case, was a way of running out the clock. By 2019, the filibuster rarely resulted in real debate or hours-long speeches. Instead it served as a warning to other members that the legislation would

The Civil Rights Act was subjected to such a filibuster, but some of the discussion indicates how deeply King's interpretation of the Beloved Community, based on his religious interpretation of the American founding, had reframed the debate. Civil rights had become not just a legal or constitutional issue but a religious imperative. Several senators deployed Christian language and concepts to argue in favor of the legislation, while the opposition denounced mixing religion and politics.[56]

The Senate invoked cloture to end filibuster, passed the motion, and voted on June 19, 1964, seventy-three for and twenty-seven against the bill, thus sending it to Johnson to sign. He did so while King and other African American civil rights activists looked on.

King understood the Civil Rights Act of 1964 as the major step forward for the Beloved Community. In ways similar to those of the churches of Montgomery, African Americans in other parts of the country had engaged in nonviolent direct action to open the hearts of white Americans to the need for racial justice. Some white Americans then marched with their black brothers and sisters to fight to end political and economic segregation. These efforts moved from the municipal to the state and finally to the national level, and King noted that emancipated African nations were doing the same.[57]

Falling Short of the Promises to God

The passage of the Civil Rights Act of 1964 gave new hope to African Americans, who sought to register to vote and accelerate efforts at integration. But they often faced hardened white opposition to both, sometimes with lethal violence that was left unpunished by intimidated or complicit white juries.[58] To shore up the federal authority to enforce voting rights, King organized a march from Selma to Montgomery in Alabama to demonstrate African American demands

---

require more than a simple majority to pass, thus diminishing the possibility of the bill reaching the Senate floor at all.

56. Patterson, *Religion in the Public Square*, 105–12.

57. King, "The Rising Tide of Racial Consciousness," in *Testament of Hope*, 146.

58. Charles Marsh, *God's Long Summer: Stories of Faith and Civil Rights* (Princeton: Princeton University, 1997), 49–81.

to end voter suppression efforts like literacy tests and poll taxes.[59] The civil rights marchers confronted Alabama state troopers at the Edmund Pettis Bridge. Two efforts to cross the bridge failed. The first effort, known as "Bloody Sunday," was on March 7, 1965, when troopers attacked marchers with tear gas and truncheons, beating a co-organizer, Amelia Boynton, unconscious in the process. The second effort on March 9 succeeded because of a federal injunction protecting the marchers, but white supremacists raided the group at night and killed James Reeb, a Unitarian minister from Boston. The third effort began under the protection of a federally led Alabama National Guard and FBI agents.

Following the march to Montgomery, there was division over King's leadership of the civil rights movement, which at this point was a decade old. Younger activists in the SNCC, led by Stokely Carmichael, had grown tired of King's emphasis on sacrificial love as the foundation for racial integration. They offered "Black Power" instead as a source for racial solidarity or "black nationalism" in which African Americans replaced racial integration with the goal of forming their own autonomous racial communities, political institutions, and customs.[60] During the March to Montgomery, King was still able to preserve some semblance of unity among activists

---

59. Literacy tests in practice were effectively gauntlets in which even the slightest mistake would cause an African American voter to lose access to the ballot, while white voters passed even when demonstrating very poor results. Often African Americans received notifications that they had failed from examiners who had only a very general grasp of the English language. Poll taxes simply penalized African Americans for being poor, and that poverty was the result of the very segregation in schools, trades, and professions that African Americans were demonstrating against. These "structural" factors gave rise to the charge of "structural racism" which, though perhaps applied too hastily or broadly in today's politics, began with battles against Jim Crow in the American South.

60. Prior to finding its home in SNCC, Black Power had been an essential part of Malcolm X's political thought, both before and after his departure from the Nation of Islam. King had used the Nation of Islam and its founder, Elijah Muhammad, as examples of what happens when white Christians and Jews fail to heed God's call to sacrificial love. The eventual rise of Black Power and its success in pushing King to the margins confirms, in part, these warnings. King insisted that the time was near and patience was wearing thin: white supremacy either had to go or violence would worsen. The Watts Riots of 1965 seemed to

and helped generate grassroots support for the Voting Rights Act of 1965, which passed through both Houses of Congress in months. Johnson signed it on August 6, 1965. Five days later, the Watts Riots in Los Angeles, California, began nearly a week of general unrest that signaled the beginning of the end for the kind of civil rights activism King had led since the Montgomery bus boycott.

SNCC activists had long chafed under King, viewing him as soft, preening, and hypocritical. The acrimony began in 1960 when King proved reluctant to participate in "sit-ins"—the nonviolent direct action technique of African Americans to enter segregated lunch counters and malt shops and demand service. SNCC activists called on King to participate, but King's role as SCLC fundraiser and government liaison made his participation risky.[61] What if the protests went wrong and undermined King's position? What if the police used the sit-ins as an opportunity to kill him?[62] King's reluctance earned him the mocking title "De Lawd" among the SNCC detractors, who gained some sympathy from communities where the SCLC had previously visited.[63] When King left places like Albany or Birmingham, so did the press, leaving black communities exposed once again to local white supremacist reprisal. Moreover, King had a doctorate, came from an upper-middle class family, and frequently spoke in

---

confirm King's prophecy, even as he was unable to win back leadership despite making more radical political appeals.

61. Levingston, *Kennedy and King*, 71–92.

62. King opted to participate and was arrested and put in an Atlanta jail. This incident was the one that eventually led the Kennedy campaign to intervene to have King freed to show their support for African Americans civil rights. Some in the campaign, however, defied Robert Kennedy's refusal to publicize their intervention and surreptitiously published the now famous "blue book" detailing appeals to black churches the Sunday before the election. The timing was key, since the campaign wanted to prevent white Southern Democrats from finding out beforehand and perhaps voting for Kennedy's Republican opponent, Vice President Richard Nixon, or simply refusing to turn out at all. See Levingston, *Kennedy and King*, 99–100.

63. Adam Fairclough, *Martin Luther King, Jr.* (Athens: University of Georgia Press, 1995), 70; Levingston, *Kennedy and King*, 207–56; Nicholas Bryant, *The Bystander: John F. Kennedy and the Struggle for Black Equality* (New York: Basic Books, 2006), Kindle, 4,023–4,416.

high-toned language. All of this was fitting for the son of an accomplished black preacher in the South, but in the northern cities it was considerably less familiar or welcome. These differences contributed to King's struggle to organize in places like Chicago the way that he had in Birmingham, even though both were industrialized cities. These differences were also why the 1966 Chicago Freedom Movement was much less successful than the Birmingham march, with King only able to extract from Mayor Richard J. Daley a few concessions on public housing and expanded mortgage opportunities for African American homebuyers—concessions that were later rescinded.[64]

However, as Jacqueline Rivers has argued, one of the chief sources for King's decline was his sexual infidelity.[65] As King himself knew, he was under constant FBI surveillance, which had recorded his repeated acts of adultery. Recently King biographer David Garrow confirmed that the FBI had evidence of King watching as an associate forced himself on a woman, and King did nothing to stop him.[66] Those who worked in civil rights at the time had at least heard rumors of King's sexual infidelity, which ate away at his moral witness against segregation. After all, how could King preach about the American covenant of sacrificial love when he could not keep his marriage covenant?

Arguably, the growing surveillance evidence weakened King's influence with President Johnson, although their 1967 conflict over the Vietnam War probably did more to harm that relationship than anything else. Many wonder how King could be a civil rights hero and at the same time an apparently indifferent witness to sexual assault. Christians, on the other hand, also understand that human beings are sinful creatures capable of great good and great evil.

---

64. Vincent Harding, "Introduction," in *Where Do We Go from Here*, xii–xiv; Martin Luther King, Jr., "Press Conference at Liberty Baptist Church, March 24, 1967," Martin Luther King, Jr. Papers, 1950–1968, Martin Luther King, Jr. Center for Nonviolent Social Change, Atlanta, Georgia.

65. Jacqueline Rivers, "The Political Theology of Martin Luther King, Jr.," Loeb Institute for Religious Freedom, George Washington University, October 11, 2018; https://loeb.columbian.gwu.edu/political-theology-martin-luther-king-jr.

66. David J. Garrow, "The Troubling Legacy of Martin Luther King," *Standpoint*, May 30, 2019, https://standpointmag.co.uk/issues/june-2019/the-troubling-legacy-of-martin-luther-king/.

Cain slew his brother out of envy. David sent a married woman's husband to die in battle after staying in the city to seduce his wife. Judas betrayed Jesus, and then Peter denied him three times during the Passion. The truth is that King was a hero for civil rights, a powerful preacher of the gospel, and a grievous sinner. He sinned against his wife with his affairs, and he sinned against this woman by not stopping the assault. One hopes that she found spiritual and medical assistance after her survival, even if she did not apparently get the justice she deserved. For all the good King did, he should not be canonized, but neither should he be thrown out of the history of the civil rights movement. Instead, his example should be a warning against idolizing political figures. As Psalm 146:3 (KJV) tells us, "Put not your trust in princes" or, for that matter, Kings.

For those who remember only King's speech before the Lincoln Memorial in 1963, it might be surprising to learn that King's view of economics was, in modern terms, that of a democratic socialist. King's last campaign in the SCLC was the Poor People's Campaign, which emphasized the need to provide economic relief to poor Americans, especially African Americans, who had been left out of the post-war economic boom. Part of that effort, for King, was working to integrate and strengthen labor unions—the reason for his support of the Memphis sanitation workers strike. In his final book, *Where Do We Go from Here: Chaos or Community?*, as well as in the posthumously published, "Showdown for Nonviolence," King revealed how radical an economic plan he thought was necessary for the federal government to right the wrongs of African American economic exploitation. Desegregation and voting rights protection were not enough; federal redistribution was required to pull up struggling black communities.[67] Advocates for limited government and free markets may see King's policy position as wrong-headed, but it is important to note that King's call for redistribution was merely an extension of the logic of Johnson's War on Poverty and hoped to capture some of the economic gains from even earlier policies that had done much to improve the quality of life in the white American middle class. In retrospect, it appears that one of the most startling differences between King and many

---

67. King, *Where Do We Go from Here*, 143–75; King, "Showdown from Nonviolence," in *Testament of Hope*, 64–72.

of his modern readers was his faith in the expertise and efficiency of the federal government to remedy the economic impact of Jim Crow on African Americans. Nonetheless, some of his policy recommendations have seen renewed interest, such as the guaranteed income.[68] Whatever the merits of King's economic policy recommendations, however, they were just as much part of his covenant foundation for America. Many conservatives admire King for his commitment to the principles of the Declaration of Independence and his gospel message for racial justice, but they must also wrestle with King's Social Gospel approach to economic redistribution.[69]

Conclusion: Mine Eyes Have Seen the Glory of the Coming of the Lord

One of the most powerful moments of King's public ministry was on April 3, 1968, the night before James Earl Ray shot him through the face and spine, eventually killing him. That night, King gave the speech titled "I See the Promised Land" in the Bishop Charles Mason Temple in Memphis, Tennessee, where he ended by meditating on his death.[70] A recording of the speech exists today, and anyone seeking to learn from King must listen to it.[71] King combines pieces of several prior speeches, but he later adds a sense that he will not see the end of the civil rights movement. Exhausted from travel and raw with emotion, King dwells on his past successes a little too long, as if wanting to give a full account of his ministry. In the process,

---

68. King, *Where Do We Go from Here*, 171–75.

69. During King's public ministry many of his opponents, including FBI Director J. Edgar Hoover, were convinced that King was a communist agent or fellow traveler, most of all because of his association with Rustin, who had once been a member of the Communist Party of the United States of America. King was not a communist and preached against communism, but the accusation persists in certain corners. King was simply in his economic thinking to the left of center.

70. King, "I See the Promised Land," in *Testament of Hope*, 279–86. See also Joseph Rosenbloom, *Redemption: Martin Luther King, Jr.'s Last 31 Hours* (Boston: Beacon, 2018).

71. The speech is also called "I've Been to the Mountaintop": https://www.americanrhetoric.com/speeches/mlkivebeentothemountaintop.htm.

he reminds the audience that Moses brought the Israelites to the promised land because the people of Israel were united.[72] But in a reference to the frayed alliances of civil rights organization, King pleaded, "We've got to stay together and maintain unity. You know, whenever Pharaoh wanted to prolong the period of slavery in Egypt, he had a favorite, favorite formula for doing it.... He kept the slaves fighting among themselves."[73] By the end of the speech, just after King pondered his near-fatal stabbing (1958) and recent threats from "sick white brothers" in Memphis, he could barely contain his emotions.[74] King then returned to the Exodus narrative:

> And He's allowed me to go up to the mountain. And I've looked over. And I've seen the promised land. I may not get there with you. But I want you to know tonight, that we, as a people, will get to the promised land. And I'm happy, tonight. I'm not worried about anything. I'm not fearing any man. Mine eyes have seen the glory of the coming of the Lord.[75]

King understood the gravity of his failures. God would take Americans to the promised land, but like Moses who disobeyed Yahweh at the waters of Meribah, King knew he did not deserve to go with them. King had preached the covenant, and he had breached it. Yet by God's mercy King was granted a vision of the Beloved Community built on loving sacrifice to one another. This great American leader, flawed Christian that he was, would probably want us to turn our hearts to God's eternal love, remembering both King's courage to inspire us and his sin to chasten us.

---

72. King frequently used the Exodus to compare the plight of African Americans to the Israelites. In this respect, he was part of a long tradition of black preachers. See Eddie S. Glaude, Jr., *Exodus! Religion, Race, and Nation in Early Nineteenth-Century Black America* (Chicago: University of Chicago Press, 2000); Gary S. Selby, *Martin Luther King and the Rhetoric of Freedom: The Exodus Narrative in America's Struggle for Civil Rights* (Waco: Baylor University Press, 2008).

73. King, "I See the Promised Land," 280–81.

74. King, "I See the Promised Land," 286.

75. King, "I See the Promised Land," 286.

Part 2

RACE, COVENANT, AND CONTEMPORARY AMERICAN SOCIETY

5

THE IDENTITY POLITICS CRITIQUE OF THE AMERICAN REPUBLIC

Joshua Mitchell

Are the conceptual resources that were brought to bear during the founding of the American Republic adequate to address the legacy of the wound of slavery in America? The admission of slavery into the Republic in the first place and—notwithstanding the 620,000 lives that were extinguished putting an end to its legal justification in 1865—the inability to resolve the matter in the Jim Crow Era and afterwards suggest to the party of the Left that they were not. The party of the Right proposes that the conceptual resources were fully adequate to produce a color-blind liberal order, which Lincoln's second founding vindicated in principle if not yet in fact. Slavery was less endorsed than accommodated at the first founding, as a necessary precondition of the existence of the Union. The Union's slavery problem would be worked out later. The party of the Left today makes the case that America has been, and will always be, suffused with systemic racism, which the founding either justified or could not overcome. The party of the Right makes the case for a capacious, liberal founding, needing no supplementary ideas to heal the wound of slavery, which was incidental to the founding rather than inscribed in it.

It is unlikely that this partisan squabble between Left and Right will be settled by further historical research into the American founding. The debate is, finally, a contemporary one, very much determined by the raging political battle of our times, namely, between what we will call here the liberal politics of competence and the identity politics of innocence. The former dates back before the founders; the latter is quite new, dating back perhaps several decades, though its intellectual origins lie further back—within Christianity itself, as we will discover. The question of the standing of slavery at the founding of the American Republic is, for us today, a question about which of these two quite different accounts of politics is to guide us. Our future assessment of the founding will hinge on which prevails. We will consider each one in turn.

The liberal politics of competence does not emerge through one author alone, though we might look to portions of Kant[1] and to all of John Locke. It is given its fullest expression two generations after the founding in the writings of Alexis de Tocqueville. For each of these authors, and for all who have contributed to the development of liberal thought, modesty informs their understanding of who humans are, what they know of themselves, what they know of others, and what they are able to accomplish in history. Individuals build a world less on the authority and commandments of others than through self-interest; and they do this with a view to achieving well-being within the confines of a middle class commercial republic. Whatever their limits, America's founding fathers began with these liberal premises. Their intellectual inheritance surely had something to do with this. More than this, however, was the providential fact that their distance from England made the development of liberal competence necessary. Local communities came first; the national government came second. Reliance on the state—indeed, the replacement of liberal competence by the administrative competence of the state—would come along only in the twentieth century. In John Marshall's *The Life of George*

---

1. In Kant's view, against their will humans are thrown into never-ending competition with others—the end of which is not happiness but an achieved competence that alone grants humans the dignity they earn. See Immanuel Kant, "Idea for a Universal History with a Cosmopolitan Intent," in *On History*, ed. Lewis White Beck (New York: Macmillan, 1963), third and fourth theses, 13–16.

Washington, we find an ennobling portrait of the character this providential fact produces: unassuming, diligent, honorable, capable of difficult labor for a noble cause, and animated by action rather than enthralled by sophistry.[2] We need explore no further than the table of contents of Thomas Jefferson's *Notes on the State of Virginia* to discover the eager, steward-like attention to the resources at hand, to the laws that make their use just, and to the liberal character that makes those resources and laws profitable.[3] Early in Alexis de Tocqueville's *Democracy in America*, we find the searing distinction between what Tocqueville calls "the manly and legitimate passion for equality,"[4] which he thought fitting of the American character, and the secret longing for servitude that he worried would emerge later.

For Kant, Washington, Jefferson, and Tocqueville, as for all liberals, an earnest and competent engagement with the present is necessary because no one can know the future. That is why there must be interminable arguments about the content and contour of the present—and why markets, elections, and vibrant social institutions provide provisional answers about the future, but no final verdict. Justice is an ongoing question, not a definitive answer that closes off further argument. Each and every moment, no matter how fixed it may seem, is a temporary equilibrium, inviting adjustment, compromise, and action. The future emerges. Because the future cannot be known until it actually arrives, liberals doubt that the far-seeing plans of "experts" get them there any better, or get them there at all.[5] Liberals are even more dubious of claims by "experts" that no further improvement is possible. For the liberal, there is

---

2. See John Marshall, *The Life of George Washington*, ed. Robert Falkner and Paul Carrese (Indianapolis: Liberty Fund, 2000), especially 465–69.

3. See Thomas Jefferson, *Notes on the State of Virginia*, ed. William Peden (New York: W. W. Norton, 1982).

4. See Alexis de Tocqueville, *Democracy in America*, ed. J. P. Mayer, vol. 1 (New York: Harper & Row, 1969), 57: "There is indeed a manly and legitimate passion for equality which rouses in all men a desire to be strong and respected."

5. See Adam Smith, *The Wealth of Nations*, vol. 1 (Chicago: University of Chicago Press, 1976), 17: "[the production of wealth is] not the effect of human wisdom." That is, no one or no small group can know, in advance, how to employ capital and labor most productively.

no post-competitive, post-political age in which the global task is to redistribute wealth and political power under a settled but never-defined schema of "social justice," overseen by global managers.[6] The version of it that global managers offer, no matter how capacious, will always be sterile. The liberal understands that these schemes always end in wretchedness, because they supplant, with abstract theories, the living facts on the ground by which the plurality of human associations has emerged and actually operates.[7]

Not only can liberals not know the future, they cannot fully know themselves.[8] They search, therefore, for a light in the darkness, for a way to find the certainty about who they are that evades them. Having an "identity" purports to offer that certainty. But the liberal is impatient with this imaginary indulgence. Imagined markers of identity are, at best, a shorthand and a convenient point of departure, perhaps a way to begin a conversation, but by no means a way to end one—as we will discover the identity politics of innocence almost invariably does. Once liberal citizens enter into conversation with their fellows, they discover that their shorthand account of themselves is woefully inadequate, and that shorthand accounts are generally obstacles to improving their lot together because they

---

6. See Joshua Mitchell, "Age of Exhaustion," *The American Interest* 11, no. 2 (November/December 2015): 53–64, https://www.the-american-interest.com/2015/10/10/age-of-exhaustion/.

7. The wreckage from twentieth-century social engineering schemes is well known. The most fragile communities are the first to succumb. See Robert L. Woodson, Sr., *The Triumphs of Joseph* (New York: Free Press, 1998), 12: "There are powerful social, economic, and political institutions that have a proprietary interest in continued existence of the problems of the poor, the denial of solutions, and the portrayal of low-income people as victims in need of defense and rescue. These powerful interest groups include members of the civil rights establishment, a massive poverty industry that owes its existence to the problems of the poor, and politicians who are aligned with them. They are the modern-day equivalents of the Pharaoh's court counselors who view our Joseph's ability to heal people and solve their problems as a threat to their domain of 'expertise.'" Woodson's argument is that local communities have within themselves the resources to heal their wounds.

8. Augustine, *Confessions*, trans. Henry Chadwick (Oxford: Oxford University Press, 1991), bk. 4, 57; see also bk. 10, 208: "I have become a problem to myself." See also Tocqueville, *Democracy in America*, 2:487.

declare not what citizens might do together, but rather why they are separate and must remain so.

Liberals presume, moreover, that liberal citizens do not really know each other. Unless they engage in regular, real-time, conversations with one another, a caricatured depiction of their fellow citizens will emerge in their imagination,[9] which will grow proportionally more egregious the more citizens grow apart. When they do not need each other in order to secure their well-being, when the state promises cradle-to-grave security, what reason do citizens have to cast the caring glance toward one another and so rein in their imagination? Without that glance, political polarization increases. By every measure where imagined distinctions could become more acute—political, economic, religious, cultural, ethnic, national, sexual—they do become more acute. Without practical engagement, citizens lose the art of engaging; if their imagination temporarily rests, it is not because they have been put at ease by the work they are doing with their fellows, but because they have excised their fellows from their lives altogether. Is it any wonder, in our own day, that isolated citizens begin to imagine that they are pure and others are stained, as the identity politics of innocence suggests?

Liberals grant humans no such purity. The much-maligned John Locke, by many accounts the father of liberal thought, built his defense of property, of limited government, and of toleration on the basis of what happened to Adam after his ejection from Edenic innocence. Most scholars today see Locke's invocation of Adam as a quaint device through which he developed a purportedly secular liberalism. This is a grievous mistake which must be rethought in light of our problem, namely, the prospective eclipse of the politics of competence by the identity politics of innocence. It was Locke who first articulated the liberal politics of competence, as we have called it here, in which citizens build a world together through their labors and ask government to stand by and protect those labors. Locke was

---

9. So subject to corruption is human imagination that the Hebrew Bible offers it as the cause of the great flood. See Gen. 6:5: "And God saw that the wickedness of man was great in the earth, and that every imagination of the thoughts of his heart was only evil continually." See also Rom. 1:21. All biblical references are to the KJV.

not oblivious to the categories of stain and purity, of transgression and innocence, on which identity politics depends; on the contrary, he thought that Christianity had already resolved the issue of innocence and transgression. His liberal politics was possible only because Christianity already had done this:

> I have set down all these texts out of St. Paul, that in them might be seen his own explication of what he says here, viz. that our Saviour, by his death, atoned for our sins, and so we were innocent, and thereby freed from the punishment due to sin.[10]

As we can see from Locke, liberalism's quintessential political philosopher, the liberal politics of competence, unlike the identity politics of innocence, presumes a divine resolution to the problem of transgression, not a mortal one.

We have anticipated the liberal critique of the identity politics of innocence. To get a sense of what the latter involves, let us step back and make a simple observation that Americans understand from their everyday experience: we are a rough-knit community of individuals, forever reinventing ourselves and losing sight of our past. Taking the long view, this is a rather exceptional state of affairs. For the most part, the human race has divided into nations with long and binding histories. In the Hebrew Bible, there is mention of seventy nations.[11] In America we often confuse the terms *nation* and *state*, and lose sight of the meaning of "nation" altogether. The state we understand: We belong to our state because we are citizens who have never-ending arguments about representation, law, consent, voting, legitimate authority, and so forth. We must constantly think and talk about these issues to bring the state to life and to sustain it. Because of the ongoing need among citizens to think and talk with one another, the state is a fragile affair, held together moment to moment, as the long and turbulent history of the United States attests. The state can be undone.

The nation is different. The Latin word *natio* from which we derive "nation" literally means birth. We consent to being a citizen of our

---

10. John Locke, *A Paraphrase and Notes on the Epistles of St. Paul*, vol. 7 *The Works of John Locke*, 12th ed. (London: Rivington, 1824), 314n‡.

11. See Gen. 10:1–32.

state, but we consent neither to the fact of our own birth nor to its terms.[12] Some of us were born here in the United States, for example; others were not. Some of us can trace our lineage back many generations. Those of us who cannot often carry the weight of our more ancient inheritances from another nation for several generations, which with the passing years is lifted as we come to feel ourselves more and more "American."

Exactly when the weight of an inheritance lifts from our shoulders is not easy to establish. Reasonable people will disagree. One of the main characteristics of modern life, in fact, is that our inheritance is in perpetual danger of being overshadowed. Tocqueville, the great French philosopher who visited America in the early nineteenth century, saw the problem long ago. "Americans cleave to the things of this world as if assured that they will never die, and yet are in such a rush to snatch any that come within their reach, as if expecting to stop living before they have relished them. They clutch everything but hold nothing fast, and so lose grip as they hurry after some new delight."[13]

It is worth remembering, especially in America, that in other parts of the world, nations—inheritances—are still very much alive and binding. Because equality is so important to us in America, we tend to think of other people around the globe as persons without predicates who have no inheritance and who are "just like us." Only in America. In the rest of the world, on the contrary, there are nations. Inheritance still binds. Reasonable people will disagree about how intact that inheritance is, and even about what that inheritance is—but in America we often unreasonably conclude that inheritance is not binding at all.

Throughout history, then, the human race has divided into nations, into different kinds of peoples, having different inheritances. As recently as the 1960s, we identified ourselves as distinct kinds of people. As we entered the 1990s, however, a new term inexplicably

---

12. Like our genetic make-up, along with all the visible markers of that make-up, our initial membership in a nation is not a matter we agree to, but rather abide by.

13. Tocqueville, *Democracy in America*, 2:536. Cf. Prov. 22:28: "Remove not the ancient landmark, which thy fathers have set."

appeared in our everyday vocabulary: *identity*. That term is now used nearly everywhere—sometimes consciously, sometimes simply because it is around and available. In its more innocent and innocuous usage, the term *identity* is the upgrade and fashionable equivalent of what we once recognized as kind. To be American today is to have an American identity. With this meaning in mind, when critics suggest that the term is unnecessary or pernicious, the usual response is that people have had identities for all of human history, so it is impossible to eliminate the term. This response is understandable—but only when identity is synonymous with kind, and has no further meaning.[14]

Identity has a second meaning, however, which is fundamentally different from kind, one without which the term probably never would have taken hold in the 1990s in the first place. This other meaning is not so much a specification of kind as it is a specification of a relationship. More importantly, the relationship is of a specific type with discernible religious overtones: the unpayable debt one kind owes another. Moreover, transgressor and innocent confront one another with this relationship not just for the moment of their encounter but permanently. Like the stain of original sin that marks Adam and all his progeny, the transgressor is permanently marked. Transgressors may have done nothing to contribute to transgressions—slave ownership by distant relatives, for example—that predated them by decades or even centuries. Little matter. They stand for the sum of the transgressions linked to their identity. Pressing Christian imagery further, and distorting it at the same time, just as Christ the transgressor stands in and covers over[15] the stains of

---

14. See Mark Lilla, *The Once and Future Liberal: After Identity Politics* (New York: Harper, 2017). Lilla's account of identity politics is of this sort. His complaint to the left is that the Democratic Party has fractured into multiple kinds, and that, unlike the old (pre-1968) Democratic Party, there is nothing that can gather these kinds together.

15. "Covering over" has biblical overtones that cannot be ignored. See Ps. 91:4: "He shall cover thee with his feathers, and under his wings shalt thou trust." God "covers" the brokenness of humanity. In the New Testament, the covering takes the form of the blood of Christ, which by virtue of covering sinners washes their sins away. See 1 John 1:7: "and the blood of Jesus Christ His Son cleanseth us from all sin." In identity politics, the offering is the white

those who claim they are innocent but are not, so no judgment against their identity may be rendered.

This second understanding of identity is more often what we mean today when we speak about identity politics. Identity politics has no single proponent; it is less a single theory than a large genus within which all theories of victimhood are species, because all of them invoke the relationship between transgression and innocence.

Identity politics began penetrating our vernacular in the 1990s, but since that time and at an ever-escalating pace, more and more groups have self-consciously claimed that they, too, have an identity—with a view to revealing to an unseeing, scapegoating[16] society the transgressions that they, the innocent, have endured.

In a quasi-religious world such as ours, innocent victims alone are hallowed; they alone receive what could be called debt-point recognition. The rest—however much their legal, economic, or social status might otherwise indicate—have no legitimate voice. Indeed, their penance as transgressors is to listen to the innocents,[17] and their lay responsibility in the identity politics liturgy is to assent to the right of the innocents to tear down the civilizational temple their transgressors have built over the centuries—paid for not simply with money but with the unearned suffering of the innocent scapegoats. The past belongs to the transgressors, who today are an archaic

---

heterosexual man, whose sacrificial blood covers the sins of all others, so that they may become innocents.

16. The social and theological ramifications of the "scapegoat" have been developed and illuminated nowhere more profoundly than in Rene Girard, *I See Satan Fall Like Lightning*, trans. James G. Williams. (Maryknoll, NY: Orbis Books, 1999). Much of what follows relies on the framework Girard lays out. The Hebrew root of the idea warrants our immediate attention. Leviticus 16:1–34 are the passages in which the scapegoat first appears. The scapegoat takes upon itself the sin of the entire community, and it then is sent out into the desert so that the community may be made pure and reconciled.

17. Emblematic of this demand for recognition by innocent victims is the exchange chronicled on the Yale University courtyard, on November 15, 2015. See https://www.youtube.com/watch?v=iAr6LYC-xpE. See also Michael Brendan Dougherty, "The Church of Grievance," in *National Review Online*, April 26, 2018, https://www.nationalreview.com/magazine/2018/05/14/victim-mentality-identity-politics-dominate-modern-left/.

holdover and an embarrassment. The future—politically, economically, and socially—belongs to the innocents. Little wonder that the prime transgressors—white heterosexual men—who in the world that identity politics constructs can have nothing important to say,[18] eventually wonder if they too have been victims, and begin cataloging their wounds. Hence the recent emergence of what might be called the "Men's Me Too Movement," which presumes that the right to speak to and with other innocent victims hangs on the unearned suffering men have also endured through the ages.[19]

Identity politics in America emerged because of the collapse of the Mainline Protestant churches, which shunted the idea of transgression and innocence from religion into politics. It emerged because of the extension to other groups, after the civil rights era, of the African American template of innocence, which served political

---

18. In 1988, Stanford became the first top-tier US university to remove "dead white men" from its core curriculum. Other universities followed. Today, teaching the Western Canon remains under assault because of the writings of the dead white men in it.

19. The emerging list of men's grievances are legion. With respect to the criminal justice system: men have a lower chance of posting bail than women; men go to prison at a higher rate, and are treated worse in prison than are women; men are punished more harshly for the same crimes; men have higher rates of solitary confinement; and men serve a higher percentage of their prison sentence. With respect to divorce: adjusted for income, men make higher alimony payments; and men receive a lower rate of custody of children after divorce. With respect to education: men underachieve in K–12; and men attend college at a lower rate and graduate at a lower rate. With respect to death: men have a lower life expectancy, by five years, in most developed countries; men are twenty times more likely to die in a work-related injury; men have a higher rate of suicide; and men are more likely to die from violent gun and knife crime. With respect to physical violence: men endure a higher rate of corporal punishment in childhood. With respect to war: men are forced by law and by societal pressure to fight and die in war; male "gendercide" has been practiced throughout history as a way of subduing populations; and as veterans, men suffer higher rates of homelessness, suicide, PTSD, and drug addiction. With respect to employment: men are "forced" to work for pay in a capitalist economy more than are women; women are concerned with breaking through the "glass ceiling," yet almost all of the thankless work done "below ground"—in mining, utilities, fishing, and excavation—is done by men. For an even more comprehensive account of the victimhood of men, see http://www.realsexism.com/.

brokers who benefitted from speaking on all of their behalf. And it emerged because of the discovery, by the academic Left in America, of European postmodern thought, which provided a framework more powerful than Marxism for attacking the legitimacy of historical inheritance. Identity politics has now incorporated itself into the heart of the Democratic Party. The Democratic Party is not, however, the source of identity politics. To justify being heard in America today, we must demonstrate our special standing as an innocent victim. Having demonstrated that, we can take our legitimate place in the political firmament and become activists, committed—in our hearts, but seldom in our daily actions—to "social justice." Most importantly, identity politics seeks to resolve the problem of stain,[20] and establishes innocence by scapegoating a mortal group.

Does scapegoating a specific mortal group help establish the publicly stated goal of identity politics, namely achieving equality? Identity politics purges and humiliates.[21] It does not make room for the innocents among the transgressors; rather, it purges the

---

20. Eric Voegelin famously wrote that Marxism immanentized the eschaton. See Eric Voegelin, *The New Science of Politics* (Chicago: University of Chicago Press, 1952), 124–25. Identity politics immanentizes the scapegoat. Late in his life (in 1894), after five decades of struggling to make sense of the wound of slavery and concerned about this impulse to scapegoat groups, Frederick Douglass wrote: "Since emancipation we hear much said of our modern colored leaders in commendation of race pride, race love, race effort, race superiority, race men and the like.... In all this talk of race, the motive may be good, but the method is bad. It is an effort to cast out Satan by Beelzebub. The evils which are now crushing the Negro to earth have their root and sap, their force and mainspring, in this narrow spirit of race and color and the Negro has no more right to excuse or to foster it than men of any other race.... Not as Ethiopians, not as Caucasians, not as Mongolians, not as Afro–Americans, or Anglo–American are we addressed but as men. God and nature speak to our manhood and manhood alone." See Frederick Douglass, "The Blessings of Liberty and Education," in *The Frederick Douglass Papers: Series One*, ed. John W. Blassingame and John R. McKivigan, vol. 5 (New Haven: Yale University Press, 1979–1992), 625.

21. The purpose of Roman crucifixion was to humiliate the victim. In Christian theology, Christ moves from humiliation to exaltation, from Good Friday to Easter Sunday. In identity politics, there is no exaltation for the scapegoat, only humiliation.

transgressors and then requires another group of innocents to step in and take their place.

But equality cannot be achieved in this way. It can only be achieved through radical asymmetry—not between one mortal identity and another, but between God and man. Only if the scapegoat is divine[22] can citizens look upon each other as equals,[23] and thereafter build a world together. Locke presumed this. In such a radically asymmetrical relationship, all mortals are broken, all mortals stained, and none are redeemable by scapegoating another kind. In short, within this radically asymmetrical relationship, the problem of humans is not a group problem. Humanity's transgression, inherited from Adam, runs deeper than the inheritance of kind bequeathed by father and mother. Not incidentally does the New Testament proclaim that the follower of Christ must leave father and mother,[24] or that kinds are overcome entirely in Christ,[25] or that disciples are to "go therefore and make disciples of all nations" (Matt. 28:18–19). No Divine scapegoat, no mortal equality.

No American citizens have been betrayed more by identity politics than have African Americans, whose special standing in the deep wound of American slavery has been used unabashedly as a template for all other supposed innocents who now make their own claims. Civil rights, women's rights, gay rights, transsexual rights: are these not all fungible variants on the same theme of transgression and innocence? Asked figuratively to step back, while new franchise-expanding innocents are invited to occupy the front seats of the Democratic Party bus, African Americans are expected to sit tight, without com-

---

22. Alternatively, the scapegoat can be an animal. See Lev. 16:1–34.

23. Might money provide the basis for equality? Money promises to do this, as Voltaire noted long ago. See Voltaire, *Letters on England*, trans. Leonard Tancock (New York: Penguin, 1980), 41. When money becomes the measure of all things, however, it produces pernicious inequalities, as writers from Plato to Marx have noted. See Plato, *Republic*, trans. Richard W. Sterling and William C. Scott, bk. 4 (New York: W. W. Norton, 1985), 423a); Karl Marx, "Manifesto of the Communist Party," in *The Marx-Engels Reader*, ed. Robert Tucker (New York: W. W. Norton, 1978), 475–76.

24. See Matt. 19:29; Mark 10:29; Luke 18:29.

25. See Gal. 3:28: "There is neither Jew nor Greek, there is neither bond nor free, there is neither male not female; for ye are all on in Christ Jesus."

plaining about where the bus is going or how much it is costing them —or at least costing a large number of them. Identity politics needs to render African Americans not as struggling but competent liberal citizens whose history evinces extraordinary and reproducible models of success, but rather as perennially innocent victims. For that reason, the history of their successes against formidable odds must be erased, without regard for those African Americans most harmed by that erasure. In its stead has been placed a new history and a new formula for benefiting not all African Americans but only that smaller group among them whose fortune and hard work have prepared them to take full advantage of the opportunities that now come their way. Along the way, the tacit understanding is that they will adhere to the account of their plight that identity politics promulgates.

> The Guardians of Grievance, the cohort of advisors that are today's version of W. E. B. Du Bois' "talented tenth" ... [have revised history to focus] almost exclusively on the degradation whites have imposed on blacks and the accomplishments of the civil rights leadership's efforts since the sixties. Conveniently airbrushed from the portrait of black America are the remarkable models of self-help—accomplishments of black entrepreneurs and mutual aid societies during eras of the most brutal racial repression and slavery. Lost is the legacy of personal responsibility and principle-based entrepreneurship that could provide today's youth with a pride in their heritage and an adaptable model that could guide their futures. The selective history that is transmitted to our young people is, simply put, that blacks came to this country on slave ships; from there they went to plantations and slavery; from the plantations to the ghetto, and, finally, to welfare.[26]

---

26. Woodson, *Triumphs of Joseph*, 51–52. See also Robert Woodson, Sr., "A Betrayal of Martin Luther King," *The Hill*, January 20, 2019, https://thehill.com/opinion/civil-rights/426017-a-betrayal-of-martin-luther-king: "The surest way to sabotage the prospects of blacks is to convince them that they have no agency and, therefore, no responsibility and no hope. This is insulting to the memory of Dr. King and immoral in its continued intellectual incarceration of people into a mindset of victimhood, rather than one of achievement."

In the world of identity which politics constructs, oppressive social forces loom large and human freedom looms small.[27] Have not the transgressors systematically scapegoated the innocents and kept them from sharing in the bounty of America? The history of slavery and its aftermath confirms this wretched fact. "Systemic racism" is the cause of the disproportion.[28] The attainment of proportional representation of innocents in every field of endeavor will overcome this hovering, shameful legacy. White privilege is the stumbling block; identity politics is the gospel good news.

Only a blind man would dismiss these impassioned claims out of hand. Grim wounds from our nation's history have not entirely healed.[29] No one knows the path to conciliation we must take—dare

---

27. Tocqueville thought that as citizens in the democratic age become more lonely and isolated, they will be enticed by histories that inform them that they are caught up in vast social forces which they are powerless to alter. Tocqueville, *Democracy in America*, 2:496: "Classical historians taught men how to command; those of our own time teach next to nothing but how to obey [social forces]. In their writings, the author often figures large, but humanity is always tiny." Marx's theory of the necessary historical development of communism is a fine example of the sort of history Tocqueville criticizes.

28. What then are we to make of certain minorities—"Asian" and "East Indian" Americans—that are overrepresented in many fields of endeavor? Should the logic of identity politics be applied to them as well, which would require quotas that work against their success? Harvard University, the City on the Hill for identity politics, is under legal scrutiny for doing just that for decades. See Anemona Hartocollis, "Asian-Americans Suing Harvard Say Admissions Files Show Discrimination," *New York Times*, April 4, 2018, https://www.nytimes.com/2018/04/04/us/harvard-asian-admission.html.

29. The portion of Tocqueville's *Democracy in America* most difficult to read and to teach is the portion about slavery (vol. 1, 316–20; 341–363). Rejecting the racialist arguments of his day, Tocqueville thought through slavery using as his model the Egyptian captivity of the Israelites. His reference to the slave's satisfaction with "his master's hearth" (317) harkens to the Hebrew Bible's account of the longing of the Israelites wandering in the desert to return and sit "by the flesh pots ... when we did eat bread to the full" (Exod. 16:3). Later, Tocqueville notes that "the Negroes will be unlucky remnants, a poor wandering tribe lost amid the huge nation that is master of the land" (vol. 2, 351)—an allusion to Josh. 14:10; Ps. 107:4; Isa. 16:8; Ezek. 34:6). Tocqueville's insight is that slavery and mastery are habits, which altering legal arrangements will not immediately erase. That is why the wound of slavery would take so long to

we say it—to fulfill our national covenant. The self-certain path identity politics insists we tread assuages White Liberal Guilt, empowers innocent patronage brokers who themselves claim to speak for the innocents, showers some African Americans with enviable opportunities, and leaves a larger number behind. Every community needs to provide exemplars for the next generation, whose members then dutifully superimpose what they have gleaned from them upon an uncertain future, so that their world becomes just familiar enough to live in and build up. With a view to providing new, lifegiving exemplars, identity politics introduces African Americans into domains in society they have yet to occupy in appreciable numbers. A liberal, committed to robust pluralism, will register the problem of "white privilege"—but then ask: "Is there no recognition of the paradox at the very heart of the justification identity politics offers for doing this?" That is, it is assumed that African Americans are innocents, without a proud historical record of competence that provides exemplars with which to build a world, and intercession (it is assumed by identity politics) is necessary in every domain to achieve proportionality. But why is this assumed? Why are we not told of the African American exemplars who have shown themselves competent in every social domain?

Now set aside the wrenching collateral damage some African Americans suffer because they do not yet have the requisite habits and academic preparation needed to succeed in these new domains[30]—or worse, suffer because they do have them, but do not have the financial

---

heal in America. After the Israelites had been released from Egyptian bondage, their habits did not immediately change. The Hebrew account is that only God, mediated through Moses, can fully release man from slavery and bring him to the promised land—a theme echoed from the African American pulpit right from the beginning. When Martin Luther King, Jr. said, on the steps of the Lincoln memorial, "I may not get there with you," he was alerting his listener-parishioners to this biblical account and reminding them that Moses himself did not cross over into the promised land (see Deut. 34:5). King's "I Have a Dream" speech of August 28, 1963, is the high-water mark of publicly pronounced American covenantal theology in the twentieth century.

30. See Richard H. Sander and Stuart Taylor, Jr., *Mismatch: How Affirmative Action Hurts Students It's Intended to Help, and Why Universities Won't Admit It* (New York: Basic Books, 2012).

wherewithal to finish their program or pay for it later? How can the large numbers of African Americans who remain after this painful winnowing, who will never be privy to the intercession identity politics promises, build a world together, sometimes in broken neighborhoods they may never leave? The history of African American exemplars, which they most need to build their world, a history that exemplifies competence and pride, is inadmissible. The goal of identity politics is to provide new exemplars for innocents who have never had them. But to become competent liberal citizens rather than dependents of the state, those who cannot meet the eligibility requirements need the old exemplars that identity politics erases. Therein lies the paradox. Identity politics must remove old exemplars in order to justify creating new ones. It thereby sacrifices the prospects of "the least among us"[31] for the benefit of other African Americans, many of whom would now rise without the extra assistance that programmatic interventions by government provide.

Surely, there is a better way to heal our national wound. Much good has come from constructively opening different domains within society to African Americans. Robust pluralism requires nothing less, and it is long overdue. If, however, the consequence of the way we are currently achieving this result is the penury of other African Americans who become permanent dependents of the state—to be pointed to as proof of the innocent victim status that justifies identity politics policies in the first place—then we have not healed the wound, we have poured salt into it. Without encouraging liberal competence among all our citizens, this wound will never heal.

> The inner-city poor furnish the statistical base for the proposals [for racial proportionality], but the benefits go primarily to the already well-off. Black executives who already hold good jobs get promoted to better ones; blacks who already sit on important corporate boards get another directorship. And the people who provide the statistical base get nothing.[32]

---

31. See Matt. 25:40.

32. William Raspberry, "When Push Comes to Shove," *Washington Post*, August 29, 1990, A25. Cited in Woodson, *Triumphs of Joseph*, 21.

Identity politics, we have suggested, requires a transgressor who covers over the transgressions of the (supposed) innocents so that the stains of those innocents may remain hidden. The deeper, Christian foundation of identity politics would have it that all are stained, and that no mortal group can relieve us of our burden. Theologically compelling though this account may be, if all are stained, then no distinctions or judgments about specific historically inflicted wounds can be made. If all are stained, then our culpability can never be mitigated or erased by the wounds we have received at the hands of others. With this insight, we stumble toward a theology of the cross, on the basis of which we would conclude that the glory of God is revealed through the afflictions that we have patiently endured, irrespective of the fact that the transgressions of others have been their source.

> And as Jesus passed by, he saw a man which was blind from his birth. And his disciples asked him, saying, Master, who did sin, this man, or his parents, that he was born blind?
> Jesus answered, Neither hath this man sinned, nor his parents: but that the works of God should be made manifest in him. (John 9:1–3)

Looking down from the divine heights, this may be true; but from man's point of view, it is not. Distinctions must be made. Some have been harmed by the transgressions of others. "Why must I look to my own culpability when I have suffered at the hands of another?" So ask merely mortal humans—who then settle in with their wound and go no further.

The legacy of the wound of slavery in America will not be overcome unless both the Christian and the merely mortal view are given their due. The haunting, paradoxical truth is that we grow and are deepened by suffering—and that we must mitigate harm and the suffering transgression causes by balancing the ledger book of justice and holding transgressors accountable. More mysteriously still, without the correction that suffering provides, man's monstrous pride, which makes him see every other cause but his own, precludes the scales of justice from ever balancing.

If the scales of justice in America are to be balanced, however, who are the transgressors? And who are the innocents? There is no slavery in America today on the basis of which we can identify specific parties to the crime. Slavery ended in 1865. If reparations are to be offered, to whom, and on what basis? By whom, and on what basis? If only these matters could be established! Yet they cannot. And if they could be, what then? Would the account be settled once the checks have cleared?

Our problem is more intransigent, more ineffable. America lives with the legacy of slavery—an aftermath in which suspicions linger and trust is too often lacking. This has left America in limbo, neither indelibly stained nor without spot or blemish. This difficult intermediary condition must be given its due. The party of the Left tells us that America is indelibly stained, and that citizens must stand back and let government programs do their work. The party of the Right tells us we are without spot or blemish, and that citizens need do nothing at all. Both parties agree: citizens themselves are of no account in this matter. That is wrong. The truth is that the legacy of the wound of slavery must be addressed as all deep wounds must be addressed: with long and patient labor, animated by good will and a prayerful longing to heal what has been broken. Only through the liberal politics of competence can this be done. The identity politics of innocence, which calls out transgression and declares innocence but goes no further, cannot accomplish this. Nor, really, does it intend to.

Words echo in our dreams; and in the morning we awaken to a world that is still stiff and unaltered. The identity politics of innocence promulgates those dreams. In the Hebrew Bible, Joseph is sold by his brothers into Egyptian slavery; then, through demonstrated competence, he helps restore his people.[33] Therein lies the way forward.

> The Josephs of our own day do not need charity. They need to be considered as "friends." The relationship of friends in every arena of society, working to pursue common goals, is a relationship that will allow Americans to heal and prosper.[34]

---

33. See Gen. 37:2–50:26.

34. Woodson, *Triumphs of Joseph*, 137. See also Shelby Steele, "The Right and the Moral High Ground," *Wall Street Journal*, March 31, 2019, https://www.wsj.com/articles/the-right-and-the-moral-high-ground-11554057729?mod=e2two.

Wounds are healed by doing, not by sayings that give citizens comforting dreams. There are no shortcuts. Let us all be those Josephs—or find them, work with them, and give them all the support we are able to provide.

6

RACE AND ECONOMICS: THE QUESTION OF HUMAN AGENCY

W. B. Allen

The image most frequently employed in the Bible to convey the idea of felicity in this world invokes the eudaemonia of repose under "one's own vine and fig tree." That image powerfully conveys the full measure of the means and fruits of economic endeavor. Taken as a suggestion of undisturbed enjoyment (peace and prosperity), it is only partly correct. To take the full measure of the promise one must reflect on the special importance of the reference to the vine and the fig.

Harvesting the fruit of the vine and the fig tree requires first of all undertaking the rigorous labor of planting, cultivating, and tending. God, in other words, did not promise to provide material security. He promised rather to reward the effort to merit material security, while endowing us from the beginning with the power to exert such effort. It should be well known that the development of grapes and figs in the abundance fit to provide secure enjoyment demands, first, a labor that will require as long as five years before the plantings will bear the fruit that is wanted. Therefore in order to enjoy repose under one's own vine and fig tree, one must first work to make the vine and fig tree fruitful—which takes a long time.

This understanding of the biblical promise relates directly to our approach to capture the measure of economic promise in the contemporary world, and especially in the context of race and economics. For it is arguable that in no other dimension of current economic thinking has common opinion been more misguided. Indeed, I would say further that in no other dimension of current thinking has common opinion been more deliberately misled. In a word, we have experienced the persistent and distorting teaching that the effective use of liberty depends upon the prior guarantee of material security. That teaching has been systematically inculcated by inflcuential leaders from Franklin D. Roosevelt through Lyndon Johnson and Martin Luther King, Jr. Although the theoretical foundations of the teaching originate with the progenitors of neo-progressive ideology in the early twentieth century, the effective dissemination of the teaching flowed from the efforts of later icons of reform.

Roosevelt set the tone beginning with his 1932 Commonwealth Club address,[1] and continuing through his State of the Union messages of 1941[2] and 1944. In this series of public statements, he developed the arguments that—

1. True individual freedom cannot exist without economic security and independence: "Necessitous men are not free men."[3]

2. Certain economic truths have become accepted as self-evident:
   "We have accepted, so to speak, a second Bill of Rights ... a new basis of security and prosperity."[4]

---

1. Samuel I. Rosenman and William D. Hassett, eds., *The Public Papers and Addresses of Franklin D. Roosevelt, Volume One: The Genesis of the New Deal, 1928–1932* (New York: Random House, 1950), 742–55, https://teachingamericanhistory.org/library/document/commonwealth-club-address/.

2. Franklin Delano Roosevelt, "January 6, 1941: State of the Union Address (Four Freedoms)," Miller Center, University of Virginia, https://millercenter.org/the-presidency/presidential-speeches/january-6-1941-state-union-four-freedoms.

3. Franklin Delano Roosevelt, "January 11, 1944: Fireside Chat 28: On the State of the Union," Miller Center, University of Virginia, https://millercenter.org/the-presidency/presidential-speeches/january-11-1944-fireside-chat-28-state-union.

4. Roosevelt, "January 11, 1944: Fireside Chat 28."

Roosevelt's reformulation of the meaning of human rights for the United States attained its consummate formulation in the 1948 United Nations Declaration of Human Rights, which bore his direct imprint: "The right to a standard of living adequate for the health and well-being of oneself and of one's family, including food, clothing, housing, medical care and necessary social services" (Article 25). This version of every human under his or her own vine and fig tree inverts the biblical order, making eudaemonistic enjoyment a prerequisite for the free exercise of one's powers of labor—without indicating any purpose for which to labor!

These prescriptions for modern life were captured in Lyndon Johnson's 1965 declaration that, in order for "20 million Negroes" to have

> the chance ... to learn and grow, to work and share in society, to develop their abilities—physical, mental and spiritual—and to pursue their individual happiness, equal opportunity is essential, but not enough, not enough. Men and women of all races are born with the same range of abilities. But ability is not just the product of birth. Ability is stretched or stunted by the family that you live with, and the neighborhood you live in—by the school you go to and the poverty or the richness of your surroundings. It is the product of a hundred unseen forces playing upon the little infant, the child, and finally the man.[5]

Implicit in this argument is the mistaken hypothesis that economics is not color blind, with the result that racial variations in economic performance can be traced to the systemic dynamics of the economic system. That hypothesis is false. While people are not color blind, economics is. When people divert economic dynamics to the harm of disfavored minorities, it is human intervention rather than economics that is at fault. We see this plainly in the transition from Theodore Roosevelt's initial attempts to de-segregate the federal workforce to Woodrow Wilson's aggressive re-segregation of the federal work force. The fact that Wilson's neo-progressivism

---

5. Lyndon Baines Johnson, "June 4, 1965: Remarks at the Howard University Commencement," Miller Center, University of Virginia, https://millercenter.org/the-presidency/presidential-speeches/june-4-1965-remarks-howard-university-commencement.

was deliberately coordinated with the legally imposed practice of Jim Crow had far more to do with stunting black economic progress than anything intrinsic to free-market economics. When neo-progressives subsequently blamed the economic system, this only obscured the real cause of the frustrated dreams of American blacks in general.

King's "Dilemma of the Negro Americans"

One casualty of this misdirected suspicion proved to be Martin Luther King, Jr., who was incontestably the foremost public figure in the United States at the time he broached the most important question confronting the nation. This was the question of his book, *Where Do We Go from Here: Chaos or Community?*[6] In raising that question as he did, he implied that he would deliver what the nation most needed at that moment. King's judgment was that community was the appropriate answer to the question. Arguably, every significant issue of race and culture that Americans have since discussed was raised at some point by King. My contention is that, if in the meantime we have inherited chaos rather than community, we must ask whether it has something to do with the responses he provided to his own question. In other words, if the economic lot of blacks in America today is far less than what it should be, we might look at the ways King answered the question.

Several possibilities confront us. Either (1) King responded correctly with an adequate view of community, and his wisdom went unheeded; or (2) King responded incorrectly, and his error passed for wisdom in the nation, entailing natural consequences; or (3) variations of each of these came to pass and intersected with other cultural forces.

King looked for moral strength in a mystical and mythical "capacity for hardships" in American blacks to forge the path toward the end of full integration into American society. "It is on this strength that society must now begin to build."[7] At that point he jettisoned any potential for the claims of freedom and self-government as sufficient to ground the appeal for wholesale inclusion in American society:

---

6. Martin Luther King, Jr., *Where Do We Go from Here: Chaos or Community?* (1967; repr. Boston: Beacon, 2010).

7. King, *Where Do We Go from Here*, 116.

"This is no time for romantic illusions and empty philosophical debates about freedom. This is a time for action."[8] His explanation for this was pragmatic: The difficulties American blacks faced in 1967 (when he wrote) were cultural and inherited, he believed, and only liberation from the weight of that inherited tradition could supply the life change that American blacks needed. The discovery of a cultural or institutional basis for black disadvantages provided for King the "most optimistic" part of the story. By his lights, culture could be turned from the work of destruction to the work of reconstruction.

> [T]he causes for [the black community's] present crisis are culturally and socially induced. What man has torn down, he can rebuild. At the root of the difficulty in Negro life today is pervasive and persistent economic want. To grow from within, the Negro family—and especially the Negro man—needs only fair opportunity for jobs, education, housing and access to culture. To be strengthened from the outside requires protection from the grim exploitation that has haunted the Negro for three hundred years.[9]

This "optimistic" conclusion comes eight pages into an analysis which opened with the observation that the "dilemma of white America is the source and cause of the dilemma of Negro America."[10] King's two Americas, setting the tone for the 1968 Kerner Commission Report,[11] relate to one another only as "oppressor" and "oppressed" are related to one another. For American blacks, the connection between their pain ("the central quality" of their life) and their hopes is a necessary intervention from "outside" to transform oppression into salvation. Without that intervention, there would be no escape from America's lack of true community.

"Being a Negro in America means being scarred by a history of slavery and family disorganization," King wrote, weaving the real-

---

8. King, *Where Do We Go from Here*, 68.
9. King, *Where Do We Go from Here*, 128.
10. King, *Where Do We Go from Here*, 121.
11. *Report of the National Advisory Commission on Civil Disorders* (New York: Bantam, 1968), https://archive.org/details/reportofnation00unit/page/630/mode/2up.

ity of three hundred years into an accumulated burden in 1967 and presenting an account of the abstract "Negro family" as if it were an autobiography.[12] In these early pages, the reader cannot escape the obvious implication that, respecting "negroes," the "content of their character" is a product of suffering, impotence, and impoverishment. Neither in recounting the tales of woe or the magical survival of American blacks does King ever turn to any intrinsic human capacities or strengths, either in explanation of past achievements or in projecting future achievements. Culture, it seems, is the only force that has formed black character—and the only force that will liberate blacks.

Since for King the warp of cultures in America is color, one might anticipate that the weave would be character, as in the expression that people are to be judged "not by the color of their skin, but by the content of their character."[13] That would mean that the cultural change one seeks is not so much color blindness, which would be merely a consequence of paying primary attention to character, but rather that sensitivity to character which would merge two cultures into one. To change the culture, one must teach the society how to make judgments of character. According to King, however, American blacks cannot take on that task themselves, for they live under the spell of "color shock"—the concept that their rejection is due to something they cannot change.

> [I]t constitutes a major emotional crisis. It is accompanied by a sort of fatiguing, wearisome hopelessness. If one is rejected because he is uneducated, he can at least be consoled by the fact that it may be possible for him to get an education. If one is rejected because he is low on the economic ladder, he can at least dream of the day that he will rise from his dungeon of economic deprivation. If one is rejected because he speaks with an accent, he can at least, if he desires, work to bring his speech in line with the dominant group. If, however, one is rejected because of his color, he must face the anguishing fact

---

12. King, *Where Do We Go from Here*, 122.

13. Martin Luther King, Jr., "I Have a Dream," August 28, 1963, https://www.archives.gov/files/press/exhibits/dream-speech.pdf.

that he is being rejected because of something in himself that cannot be changed.[14]

Famously, each of King's hypotheticals served in the earlier part of this century as the catechism black families carefully rehearsed in their children (including, I dare say, the family of the elder King who instructed King, Jr.). For example, they were surely taught the value of advancement through education. The conclusion, however, that skills and character which one might change have been subordinated to the overriding importance of "color shock" relegates the earlier catechism to a second-order necessity. A day may come when one can counsel poor men to "try harder," if ever the society can rid itself of "color shock."

Paradoxically, King seemed to believe that would not happen. As long as blacks were mired in poor education, poverty, and social disadvantage, these things "proved" that color shock was a long way from being eradicated. So in the meantime, "wearisome hopelessness" was inevitable for blacks. It would be impossible for them to attempt cultural or economic improvement as long as they were poor and disadvantaged. Their poverty and disadvantage were proofs of white racism, which showed that color shock was deeply entrenched. It was a vicious circle: black disadvantage proved white racism, which made black efforts to escape disadvantage futile, while lack of effort reinforced white perception of black inferiority, which in turn only reinforced white racism. King's remedy actually perpetuated the problem.

King wrote little about character in American blacks except to exculpate crimes by citing the "environment" and "victimization." It may be a dramatic illustration of the path taken in his book (and life) that he focused, as did many others, on the disproportionate number of American blacks who served in Vietnam as an injustice, while saying nothing of blacks' disproportionate heroism, their disproportionate sense of duty, and their disproportionate inclination to volunteer.

---

14. King, *Where Do We Go from Here*, 131.

But King did not neglect character entirely. When he enumerated five recommended responses to "the Negro's dilemma,"[15] he began with his closest invocation of character, "a rugged sense of somebodyness." To overcome a "feeling of being less than human, the Negro must assert for all to hear and see a majestic sense of his worth."[16] Naturally, mere self-assertion is not a substitute for solid accomplishment. Moreover, it may be the case that a premature self-assertion may subvert the genuine foundations of accomplishment, which alone engender self-respect.

Nonetheless, King evidently means in this appeal to inculcate a sense of need for such fundamental virtues as industry, courage, and moderation. In this regard, it is impossible to explain why his spirited defense of real life in the ghetto—where there are "churches as well as bars" "stable families ... as well as illegitimacies," and "ninety percent of the young people who never come in conflict with the law"[17]—did not provide him substantial opportunity to sermonize on opportunities for emulation in the pursuit of "somebodyness." Praiseworthy elements of character must surely inform the "striving" and "hoping" which he describes in that context. It appears that King did not enlarge on these themes because they did not support the ultimate response he had fashioned for the main question.

The remaining responses to "the Negro's dilemma" are "group unity," a "constructive use of the [limited] freedom we already possess," union "around powerful action programs," and "enlarging the whole society and giving it a new sense of [progressive] values."[18] These prescriptions for "social change" merge in a single consideration, which King develops in his final chapter, "The World House." There he describes the emergence of a political movement transcend-

---

15. King, *Where Do We Go from Here*, 142. "[T]he Negro is called upon to be as resourceful as those who have not known such oppression and exploitation. This is the Negro's dilemma. He who starts behind in a race must forever remain behind or run faster than the man in front. What a dilemma! *It is a call to do the impossible.* It is enough to cause the Negro to give up in despair." [Emphasis added.]

16. King, *Where Do We Go from Here*, 144–45.

17. King, *Where Do We Go from Here*, 134.

18. King, *Where Do We Go from Here*, 142.

ing the United States and animating a global movement toward social democracy.[19]

That ultimate political movement is the international analogue to the indigenous political movement King envisioned for United States, where he would nurture a five-point program that argues, "More and more, the civil rights movement will have to engage in the task of organizing people into permanent groups to protect their own interests."[20] As described, this movement would consist of blacks, northern liberal Democrats, labor unions, and an ever-widening circle of oppressed peoples. King was convinced that "there is a need for a radical restructuring of the architecture of American society."[21] The word *architecture* was deliberate, for King had in mind a new design based on fundamental principles rather than incidental circumstances.

King said little else about character, for three reasons. First, he placed no faith in the character of American whites. Second, he expected no rewards for exertions of character by American blacks. He was not interested in a "new black middle class" and never counseled the poor to follow the middle class. Third, a focus on character within a given community would be inconsistent with his mission to transcend that community for the sake of a new community built on entirely different grounds.

Although King acknowledged that "we are also Americans," that identity was a decidedly subordinate moral consideration in the analysis. The fact that "our destiny is tied up with the destiny of America"[22] did not commit American blacks to an American destiny which was intrinsic to its foundation. For King, American racism could be negated ultimately only by the negation of the moral soil from which it sprouted. It was as if racism was native to America's soil rather than an excrescence of that soil, and it would need a new soil.

---

19. King, *Where Do We Go from Here*, 142.
20. King, *Where Do We Go from Here*, 154–55.
21. King, *Where Do We Go from Here*, 157.
22. King, *Where Do We Go from Here*, 62.

> [H]istorians in future years will have to say there lived a great people—a black people—who bore their burdens of oppression in the heat of many days and who, through tenacity and creative commitment, injected new meaning into the veins of American life.[23]

Martin Luther King, Jr. answered his rhetorical question "chaos or community" by dreaming of founding a new community. The unjust treatment he accorded George Washington, ignoring Washington's moral anguish about slavery and denying Washington's liberation of his slaves in his will, may be attributed to King's own ambition to rival Washington as a founder. But King failed where Washington succeeded. It remains for us to figure out why.

Martin Luther King, Jr.'s Failure

Let me repeat my observation that there are few if any questions about race and culture that we entertain in 2019 which had not been considered, in some manner, by King in 1967. Nor would many deny that black communities deteriorated culturally in the three decades after his death, when his influence hardly diminished. Nothing illustrates this deterioration better than the emergence of "hate speech" proscriptions that exempt black folk. It was once common in the homes of American blacks whom I knew to admonish youths to avoid terms such as *nigger* in referring to one another. Such precepts continued into the 1960s. But since then they have disappeared almost altogether. I submit that they have disappeared because of the successful invocation of the false notion of a black culture and the correlative exculpation of blacks for all sorts of "bad behavior" on the grounds of their "victim" status. King's opting to shape community among blacks rather than to shape a community on American principles is the immediate moral cause of this enormous transformation in our society. One could add that this approach has also affected the economic status of large parts of the black community that have accepted King's presuppositions about liberty and security.

---

23. King, *Where Do We Go from Here*, 158.

Not blacks alone but also many whites have fallen prey to King's misguided principles For many, it was easy to transition from thinking of blacks as different and inferior to thinking of blacks as unassimilably different. This move released mental and moral energy which otherwise could have been used to build community. For guilty consciences anxious to escape responsibility, but at a loss as to what course to pursue, the idea that one could embrace "diversity" or "multiculturalism" (or the idea of a separate black community which merited respect as distinct) provided a natural outlet. Then it was no longer necessary to ask whether America had succeeded in fulfilling its principles on its own terms.

Of course, the nettlesome question of economic and social inequality remained—at least the inequality that could not be reduced to cultural difference. Since it is impossible to measure the connection between economic progress and respect for cultural difference, it follows that diminishing inequalities constitute no evidence at all of a need for special treatment for American blacks. In fact, thinking this way is actually paradoxical. Let me explain.

It is commonly supposed that special programs for blacks are justified by their "history" and not their present circumstances. That means one cannot demand either personal or cultural accommodations to American society to show the effects of the special programs. So the question of "progress" is impossible to measure. All that is left is the standard of "representation" as a totem to express King's goals. This is why we often hear of "underrepresented minorities" in the workplace, in schools, and in government offices, appointed and elective. What is actually meant, however, remains vague. As long as a single minority individual anywhere might be said to be less advantageously situated than he or she might wish, it will be said that minorities are underrepresented. And it will be impossible to criticize minority culture—especially black culture—or to talk about what will bring genuine economic improvement to black communities. The paradox, then, is that presumptions about what is needed for black progress are the very things that stymie black progress.

Nothing the nation does, including "massive government expenditures," can ever genuinely satisfy the demands that King made for a new American community without its American roots. But what *is* possible for the United States today is to discover a way to reconnect ideas of American community with both expectations of as well as obligations to American blacks. But this cannot be accomplished without refuting and overturning the cultural exceptionalism built by King and others. The most recent evidence of that cultural exceptionalism is on display in the "1619 Project" that has gained wide currency and is on prominent display in a glossy *New York Times Magazine* presentation.[24] The upshot of the project is the argument that the contributions of enslaved Africans are mainly responsible for American prosperity.

Let's begin by asking the obvious question: Is it true that American blacks in 2019 (or 1967 for that matter) reflect in their characters, habits, attitudes, and prospects the full weight of three hundred years of suffering by American blacks? Take an individual black, born in this generation. In what way does he or she bear the weight of three hundred years of black experience? Are his or her natural endowments irrelevant? His or her family circumstances? His or her friends? The accidents that befell him or her in the course of his or her life? What about the three hundred and sixty years of broader American experience and the much longer European experience stretching back to prehistory? When calculating the impact of the past on just one person, what sense does it make to focus on the experience of slavery? He wears no stripes on his back! My point is that it is an entire fiction that black people today still feel the pains of the past.

I will make this more personal. Family lore has it that my great-grandfather freely emigrated from the West Indies to the United States shortly before the onset of the War for the Union in 1861. He had been enticed by an offer of economic opportunity—that is, he was recruited to be a foreman on a large farm in the South. By that time, of course, it had become increasingly difficult to smuggle slaves into the country in violation of the law, but evasions remained possible. When, therefore, Great-Grandfather Sidiphus arrived in the United States and discovered that he was just another slave, one of those evasions was revealed.

---

24. See W. B. Allen, "The *New York Times* Resurrects the Positive Good Slavery Argument," *Law & Liberty*, October 2, 2019, https://www.lawliberty.org/2019/10/02/the-new-york-times-resurrects-the-positive-good-slavery-argument/.

The point of this story is not that of fraud and betrayal—both of which were very real. Nor is it to invoke the oppression of slavery, though that was very real. It is rather to raise the very poignant question of whether Sidiphus's initiative in seeking out opportunities of economic advance for himself and his later family was justified by the results. At first glance, it may not appear so. But when one reflects that his enslavement was not long-lived, that the country to which he looked as a land of opportunity soon liberated its slaves, and that he did eventually build a family, a large family that experienced the disadvantages of living as a despised minority among people who sought to foreclose opportunities to prosper, but, finally, also produced offspring who advanced to the highest levels of achievement and responsible office in the country, one must ask whether Sidiphus indeed made a mistake. It turned out that the economic opportunity he sought did indeed redound to the benefit of his posterity—and others besides. Moreover, that fact seems to have a direct relationship to the design and effect of American institutions and beliefs. This means, in sum, that our picture of the past must reflect multiple pathways and outcomes and not merely simplistic blacks and whites. And that great fact has been missed by far too many thought leaders in the late twentieth- and early twenty-first centuries.

Race has long been a problem in the United States in ways adequately explained in various technical writings, including some of my own. It has not, however, been proven that race is an integral part of American culture. It is a logical error to confuse what is pervasive with what is integral. And it is a moral error to derive necessary conclusions from accidental determinants. The conclusion that racism is intrinsic or integral to American principle constitutes such a moral error.

On the basis of this moral error Martin Luther King, Jr., and others besides, have created a fiction of black culture and community that serves a single purpose—namely, to extract American blacks from the warp and woof of an American culture regarded as fatally flawed. The reality in the United States has been and remains plural communities fused (and continuing to fuse) into a single American culture. There exist plural black communities, no less than plural white communities—despite the reality that black communities in the main have not been constituted by family migrations as white communities typically have been. The relatively successful effort to flatten the plural black communities into a single conception of *the* black community represents a significant political accomplishment, which has done little to alter the social landscape. On that social landscape, accordingly, one still witnesses the leading dynamic of American culture—assimilation—occurring under the lengthening shadow of a changing political reality. That changing political reality means we might reasonably wonder how long the American dynamic will persevere, as the supporting political fretwork continues to evolve to accommodate the goals of King's "revolution." Must it ever after be regarded as settled that political representation consists in identity group participation? Or will it again become possible to imagine political representation as the representation of individuals? Assimilation has occurred heretofore on the basis of the latter dynamic—individual representation—which operated to attenuate group loyalties. The current trajectory of group representation, however, heightens the political significance of group loyalties.

I have written above of the disappearance of certain social practices in the black families that I knew. Others speak and have routinely written (dating at least from the Moynihan Report[25]) of the disappearance of supportive social institutions and practices in black communities plagued by crime, illegitimacy, and other dysfunctions. All evidence suggests a social migration toward the new political standard of participation in society, a standard that distinguishes groups and group rights and that measures social obligation strictly in relation to group identity. More and more, then, I am judged not as an individual but as a "black" person. This is a disintegration of that larger patriotism which is founded in the *individual*'s rights. The lesser patriotism—the group identity—undermines the larger patriotism.

My argument about undermining American patriotism would not make sense if it were true that American principles fail to secure any reasonable prospect of pervasive liberty, and provide no foundation for genuine community and prosperity. I think they do, but I also think that we have not given them a chance to be tested adequately

---

25. Lee Rainwater and William L. Yancey, *The Moynihan Report and the Politics of Controversy* (Cambridge: MIT Press, 1967).

on this question of race. For King, and nearly all who followed him, have preferred the lesser patriotism of black identity rather than the larger patriotism of individual identity rooted in American principles. Not since the beginning of the civil rights movement have we tried to test those principles. Ironic, isn't it? The civil rights movement may inadvertently have spawned the most serious obstacle to the progress of American blacks in our time. This is the paradox I mentioned earlier. Black leaders have turned to group identity rather than individual identity and American principles of assimilation. The result has been cultural stagnation for some black communities. Just as Americans discovered in the Revolution of 1776 that they could not see the end of their journey unless they committed themselves to the point where they could not turn back, both black and white Americans must commit themselves to the project of *American* identity before they can experience the results of that project.

Therefore the task to renew the appeal of American community and the legitimacy of assimilation—including standards of decent behavior—falls not to American blacks or whites per se but to every American. For King's failed response to the great crisis draws the chaos nearer with each revolution of our political solar system.

The way forward is not too difficult to discern. We should learn from the course followed by King rather than follow it. King discarded a history of accomplishment for a paean of victimization. He neglected even his own middle class biography to weave a story of deprivation into the lineage of every black. Sadly, King committed black people to subjugation to cultural identity in purchase of political cachet.

Elsewhere I have written that George Washington's success may be attributed to the fact that he preferred justice to patriotism.[26] Certainly it is true, one may insist, that King preached justice above patriotism. But why, then, may he not be regarded as equally successful? The answer comes in two parts. First, what one preaches does not always reveal one's purpose. Second, even if one grants as I do that King preached justice, everything must hinge on the question of presumptions about the requirements of justice. Getting them wrong will cause even a noble intent to miscarry.

---

26. W. B. Allen, *George Washington: America's First Progressive* (New York: Peter Lang, 2008).

Exploring that important question will return us to the question of the economic prospects for American blacks (or the question of race and economics in general) and, in doing so, we can follow no finer examples than those of Frederick Douglass (who closed the nineteenth century) and Booker T. Washington (who opened the twentieth) on that precise question.

Growing and Prospering While Suffering

The real test of an economic system lies in its capacity to resist the distorting effects of partial and discriminating interventions. While the logic of trade is unvarying—and color blind—the imposition of political or cultural restraint can direct it away from its natural currents. Nothing illustrates this better than the pattern of Jim Crow legislation at the end of the nineteenth century that sought to enforce segregation in public transportation. The reason such laws were required in Louisiana, Tennessee, Georgia, and elsewhere was precisely because the market operating in the absence of restraint would not sustain segregation. The emergence of Jim Crow, therefore, constitutes *prima facie* evidence of economic conditions otherwise favorable to effective participation in the market by American blacks.

That is the story told so effectively by Frederick Douglass and Ida Wells-Barnett in 1893 in the essays collected in *The Reason Why*, which challenges the Columbian Exposition's exclusion of American blacks in the story of American industrial and cultural progress. Wells declared that the neglected story "would best illustrate [America's] moral grandeur."[27]

> The exhibit of the progress made by a race in 25 years of freedom as against 250 years of slavery, would have been the greatest tribute to the greatness and progressiveness of American institutions which could have been shown the world.[28]

---

27. Ida B. Wells, Preface to Wells, ed., *The Reason Why the Colored American Is Not in the World's Columbian Exposition: The Afro-American's Contribution to Columbian Literature* (Urbana and Chicago: University of Illinois, 1893), https://digital.library.upenn.edu/women/wells/exposition/exposition.html.

28. Wells, Preface to *The Reason Why*.

What is remarkable about this claim is the context in which it is made, a context that Douglass and Wells-Barnett emphatically make plain: In the scant twenty-five years since 1865 (the war's end), the population of blacks in the United States had virtually doubled (4 million to 8 million). Moreover, that natural increase had been accompanied by extensive accomplishments in educational, agricultural, industrial, and cultural development. Census reports demonstrate in considerable detail a portrait of solid participation in the economy. They do so, however, against the backdrop of the "outrages upon the Negro in this country."[29]

Nor were they sparing in detailing those outrages, which included drastic restrictions of the franchise, coordinated exclusions from political office, deprivation of material resources, and most significantly, widespread campaigns of violence and brutalization characterized by thousands of lynchings throughout the country. In other words, the transition in only a quarter of a century from the status of a mere "commodity"—nearly imbrued chattel—to that of demonstrated humanity transpired in the ferocious heat of a furnace of rejection, a heat so intense that Douglass could maintain that "what the colored people gained by the war they have partly lost by the peace."[30]

To say that they did not wear rose-colored glasses would be an understatement. Retelling the story from 1619 to 1893, they comprehended every reversal and disappointment. Nevertheless, Douglass was able to aver,

> As to the increased resistance met with of late, let us use a little philosophy. It is best to account in a hopeful way for this reaction and even to read it as a favorable symptom. It is a proof that the Negro is not standing still. He is not dead, but alive and active. He is not drifting with the current, but manfully resisting it and fighting his way to better conditions than those of the past, and better than those which popular opinion prescribes for him. He is not contented with his surroundings but wholly dares to break away from the path and hew out a way of safety and happiness for himself in defiance of all opposing forces....

---

29. Frederick Douglass, Introduction to *The Reason Why*.
30. Douglass, Introduction to *The Reason Why*.

> The enemies of the Negro see that he is making progress and they naturally wish to stop him and keep him in just what they consider his proper place....
>
> But the Negro has said a decided no to all this, and is now by industry, economy, and education wisely raising himself to conditions of civilization and comparative well-being beyond anything formerly thought possible for him....
>
> What the Negro has to do then, is to cultivate a courageous and cheerful spirit, use philosophy and exercise patience. He must embrace every avenue open to him for the acquisition of wealth. He must educate his children and build up a character for industry, economy, intelligence and virtue. Next to victory is the glory and happiness of manfully contending for it....
>
> Our situation demands faith in ourselves, faith in the power of truth; faith in work and faith in the influence of manly character.[31]

The counsel of resistance in the face of adversity was made not in a vacuous appeal to hopefulness but in reliance upon "vine and fig" investment—hard and patient labor. That counsel, in turn, shows confidence in the power of economic self-reliance to reverse political and cultural disadvantages. The prudence of this counsel could be measured in a fair test of economic self-reliance. Booker T. Washington took up that challenge.

When Do We Reach Q. E. D.?

In 1893, Booker T. Washington delivered a series of speeches articulating the foundations of his project at Tuskegee Institute. In these addresses he explained that the purpose of his Institute was to demonstrate that "the Negro race" should be recognized as a contributor to the nation's well-being instead of "a burden, a menace to your civilization and commercial life."[32]

Washington made his arguments most comprehensively in his 1899 "Memorial Address on Abraham Lincoln," which took its place

---

31. Douglass, Introduction to *The Reason Why*.

32. Booker T. Washington, "Address Delivered at Hampton Institute," November 18, 1895, Teaching American History, https://teachingamericanhistory.org/library/document/address-delivered-at-hampton-institute/.

alongside the similar and earlier famous address by Douglass at the dedication of the Freedmen's Memorial to Lincoln. In his own address, Washington was careful to establish Lincoln as a bridge figure who can link American whites and American blacks in a common cause.[33] That cause would transcend emancipation and open a window onto the life of "unfettered freedom" for black and white alike.

> A freedom from dependence on others' labor to the independent or self-labor; freedom to transform unused and dwarfed hands into skilled and productive hands; to change labor from drudgery into that which is dignified and glorified; to change local commerce into trade with the world; to change the Negro from an ignorant man into an intelligent man; to change sympathies that were local and narrow into love and good-will for all mankind; freedom to change stagnation into growth, weakness into power; yea, to us all, your race and mine, Lincoln has been a great emancipator.[34]

This is Washington's way of transforming Jerome Ferris's painting, "Lincoln and the Contraband," (the spirit captured in Douglass's celebration of Lincoln) into a portrait of "Lincoln and the Citizens," where the dilemmas of difference are erased through the fruits of industry. It is important to observe that Washington's counsel of self-reliance (hardly surprising in a man who, as a boy, walked five hundred miles in order to obtain a higher education at Hampton Institute) conveys not exhortation to black separatism but confidence in black agency. The nexus between self-sufficiency and eventual assimilation, resting on the efficacy of the free market, presupposes that real change requires mutual respect and independence of parties rather than dependence of one party on another.

---

33. As the scholar Diana Schaub has pointed out. Schaub, "Booker T. Washington and the Lessons of Lincoln," lecture at University of Colorado-Boulder for the American National Character Project, September 19, 2019, https://www.youtube.com/watch?v=3A3V77fR7sU.

34. Booker T. Washington, "An Abraham Lincoln Memorial Address in Philadelphia," February 14, 1899, Teaching American History, https://teachingamericanhistory.org/library/document/an-abraham-lincoln-memorial-address-in-philadelphia/.

This concept was forcefully brought home to me in 2018 when I led forty-five school teachers on a tour of civil rights sites and monuments throughout the South. As we visited Selma, Alabama, we paused at Bethel A.M.E. Church, where the protesters who crossed the Edmund Pettus Bridge gathered to prepare themselves for their famous march in 1965. As we sat in the sanctuary and I was addressing the assembly on the context and endeavors of that great event, I looked up and around at the inside of that church and broke off mid-sentence. After a pause I said, "This splendid architecture was erected in the first decade of the twentieth century, in the very teeth of repressive rage—think of the lynchings all over the nation at this time."

I then asked, "Who built this building?"

We all knew. It was the black churchgoers. They had constructed an edifice of impressive beauty and solidity. Then I asked another question.

"Is it not impossible to imagine the people who could do this as somehow disabled, limited, unable to provide for themselves even in the midst of great suffering?"

The obvious answer was that it is impossible. We resolved from that moment no longer to bear the image of a people who were awaiting rescue as the characteristic image of the American black.

Between the opening and the end of the twentieth century, however, there was resistance to the approach argued by Douglass and Washington. Sociologist and writer W. E. B. Du Bois, for example, advocated political and legal rather than market initiatives. Du Bois became increasingly disenchanted with market-based exertions in the face of lynchings and race riots that seemed to put black economic independence out of reach. The burgeoning black capital and professional classes were narrowly constrained when not simply burned out or killed. And that situation was often taken as an expression of the nature of capitalism rather than what it really was—namely, extra-legal, legal, and non-economic repression.

By the middle of the twentieth century, the Douglass-Washington current reached its consummation in the 1950 release of a half-dollar coin bearing the images of George Washington Carver and Booker T. Washington. That coin symbolized the appeal of the argument for growth through economic presence. By the same time, however, not only had the arguments of Franklin D. Roosevelt—captured in the United Nations Declaration of Human Rights—gained complete purchase, but growing anti-capitalist sentiment among black leaders began to surge, eventually to crest in the creation of the national holiday for Martin Luther King, Jr. Between these two events—the release of the Carver-Washington half-dollar and the establishment of the King holiday—something was lost in American black cultures: continued confidence in the efficacy of self-reliance.

Washington's most powerful and comprehensive speech, "The Educational and Industrial Emancipation of the Negro" in February 1903, apparently lost traction during those years. In that speech Washington, like Douglass before, provided a comprehensive narrative of the American experience in which he delineated with great clarity the meaning of freedom. In that speech he powerfully weaves together the importance of independence and agency with the underlying foundation of Christian principle.

> Those are most truly free today who have passed through great discipline. Those persons in the United States who are most truly free in body, mind, morals, are those who have passed through the most severe training—those who have exercised the most patience and, at the same time, the most dogged persistence and determination.
>
> To deal more practically and directly with the affairs of my own race, I believe that both the teachings of history as well as the results of everyday observation should convince us that we shall make our most enduring progress by laying the foundation carefully, patiently in the ownership of the soil, the exercise of habits of economy, the saving of money, the securing of the most complete education of hand and head, and the cultivation of Christian virtue....
>
> I repeat here what I have often said in the south. The Negro seeks no special privileges. All that he asks is opportunity—that the same law which is made by the white man and applied to the one race be applied with equal certainty and exactness to the other.[35]

---

35. Booker T. Washington, "The Educational and Industrial Emancipation of the Negro," February 22, 1903, Teaching American History, https://teachingamericanhistory.org/library/document/the-educational-and-industrial-emancipation-of-the-negro/.

Washington was no less specific and demanding in what he sought of the dominant race: "No race can degrade another without degrading itself. No race can assist in lifting another without itself being broadened and made more Christ-like."[36]

Washington made clear that even in the face of enormous suffering, growth remains possible, as long as there is respect for individual agency. When Washington answered the question of what is to be done for the Negro, his reply was, "Let him alone." This is what he meant when he said that "freedom is enough." For the black man is no less suited to provide for himself than any other human being. Despite the cultural setbacks I have described in this chapter, the reality is that demonstrable progress is evident in the accomplishments and advances to date of the black middle class. What remains perplexing is the continuing tendency in public discourse to discount that progress and speak instead of black victimhood. In other words, history has proved what Douglass and Washington set out to demonstrate, but current conversation persistently fails to attend to that history.

This is not the place to explore in depth today's cultural preference for the counterfactual over the actual relationship between race and economics. But I can say at least this much—that we no longer assume that man's good has already been provided by his own form and constitution. We have presumed instead that what becomes of a man or woman depends upon what society will do for him or her. As a consequence, the natural and necessary instruments of peace and prosperity are systematically disregarded in favor of constructivist attempts to remake humanity by governmental means. We saw that tendency in Roosevelt and his successors. We know, too, that it lies at the heart of a secular approach to the question of humanity. Oddly, and even paradoxically, we suffer from a disposition to rely upon human self-sufficiency to create human meaning, while disregarding the evidence that the individual human is already invested with the powers needed to earn a repose "under his own vine and fig tree."

---

36. Washington, "The Educational and Industrial Emancipation."

7

EXILE AND RETURN FROM SLAVERY*

Glenn C. Loury

When thinking about the moral foundations of the American Republic, the historical fact of African slavery and the ongoing struggle of black people for inclusion within the body politic pose profound questions with biblical resonance. These are questions about responsibility, duty, rights, and mutual obligation. Such questions have bedeviled reflective observers of the American scene for centuries. They do not yield to simple formulas. A cursory review of contemporary American politics confirms that these matters have yet to be resolved. Slavery was our "original sin" but, by itself, emancipation of the slaves has not led to our national "salvation." Therefore we must ask where such nation-saving grace might be found.

I argue here as a matter of social ethics that an adequate moral reckoning with the legacy of slavery requires us Americans to replace a legalistic notion, "racial justice," with a covenantal ideal that I call "transracial humanism." By "racial justice" I mean the pursuit by victims of antiblack racism for quid-pro-quo recompense and make-whole relief. I wish to contrast this with the humanistic

---

*Parts of this chapter are adapted from my 1996 University Lecture at Boston University, "The Divided Society and the Democratic Idea."

ideal that we Americans are all one people, bound together under a national covenant and for this reason responsible to one another in a deep and ongoing way. In doing so I recognize that not all moral dilemmas are justice dilemmas; not all inequalities are evidence of unfairness; not every group disparity requires political remedy; not all historical wrongs can be rectified; and neither can all political conflicts be reconciled.

Even so, I wish to suggest, a nation can endure such unavoidable injustices, unfairness, inequality, and conflicts as may, from time to time, afflict it, if only its people would faithfully embrace the appropriate national covenant. That is, "transcendence" remains available to us in the face of "original sin," if we understand the ongoing and seemingly permanent subordination of the descendants of African slaves within America's social economy as mainly a relationship problem, and not a justice problem. To put this somewhat differently, our national salvation lies mainly in our redefining identities, not in redistributing resources.

This point has ancient resonance. The biblical story of national covenant, with its motifs of exile and return, provides a helpful analogue for the new relationships and identities that are needed. Biblical Israel was exiled twice for her unfaithfulness to the national covenant to which YHWH had called her. Especially in the second exile in Babylon, Israel was cured of her previous penchant for idolatry. She might have been guilty of other sins in her later history, but after her sixth century BCE return from Babylon, she never again lapsed into pagan idolatry. Her time in exile prompted her prophets and leaders to search their hearts for a way to return to the God of Israel.

My contention is that national covenant is a powerful religious concept that involves all persons in a society. America has experienced a kind of exile in its covenant because we have divided into "us" and "them." We have not taken ownership of the covenant for ourselves. We have permitted false conceptions of race to get us off the hook, in terms of mutual obligation. By seeing ourselves as belonging to distinct races, we have deceived ourselves into ignoring the social obligations of the covenant.

America was a slave republic at the founding. It would be another four score and seven years before the nation—which had been, in

Lincoln's immortal words, "conceived in liberty and dedicated to the proposition that all men are created equal"—would, via the seismic convulsion of a great civil war, finally rid itself of that most undemocratic of institutions. But the abolition of slavery did not resolve the conflict between our democratic ideals and the reality of social division. There remained the need to achieve an estate of equal citizenship for the descendants of African slaves, not just in theory, but also as a matter of political fact. Nearly a century more would pass before significant progress toward this objective could occur. This democratization, though well advanced, even today remains incomplete.

We have no need for a litany of statistics here. The plain fact is that black Americans are vastly overrepresented among those suffering the maladies and afflictions of social marginality, however measured. Some districts in the middle of our great cities, occupied almost exclusively by blacks, are among the most miserable, violent, and despairing places in the modern, industrial world. The prisons are filled to overflowing with black men. Blacks as a group experience lower life expectancies, higher infant mortality rates, less academic achievement, higher poverty rates, and greater unemployment than do other Americans. Historical trend lines give us no reason to anticipate that these disparities will attenuate in the near future.

Nor is this divide discernible only in the conditions of the poor. The psychological and political rifts separating Americans by race cut across class lines. Weariness is discernible in the public conversations we now endure across this chasm. Idealists of an earlier era who preached the interracial gospel of "the Beloved Community" look in hindsight to have been naive dreamers. Nevertheless, theirs was a worthy dream, I contend—one that we can and must make our reality if this breach is ever to be healed.

This is no easy task. When Americans talk about race, words such as *dilemma*, *paradox*, and *tragedy* abound. Despite the revolution in our law and politics that occurred in the 1950s and 1960s, the poisonous legacy of slavery remains with us, as do many of the doubts about the future of our political order to which that legacy has given rise. Such doubts have troubled every generation since the founding. In the early nineteenth century, Alexis de Tocqueville, surveying the future prospects for race relations in the United States, prophesied that "the presence of the blacks upon American soil" would become the cause of "great revolutions there." He was particularly struck by how "the prejudice rejecting the Negroes seems to increase in proportion to their emancipation, and inequality cuts deep into mores as it is effaced from the laws."[1] At mid-twentieth century, we find Gunnar Myrdal rediscovering this fundamental conflict between the high ideals of our political culture and those social customs that relegated Negroes to a status of second-class citizenship. His book was called, simply, *An American Dilemma*, and it came to define America's race problem in the post–WWII era.[2]

Now, as a new century unfolds, the way forward toward racial reconciliation is decidedly unclear. We Americans must entertain the possibility that the civil rights revolution, so welcome and so long overdue, did not fully vindicate the virtue of our democratic traditions. A great deal of work remains. Responsibility for doing this work falls upon all Americans. This is the work of civic inclusion—incorporating descendants of slaves fully into the commonwealth—and thereby completing a process begun by emancipation. The fact is that, despite the historic achievements of the civil rights movement, there remains a fundamental dualism at the heart of public ideals about race in America. We harbor a glaring contradiction between the ethical conviction that a person's race is an irrelevancy and the reflexive social practice of attending assiduously to racial identity. We say people should be judged by the content of their character and not the color of their skin; yet we sort, count, respond to, cavort with, and assess one another based on race. I need to say a bit more about this glaring contradiction.

Please bear in mind that I am a social scientist, not a theologian, and so will be writing principally in that voice here. The crux of my argument turns on the distinction I draw between informal social relations and formal economic transactions. With whom one chooses to associate in the private sphere is a matter of social relationships. How one treats those encounters in the commercial marketplace

---

1. Alexis de Tocqueville, *Democracy in America*, trans. George Lawrence (Garden City, NY: Anchor Books, 1969), vol. 2, 639; vol. 1, 10, 344.

2. Gunnar Myrdal, *An American Dilemma: The Negro Problem and American Democracy* (1944; repr., London and New York: Routledge, 1996).

is a question about the character of economic transactions. Ideas that people hold about "race" affect their behaviors in both spheres, but with very different consequences for the persistence of racial inequality in America.

I will begin by making two basic observations about "race" and "social capital." Some forty-plus years ago, in my doctoral dissertation at MIT, I had the good fortune to coin the term "social capital."[3] By discussing here, briefly, how I came to coin the term "social capital," I can further illuminate the contrast that I wish to draw between informal social relations and formal economic transactions as mechanisms perpetuating the subordinate position of black people in the United States. I set out in that dissertation to contrast my concept "social capital" with what economists call "human capital." Human capital theory imports into the study of human inequality an intellectual framework that had been well developed in economics to explain the investment decisions of firms—a framework that focuses on the analysis of formal economic transactions. Put simply, my point in that 1976 dissertation was that associating business with human investments is merely an analogy, not an identity—particularly if one seeks to explain persistent racial disparities. I argued that important things were overlooked in the human capital approach, things having to do with informal social relations. I called specific attention to two distinct ways in which human capital theory, as deployed by economists in the study of racial inequality, was incomplete.

Observation 1

First, I stressed that *all human development is socially situated and mediated*. That is, I argued that the development of human beings occurs inside of social institutions. It takes place between people by way of human interactions. The family, the community, the school, the peer group—these and other *cultural institutions* of human association are where human development occurs. Consequently, many resources essential to human development—the attention that a parent gives to her child, for instance—are not *alienable*. (That is

---

3. Glenn Loury, "Essays in the Theory of the Distribution of Income" (PhD diss., Massachusetts Institute of Technology, 1976).

to say, the mother's attention is a fundamental component of her relationship to her child and is inseparable from the personality of the one who provides it.) Developmental resources, for the most part, are not "commodities." That is to say, the most important influences for fostering a youngster's later-life success cannot be acquired "over-the-counter," via formal transactions that can be regulated so as to avoid racial discrimination. Neither are such resources transferrable from one child to another to assure a level developmental playing field. What I am suggesting here is that when speaking about human development, the character of relationships between people matter as much as the availability of physical resources.

Simply put, the development of human beings is not for sale. To the contrary, a structure of connections between individuals creates the context within which developmental resources are allocated to individual persons. Opportunity travels along the synapses of these social networks. For this reason, the development of human beings is not the same as corporate investment. Consequently, it need not be a good metaphor, or a good analogy, to reason as though this were so.

This idea may appeal to the non-economists among my readers: People are not machines. Their "productivities"—that is, the behavioral and cognitive capacities that bear on their social and economic functioning—are not the result of some mechanical infusion of material resources. Rather, these capacities are the byproducts of social processes mediated via networks of human affiliation and connectivity. This point was fundamentally important, I thought and still think, for understanding persistent racial disparities.

Observation 2

My second observation was that *what we are calling "race" is mainly a social, and only indirectly a biological, phenomenon*. The persistence across generations of racial differentiation between large groups of people, in an open society where individuals live in close proximity to one another, provides irrefutable indirect evidence of a profound separation between the racially defined networks of social affiliation within that society. Put directly, *there would be no "races" in the steady state of any dynamic social system unless, on a daily basis and in regard to their most intimate affairs, people paid assiduous attention to the boundaries separating themselves from racially distinct others.* That is, over time "race" would cease to exist unless people chose to act in a manner so as biologically to reproduce the variety of phenotypic expression that constitutes the substance of racial distinction.

I cannot overemphasize this point. "Race" is not a thing given in nature. Rather, it is socially produced; it is an equilibrium outcome; it is something we are making; it is endogenous. Thus, if the goal is to understand durable racial inequality, we will need to attend in some detail to the processes that cause "race" to persist as an unpleasant fact in the society under study. For such processes almost certainly will be related to the allocation of human developmental resources in that society.[4]

It is instructive to contrast a social-cognitive conception of "race" with acts of biological taxonomy—that is, sorting human beings based on presumed variations of genetic endowments across what had for eons been geographically isolated subpopulations. On an evolutionary time scale such isolation was until recently the human condition, and it may be thought to have led to the emergence of distinct "races." As we all know, use of the term *race* in this way is controversial, particularly if one aims to explain social inequalities between groups.

Thus, when scientists like noted population geneticist Luigi Cavalli-Sforza[5] or social critics like noted philosopher Anthony Appiah[6] deny that the term *race* refers to anything real, what they have in mind is this biological-taxonomic notion; and what they deny is that meaningful distinctions among human subgroups pertinent to accounting for racial inequality can be derived in this way.

My point is that using "race" as a category of social cognition is conceptually distinct from the more dubious use of the concept for

---

4. I develop this argument more fully in Glenn Loury, *The Anatomy of Racial Inequality* (Cambridge: Harvard University Press, 2002).

5. See, for example, Luigi Cavalli-Sforza, Paolo Menozzi, and Alberto Piazza, *The History and Geography of Human Genes* (Princeton: Princeton University Press, 1996).

6. Kwame Anthony Appiah, *In My Father's House: Africa in the Philosophy of Culture* (New York: Oxford University Press, 1992).

purposes of biological taxonomy: to establish the scientific invalidity of "race" demonstrates neither the irrationality nor the immorality of invoking racial classification as acts of social cognition. Therefore, it is in this social constructivist spirit that I shall employ the concept here, with an emphasis on the negative interpretative/symbolic connotations that are attached to "blackness" in the United States.

Here then is my second observation in a nutshell: The creation and reproduction of "race" as a feature of society rests upon a set of *cultural* conceptions about identity held by the people—blacks and whites alike—in that society. These are the beliefs that people hold about who they are and about the legitimacy of conducting intimate relations with racially distinct others. (By "intimate relations," I do not only mean sexual relations.) Marriage across racial lines is rare because many, indeed most, people harbor a preference for intimately associating with co-racialists. In a similar fashion, racially segregated church congregations, schools, and residential neighborhoods are commonplace because people take account of race when deciding to join or to remain in such associations. Racial designations such as "black" or "white" are not natural categories, but instead their meaning varies as one moves between cultures and across national borders.

My impulse to contrast *human* and *social* capital all those years ago was rooted in my conviction that beliefs of this kind affect the access people enjoy to those informal resources that individuals require to develop their human potential. For instance, when families form mainly within racial group lines and there is substantial inequality between groups, the opportunities for the development of children in the disadvantaged racial group will also be subpar. What I called "social capital" in 1976 was, in this view, a critical prerequisite for creating what economists referred to as "human capital." For example, the belief that I am different racially from that person to whom I am otherwise attracted may prevent me from dating, marrying, and parenting with that person. This belief, in turn, affects where I live and send my kids to school. This point is crucial, I believe, if we are to understand the persistence of racial inequality in America.

That was Glenn Loury circa 1976. By 1985, I had become a Reagan Republican! I was given in those years to emphasizing the problem of single-parent families; to talking about births out-of-wedlock among blacks; about low labor-force participation and poor educational performance; about high criminal participation and victimization rates, and so forth. My favored formulation was, there is an *enemy without*—namely racism; but there is also an *enemy within*—namely the behavior patterns inhibiting African Americans from seizing such opportunities as had come to exist. I argued that these opportunities, though not completely equal, were much more equal than had been the case before the civil rights movement. I stressed to other blacks, every chance I got, that if we were ever to achieve equality within American society, we could not simply rely on antidiscrimination laws and affirmative action; we would also have to address some of these internal patterns. Today, more than three decades later, I still believe this to be the case.

I thought then, and think now, that it is implausible in the extreme to expect that such patterns as the majority of children born to African American women being born to a woman without a husband would be reversed by government policies such as the redistribution of resources. If they were to be reversed at all, I reckoned, this would require a determined effort by African Americans ourselves to think differently about our responsibilities to our children and to one another. We needed to grasp the nettle, to face-up to our existential circumstance, to be honest about the problematic aspects of our culture, and to take responsibility by addressing them. "No one is coming to save us," I would cry out. "This is not a question of justice," I would say. Certainly it isn't fair that we—the descendants of slaves—find ourselves in this circumstance. Nevertheless, it is necessary to take on these responsibilities in view of the fact that nobody is coming and, more fundamentally, given that no one can come into our intimate gender relations, into the families and neighborhoods where our children are being raised, so as to reorder those cultural institutions in such a manner as would be more developmentally constructive. These matters are ultimately and necessarily in the hands of African Americans ourselves, I reckoned. What we are talking about here is facing up to such questions as: Who are we as a people? How, then, must we live with one another? What will we do to honor the sacrifices that our ancestors made to leave us the opportunities we now enjoy? What do we owe to our children? We are talking here, in other words, about the African American communal covenant as part of the larger American national covenant.

But that is not the only thing we are talking about here. We are also talking about the reality of racial stigma. The symbols that signify racial difference are freighted with important connotations that can have an adverse effect on a person's opportunities to develop his or her skills. Specifically, in the US context, "blackness" has meanings associated with it that are stigmatizing. This stigma inclines people to a presumption against the merits of persons bearing the mark. People start to doubt the assumption that the stigmatized one is "like us." Stigma leads an observer to be reticent about entering into intimacy with such a person. This stigma results in a social allocation of developmental resources reflecting "developmental bias." Our segregated schools, neighborhoods, and marital patterns give plain evidence of these presumptions.

Without appreciating that some bodily marks signify things—negative things, "otherness" things—that influence the chance for people bearing those marks to develop their human capacities, without seeing this, one may attribute the backwardness of these people who have been stigmatized to their "essence." One will say, in effect, "It must be something about 'those people,' not about us, that causes them to be so backward." One will eschew social, political, and moral responsibility for their plight. One will conclude that their failure to develop their human potential either reflects the absence of such potential in the first place (and we have books on the shelf making that argument), or one will decide upon this narrative: "Their failure is due to their backward culture which, sadly but inevitably—What more can we do?—causes them to lag behind." Yet they are not the authors of the stigma that engenders developmental bias against them. When we understand that the way people come to value things or make decisions is partly created via interactions in society, then their flourishing, or lack thereof, reflects on society as a whole, as well as on themselves. It reflects on an "US," not merely on a "THEM."

This reflection leads me to an important conclusion: How a society answers the question, "Who are WE?" is a fundamentally significant issue. It is certainly an important question in the United States today. Who are WE? Whose country is it? When we talk about crime, violence, school failure, urban decay, and so forth, are these matters, in the back of our minds, matters of US against THEM? Because if it is US against THEM, anything is possible. It becomes possible to say about those people languishing in the ghettos of our great cities: "That's not my country. That's some third world thing." This was actually said during the flood of New Orleans after Hurricane Katrina. But it is a lie. There have been black people in New Orleans for two hundred and fifty years. They are not aliens. They are as American as one can get, as American as anybody can be. That was US down there crawling up on the rooftops. That was US huddled in the Superdome. That was US.

These behavioral problems are a quintessentially American affair, not simply a measure of the inadequacy of "black culture." They reflect upon OUR social inadequacy, I wish to argue. Moreover, I buttress that argument by observing the incompleteness of human capital theory, by insisting that human developmental processes are socially contextualized, and by stressing the foundational role "race" plays in all of this. This is what I mean when I, as an economist, nevertheless insist on placing relations before transactions! What I am talking about now, in other words, is the American nation state's civic covenant, rightly understood.

Consider the poor inner-city dwellers who make up perhaps a quarter of the African American population. The dysfunctional behavior of many in this population is a big part of the problem here, to be sure. So, the demand of conservatives for greater personal responsibility in these quarters is both necessary and proper, I would hold. And yet, confronted with the despair, violence, and self-destructive folly of so many people, it seems to me morally superficial in the extreme to argue, as many conservatives have done, that "those people should just get their acts together; if they did, like many of the poor immigrants, we would not have such a horrific problem in our cities."

To the contrary, any morally astute response to the "social pathology" of American history's losers would have to conclude that, while we cannot change our ignoble past, we need not and must not be indifferent to contemporary suffering issuing directly from that past. THEIR culture may be implicated in their difficulties, but then so too is OUR culture complicit in their troubles. We bear collective responsibility for the form and texture of our social relations. Of course, many whites reading this may say, "I don't get it. I care about the poor kids who grow up in the inner cities with lousy schools and no fathers. But how am I a cause of that?" And, of course, no single individual can be held responsible for the behavior of a stranger. But we are connected to other people in a myriad of ways—through the organization of our communities, the character of our social policies, and the nature of our laws. Through personal and political actions, we contribute to the social conditions that shape the behavior of other people. Some of us voted for Great Society programs that may have exacerbated the problem, for example. Or, some of us advocated for tough-on-crime policies that led to a massive growth of a prison-industrial complex that adversely affected our fellow citizens. And then there are sins of omission, like not trying as Christians to discuss race and partner with black churches.

Thus while we cannot ignore the behavioral problems of this so-called underclass, we should discuss and react to them as if we were talking about our own children, neighbors, and friends, which is to say: *This is an **American** tragedy. It is a national, not merely a communal, disgrace.* Changing the definition of the American "we" is a first step toward rectifying the relational discrimination that afflicts our society. And this step will require adjusting ways of thinking on both sides (or better, all sides) of the racial divide. Achieving a well-ordered society, where all members are embraced as being among US, should be the goal. This, I claim, is the principal implication for racial reconciliation of America's national covenant.

What this means fundamentally is that we accept the continuing racial divides in our country as part of the national covenant—which means *our* nation and *our* covenant. It also means to accept the fact that the perpetuation of our racial divides means that *we*—not *they*—are in exile. And that *we*—not *they*—need to find a way to come out of exile. Were we to look at the matter in this way, it would transform how we think about and act on the problem of racial inequality in America. For instance, an assertion of racial injury in the face of the underclass crisis leads many into a political cul-de-sac.

There are two points to make in this regard. First, there are no politically feasible, racially based solutions to the problems of the urban black poor. Indeed, it is not entirely clear how these marginalized, suffering masses might yet be integrated into the commonwealth. Anyone professing to have the answer is either a fool, or a liar. Every conceivable response to this social dilemma—be it education and welfare reform, tax abatements, greater private philanthropy, improved law enforcement, or massive public works—requires significant public (if not always governmental) involvement, a major infusion of resources, and a fair amount of time. Progress depends on the creation of political majorities willing to support some such undertakings. And, if recent American electoral history teaches us anything, it is that such majorities cannot be built in an explicitly racial manner. Therefore identity politics, where Americans are defined and typecast by race, is not the answer. The majorities we need must be built across racial lines through cultural centers such as synagogues and churches.

Second, discussing social dysfunction in racial terms plays right into the hands of society's most reactionary forces, inviting the view that "those people" in the ghettos are fundamentally different, that "they" are, whether for biological or deep cultural reasons, beyond hope of redemption. Arguably, some of the ugliest (and most sophisticated) recent assaults on the proposition that "all men are created equal" can be understood as conservative reactions to the efforts of racial egalitarians to legislate their way out of the fact of lagging black achievement. The era of jujitsu politics—when blacks tried to use the relative strength of whites against them by holding up black underachievement as proof that whites had failed to extend equal rights—has definitely run its course. The typical response to such advocacy nowadays is the baldly stated "refutation" that, evidently, blacks do not have what it takes to succeed in America, as so many nonwhite immigrants have done and continue to do.

Recalling the moral foundations of the original civil rights revolution suggests a way out of this impasse. Martin Luther King, Jr. was fond of saying that "every man is heir to a legacy of worthiness." If the black inner-city poor do not now enjoy the basic human inheritance of dignity and worthiness of which King (and Jefferson) spoke, this is not primarily because they descend from slaves. Advocacy on their behalf grounded solely in that historical fact will fail. Are they not better served by invoking a transracial humanism, by urging a commitment—universally applied—to engage the intractable problems of the socially marginalized? Is it not wiser, ultimately, to present the problems of the black underclass in their essential human terms, rather than on narrow racial ground? The newly emerging recognition of similar problems among the white underclass supports my contention.

These questions give rise to the following argument: The fundamental challenges any person faces in life arise not from his or her racial condition, but from our common human condition. The social contingency of race is, in itself, but one piece of the raw material from which an individual must yet construct a life. For all of us, it is the engagement with this project of construction that brings about our development as human beings and the expression of our individual personalities. And because we share this existential problem—identical in essentials, different only in details—we can hope to transcend racial difference to gain a genuine, mutual understanding of our respective experiences and travails, and ultimately to empathize with one another. As Jean-Paul Sartre might have said, because we all confront the challenge of discovering how to live in "good faith," we are able to share love across the tribal boundaries.[7]

Empathy lies at the core of this transracial, humanistic argument. From this point of view, however closely race may correlate with social disability, citizens looking upon juvenile felons, welfare mothers, or slow learners should consider that "there but for the grace of God go I, or my brother, or my child." In more practical terms, the attainment of true democracy in our divided society requires that the white middle class see the black underclass as consisting of people who, in essence, are not so very different from themselves—all of us having been created in the image of God. Rather than asking, "What manner of people are they who languish in that way?" the public question should become, "What manner of people are we who accept such degradation in our midst?"

Unfortunately, we are a long way from achieving this democratic goal. Dramatic, persistent economic and social disparities between the races have, in the aftermath of the civil rights revolution, given rise to the (usually unspoken) question, in the minds of blacks and whites alike, as to whether blacks are capable of gaining equal status, given equality of opportunity. It is a peculiar mind that fails, in light of American history, to fathom how poisonous a question this is. And while I unequivocally believe that blacks are indeed so capable, any such assertion is a hypothesis or an axiom, not a fact. The fact is that

---

7. Jean-Paul Sartre, *Notebooks for an Ethics* (Chicago: University of Chicago Press, 1992).

blacks have something to prove, to ourselves and to what W. E. B. Du Bois once called "a world that looks on in amused contempt and pity."[8] This is not fair or right. It is simply the way things are.

Things have been this way for quite some time now. In his treatise *Slavery and Social Death*, sociologist Orlando Patterson argues persuasively that one cannot understand slavery without grasping the importance of the concept of honor. Slavery, he says, is not simply property-in-people; rather, it is "the permanent, violent domination of natally alienated and generally dishonored persons."[9] The ritualized, hierarchical relations of respect and standing between the owner and the one owned are what distinguish slavery from other systems of forced labor. As Patterson points out, this is a parasitic relationship: owners derive honor from their power over the slaves, who suffer an extreme marginality because they have no social existence except for what is mediated by their master.

But then if slavery was not mainly a legal convention, but instead an institution of ritualized hierarchy, how could emancipation—the termination of the masters' legal claims—be sufficient in itself to make slaves (and their descendants) into genuinely equal citizens? Must not the historically generated and culturally reinforced dishonor of the freed people also be overcome? If the former slave, who just yesterday stood before the nation without honor or the possibility of honor, is to become a citizen—that is, a coequal participant in the national enterprise—then must not the deeply entrenched presumptions of inferiority, of intellectual and moral inadequacy, be extinguished? And how is that to be done?

Perhaps it was the prompting of questions such as these which, over a century ago, led Booker T. Washington to observe,

> It is a mistake to assume that the Negro, who had been a slave for two hundred and fifty years, gained his freedom by the signing, on a certain date, of a certain paper by the President of the United States. It is a mistake to assume that one man

---

8. W. E. B. Du Bois, *The Souls of Black Folk* (New York: Dover, 1903), 2–3.

9. Orlando Patterson, *Slavery and Social Death: A Comparative Study* (Cambridge: Harvard University Press, 2018), 13.

can, in any true sense, give freedom to another. Freedom, in the larger and higher sense, every man must gain for himself.[10]

This quote, in our current political discourse, is remembered as a conservative's statement; and my citing it is taken as an embrace of laissez-faire. Yet nothing could be further from the truth. My point here has little to do with the transitory, partisan conflicts of our day, and everything to do with a timeless, existential challenge which black Americans have confronted—collectively, and not just as individuals—from the very beginning of our sojourn in America.

The civil rights leader Jesse Jackson (no Booker Washington, he!) used to teach young blacks the exhortation: "I am somebody," and this is certainly true. But the crucial question then becomes: "Just who are you?" Many of our fellow citizens now look down upon the carnage playing itself out on the streets of ghetto America and supply their own dark answers. The youngster's response should be: "Because I am somebody, I waste no opportunity to better myself. Because I am somebody, I respect my body by not polluting it with drugs or promiscuous sex. Because I am somebody—in my home, in my community, in my nation—I comport myself responsibly, I am accountable, I am available to serve others as well as myself." It is the doing of these fine things, not the saying of any fine words, which teaches oneself, and others, that one is somebody who has to be reckoned with.

But who will show the many hundreds of thousands of black youngsters now teetering on the brink of disaster how to be somebody? One finds a precedent for the huge task we face in the Old Testament Book of Nehemiah, which begins as follows,

> Hanani, one of my brethren, came, he and certain men of Judah; and I asked them concerning the Jews that had escaped, which were left of the captivity, and concerning Jerusalem.
>
> And they said unto me, The remnant that are left of the captivity there in the province are in great affliction and reproach; the wall of Jerusalem also is broken down, and the gates thereof are burned with fire.

---

10. Booker T. Washington, *The Story of the Negro*, vol. 2: *The Rise of the Race from Slavery* (New York: Association Press, 1909), 47–48.

> And it came to pass, when I heard these words, that I sat down and wept, and mourned certain days, and fasted, and prayed before the God of heaven. (Neh. 1:2–4 KJV)

The wall is broken down, and its gates are burned with fire. This metaphor of decay and assault is an apt one for our current ills. We are invited to think of a city without walls as one with no integrity, no structure, subject to the vagaries of any passing fad or fancy. We imagine the collapse of civil society—the absence of an internally derived sense of what a people stand for, of what they must and must not do. With the wall broken, and its gates burned, anything becomes possible.

In the biblical account, Nehemiah heroically led the Jews of Jerusalem to renewal. He went to the Persian king whom he served as cup bearer, secured provisions, and returned to Jerusalem, where he rolled up his sleeves and went to work restoring the physical integrity of the environment, but also presiding over a spiritual revival among the citizenry. (Even an economist knows that "man does not live by bread alone.") Now, let me relate this to my overarching theme, lest you think you are about to hear a sermon. (I am fully capable of sermonizing on this subject—that my second son's name is Nehemiah is no accident—but this is neither the time nor the place to begin a preaching career.) Nehemiah, a Jew, was specifically concerned about his people. His work, the reconstruction of civil society, could only be undertaken, as it were, "from the inside-out." He dealt in the specific and concrete circumstances confronting the Jews. He did not deal in mere abstractions. He made himself present among those for whom he had a special affection, toward whom he felt a special loyalty. His is not so bad a model.

In the inner-city ghettos today "the remnant there are in great affliction and reproach." For the civic wound of black alienation to be fully and finally bound, a great deal of work must be done on the ground in these communities. We blacks are connected—by bonds of history, family, conscience, and common perception in the eyes of outsiders—to those who languish in the urban slums. Black politicians, clergy, intellectuals, businessmen, and ordinary folk must therefore seek to create hope in these desolate young lives; we must work to rebuild these communities; we must become our brother's keeper.

We arrive, then, at the ultimate racial paradox: self-development, an existential necessity for blacks as an ethnic community, is in tension with the moral requirement for Americans as a democratic polity to achieve a humanism that transcends race. This tension is reflected in the dual meaning of "we" implicit in the question, "What manner of people are we who accept such degradation in our midst?" The two implied imperatives, despite their common appeals to human empathy, rest on very different grounds. One draws on ties of blood, shared history, and common faith. The other endeavors to achieve an integration of the most wretched, despised, and feared of our fellows along with the rest of us into a single political community of mutual concern. One takes the social fact of race as a given, even celebrating it. The other aims to move beyond race altogether.

This problem is closely related to an age-old conundrum in political theory—that of reconciling individual and social responsibilities. We humans, while undertaking our life projects, find ourselves constrained by social and cultural influences beyond our control. Yet if we are to live effective and dignified lives, we must behave as if we can indeed determine our fates. A long-term welfare mother must be seen as responsible for her plight and that of her children, even if it is also the case that she is being acted on by economic and social forces larger than herself. But she is not an island; she does not have complete freedom to determine her future. So, we must help her. That is our responsibility. Similarly, blacks as a group have been constrained by an ugly history of racism, some effects of which continue to manifest themselves into the current day. Yet seizing freedom "in the larger and higher sense" requires that blacks accept responsibility for our own fate, and for the values embraced by our children, even though the effects of this immoral past remain with us.

But this accepting responsibility should not be an excuse for the rest of the nation to withdraw into a posture of indifference, looking on in "amused contempt and pity." It is a basic moral truth that "those people"—who now languish in the drug-infested, economically depressed, crime-ridden central cities—are "our" people, and "we" must be in relationship with them. America's democratic pretensions—to being "a city on a hill," a beacon of hope and freedom to all the world—seem fraudulent when set alongside the lives of haplessness and despair lived by so many of those Americans who descend from slaves. So the citizens of this republic bear a responsibility to be actively engaged in changing the structures that constrain the black poor, in such a way that they can more effectively exercise their inherent and morally required capacity to choose. That "those people"—who now languish in the drug-infested, economically depressed, crime-ridden central cities—are "our" people, and that "we" must be in relationship with them, are moral truths which transcend politics.

Our situation resists pat, ideologically pure resolution. Those of us committed to seeking true democracy in this divided society shall have to engage in a fair amount of muddling-through. Our work will, however, be aided enormously if all concerned can proceed with patience, wisdom, and a spirit of generosity. Perhaps not every American is cut out for the hard, civic task of sustained engagement with this problem.

"The Negro lives on a lonely island of poverty in the midst of a vast ocean of material prosperity," Martin Luther King, Jr. said in 1963, in his prophetic "I Have a Dream" speech. This is still true, in far too great a measure. And while it is by no means the only truth, it is one that no political or intellectual movement aspiring to lead our country should be allowed to forget.

8

Undermining the Covenant of Marriage: Racial Injustice and the Black Family

Jacqueline C. Rivers

The black community in the United States has faced many formidable barriers to prosperity and human flourishing. Many of these have been structural in nature, such as the recent rise of the mass incarceration of young black men. However, the effects of other issues where structure and culture interact are widely debated. One such area whose importance has been hotly contested is the fractured family structure that is prevalent in the black community. Daniel Patrick Moynihan in his infamous report portrayed the lower-class black family as a "tangle of pathology" and at the same time attributed its failure to poor black men's lack of access to jobs that pay a living wage.[1] Many scholars, Carol Stack notably among them, have defended the extended family structure that was prevalent among poor blacks as an effective alternative to the traditional family.[2]

---

1. Daniel P. Moynihan, "The Negro Family: The Case for National Action," in *The Moynihan Report and the Politics of Controversy: A Transaction Social Science and Public Policy Report*, ed. Lee Rainwater and William L. Yancey (Cambridge: MIT Press, 1967), 47–124.

2. Carol B. Stack, *All Our Kin: Strategies for Survival in a Black Community* (New York: Harper & Row, 1974), 90–107.

This essay reflects on the state of the black family in light of how racial injustice and social transformation have undermined the practice of marriage as a covenant. During the earliest phase of African American life, slave laws prohibited blacks from entering into the covenant of marriage.[3] For a period following emancipation and during the horrors of the Jim Crow South, it became advantageous to whites to promote marriage among blacks.[4] However, as the Great Migration took blacks to the cities of the north and west, the persistent employment challenges faced by poor black men further eroded the basis of marriage.[5] More recently, extensive cultural changes in the broader society have exacerbated the problem. This complex interaction of structure and culture has produced a situation in which marriage rates among blacks at all levels of socioeconomic status lag behind those of their white counterparts.[6] Any effort to address the situation must combine initiatives to address both cultural and structural aspects of the problem.

Marriage as Covenant

Before discussing the state of the black family in detail, it is necessary to explore the idea of marriage as a covenant.[7] According to John Kippley, "Christian marriage is a covenant ... [that] entails unlimited liability and promise."[8] Unlike parents and children or other blood relations, husband and wife choose each other; in doing so they enter into a relationship which entails divinely appointed responsibilities

---

3. Orlando Patterson, *Rituals of Blood: Consequences of Slavery in Two American Centuries* (Washington: Civitas/CounterPoint, 1998), 25–37.

4. Laura Edwards, "'The Marriage Covenant Is at the Foundation of All Our Rights': The Politics of Slave Marriages in North Carolina after Emancipation," *Law and History Review* 14, no. 1 (1996): 90–94.

5. Moynihan, "The Negro Family," 47–124.

6. Ralph Richard Banks, *Is Marriage for White People?: How the African American Marriage Decline Affects Everyone* (New York: Dutton, 2011), 52–53.

7. Paul Ramsey, "Marriage Law and Biblical Covenant," *Religion and the Public Order* 1 (1963): 44–45.

8. John F. Kippley, *Sex and the Marriage Covenant: A Basis for Morality* (San Francisco: Ignatius, 2005), 15.

to care for each other unstintingly. Kippley describes this covenant as the "self-giving commitment of marriage."[9] Treatments in both the Old Testament (the marriage of Hosea and Gomer) and New Testament (Paul's analogy regarding marriage) support this notion of marriage as covenant.[10]

Elements of both the Mosaic and the Deuteronomic covenants between Yahweh and Israel are prophetically symbolized for the Hebrews in the eponymous book of Hosea by the prophet's marriage to his unfaithful wife, Gomer.[11] A similar analogy is evident in the book of Ezekiel when Yahweh compares establishing his covenant with Israel as compassionately sheltering and taking the nation in marriage (Ezek. 16:8). The symbolic parallelism clearly communicates that the marriage is intended to share the covenantal characteristics of the relationship between Yahweh and Israel.

In Deuteronomy God reminds the nation of Israel that his purpose in delivering them from Egypt was to reveal himself to them, so that they would know that he is God (Deut. 4:10–14, 32–35). This act of self-revelation is an invitation to a relationship with God that is both intimate and reverential. At the heart of the covenant is the love of Yahweh for Israel in response to their cry for rescue from oppression by the Egyptians.[12] Yet even before the Deuteronomic covenant, Yahweh's relationship with Israel is already established in his covenant with Abraham; indeed from the Abrahamic to the Mosaic to the Deuteronomic covenant there is an extension and unfolding of Yahweh's promise to greatly multiply and bless Abraham's offspring (Gen. 12:2; 22:17–18). The covenant that God established with Abraham is a declaration of his favor; it extends both to Abraham

---

9. Kippley, *Sex and the Marriage Covenant*, 7.

10. Jack O. Balswick and Judith K. Balswick, *A Model for Marriage: Covenant, Grace, Empowerment and Intimacy* (Downers Grove, IL: InterVarsity, 2006), 39–40; Kippley, *Sex and the Marriage Covenant*, 7.

11. Mordechai A. Friedman, "Israel's Response in Hosea 2:17b: 'You Are My Husband,'" *Journal of Biblical Literature* 99, no. 2 (1980): 202.

12. William D. Barrick, "The Mosaic Covenant," *Master's Seminary Journal* 10, no. 2 (1999): 213–14.

and to the nation that would spring from him.[13] One central element of all the covenants is the obligation to honor the terms of the agreement; faithful observance is a condition that Yahweh imposes upon himself. However, for Israel failure to do so entail curses; obedience results in blessings.

This faithfulness is why loyalty is a theme that runs throughout Old Testament accounts of the covenants; Yahweh is Israel's God and they are his people. He demands an exclusive relationship that is not violated by the pursuit of other gods (Exod. 20:3). Although Israel strays time and again, and is exiled for her disloyalty, Yahweh repeatedly promises that a remnant will endure.[14] God declares that his love for his people is permanent. Their relationship is marked by demands for loyalty and forgiveness for disloyalty.

Several things stand out in this divine marriage between God and his people: the bond between Yahweh and his people is rooted in love and compassion; it is marked by intimate self-revelation; it arises from the favor Yahweh shows for his people; and loyalty is at its core. In Malachi, Yahweh declares that he is a witness to the covenant of marriage between man and woman: "the LORD is the witness between you and the wife of your youth ... the wife of your marriage covenant." (Mal. 2:14 NIV). God himself is testifying to the covenant nature of the marriage union. This declaration suggests that the qualities that exemplify the covenant between God and Israel are also to define the bond between husband and wife. It is to be loving, intimate, exclusive, and permanent.

A similar picture emerges of the new covenant between Jesus and the church in Ephesians 5:21–33. In Paul's teaching, the bond between Christ and the church is the equivalent of that between husband and wife. The husband is to love his wife as Christ loved the church, giving his very life for her. He is to love her and care for her as he loves and cares for his own body. For the husband to love his wife is to love himself. His commitment to her is to equal his commitment to himself. In return, the wife is to support the leadership of her

---

13. Keith H. Essex, "The Abrahamic Covenant," *Master's Seminary Journal* 10, no. 2 (1999): 196, 197.

14. 2 Kings 19:30–31; Isa. 6:11–13; 10:22; 17:4–6; Ezek. 14:21–23; Amos 3:12; Zech. 8:7–8.

husband and to submit to him in all things. Paul explicitly draws the connection between marriage and the covenantal relationship between Christ and the church. The key element in the relationship is love and radical self-giving by both parties.[15]

Paul also implies that the relationship is exclusive and demands unswerving loyalty from the husband. Just as each man's body cannot be exchanged with another's, the wife's body is not interchangeable with any another woman's. The husband must be loyal to his wife and to her body. However, if the element of enduring loyalty is implicit in Paul's teaching, it is indubitably clear in Jesus' prohibition of divorce (Mark 10:6–9). Marriage is inviolable save for rupture arising from sexual infidelity (Matt. 5:32; 19:9) or desertion (1 Cor. 7:15). This demand for loyalty in the covenant of marriage is critical to the state of the black family.

Structural and Cultural Pressures on the Black Family

Two key factors that affect black marriages are fundamental disagreement between black men and women on issues of sexual morality and high rates of infidelity among black men.[16] Black women are far more sexually conservative than black men. While it is not uncommon for American women to be more conservative than men in this area, the gender gap is much more prominent among blacks than it is among whites or Hispanics. According to a 1998 study by Orlando Patterson, black women become sexually active later than their male co-ethnics, are more disapproving of premarital sex, and are less tolerant of extramarital affairs. Black women also tend to be more sexually conservative than their white counterparts, though the racial gaps among women are not as large as the gender gap among blacks. One important example is black women's strong disapproval of extramarital affairs: 84 percent of them say such affairs are always wrong under any circumstances. Only 70 percent of African American men hold the same position, creating a gender

---

15. Balswick and Balswick, *Model for Marriage*, 70.
16. Patterson, *Rituals of Blood*, 117; Banks, *Is Marriage for White People?*, 52–53.

gap that is twice as large as that between white men and women.[17] Higher rates of religiosity among black women relative to both black men and white women appear to be implicated in the divergence of views regarding sexual morality; 69 percent of black women report that religion influences their position on these issues, while that is true of only 50 percent of black men and 57 percent of white women.[18]

The gap on sexual issues between African American men and women extends beyond their opinions and stated commitments to their behavior. Black men not only have different sexual values than black women, they also have higher rates of infidelity whether they are married or unmarried. This pattern of infidelity was reflected in Patterson's study: 83 percent of married African American women reported never being unfaithful, compared to just 57 percent of black men.[19] In addition, black men in some neighborhoods have been found to participate in long-term relationships with multiple partners at higher rates than either black women or white men. Participation in multi-partner relationships among men was also related to lower rates of marriage among both men and women in the communities where these men lived.[20]

Other studies have found that including in the analysis factors such as the more permissive values of men accounts for the difference in the gender gap in infidelity rates. In other words, it appears that one contributor to infidelity among black men is their tendency to see extramarital affairs as morally permissible. However, this does not fully explain higher rates of infidelity among black men.[21] Other dynamics appear to influence them. Ralph Banks argues that middle class black men, who are substantially outnumbered by middle class black women, are able to forgo marriage because they are in such

---

17. Patterson, *Rituals of Blood*, 119.

18. Patterson, *Rituals of Blood*, 118.

19. Patterson, *Rituals of Blood*, 130.

20. Edward O. Laumann, *The Sexual Organization of the City* (Chicago: University of Chicago Press, 2004): 178–79.

21. Judith Treas and Deirdre Giesen, "Sexual Infidelity among Married and Cohabiting Americans," *Journal of Marriage and Family* 62, no. 1 (2000): 59.

high demand that their female peers will consent to man-sharing rather than be alone.²²

This situation may in fact capture some of the sexual dynamics among middle-class blacks; it is consistent with Treas and Giesen's finding that the availability of sex partners influences levels of infidelity.²³ It is also consistent with Patterson's findings: rates of infidelity are highest among black men in the highest and lowest income groups: "The highest income bracket of Afro-American men has the same proportion of persons with multiple partners (40 percent) as does the lowest."²⁴ This widespread infidelity among black men contributes to higher rates of divorce among blacks since black women are more likely to divorce a philandering husband than are white women.²⁵ Fifty-five percent of African Americans divorce within fifteen years of marriage compared to 42 percent of non-Hispanic whites.²⁶

It may well be that such behavior also leads to anger and bitterness in intimate relations between black men and women.²⁷ One of the key qualities of a covenantal relationship—fidelity, and the trust associated with it—is in short supply between black men and women. The factors that contribute to high rates of infidelity and the problematic nature of intimate relations between black men and women documented here are complex. However, several scholars agree that both current and historical forces, both structural and cultural influences, play roles. One major contributor has been the pattern of male/female relationships imposed on enslaved people who were not permitted by slave holders to enter into the marriage covenant at all.²⁸ Slaves could not legally be married, a fact which

---

22. Banks, *Is Marriage for White People?*, 58–59.

23. Treas and Giesen, "Sexual Infidelity," 59.

24. Patterson, *Rituals of Blood*, 128.

25. Patterson, *Rituals of Blood*, 86.

26. Paul R. Amato, "Research on Divorce: Continuing Trends and New Developments," *Journal of Marriage and Family* 72, no. 3 (2010): 651.

27. Banks, *Is Marriage for White People?*, 54–57.

28. Patterson, *Rituals of Blood*, 25–44; Andrew J. Cherlin, "American Marriage in the Early Twenty-First Century," *The Future of Children* 15, no. 2 (Fall 2005): 38; Eugene D. Genovese, *Roll, Jordan, Roll: The World the Slaves Made* (New York: Pantheon, 1974), 450–52; Edwards, "The Marriage Covenant," 90.

went a long way to inhibiting the creation of a culture based on stable marriages.

Nonetheless, it is clear that enslaved people did form deep bonds that tied them to family members.[29] The most powerful evidence is the large numbers of freedmen and women who formalized their common-law marriages after emancipation and the haste with which they did it. According to Laura Edwards, "in July 1865 ... an Episcopal minister in Warren County [North Carolina] married 150 African-American couples in just two days."[30]

However, even scholars determined to assert the agency of enslaved people, such as Eugene Genovese, acknowledge that the institution of slavery had an extremely limiting effect on slave marriages.[31] Indeed, slavery had a devastating effect on the role of husband and father: slaveholders were overwhelmingly the source of material support and had final control over virtually every aspect of the family's life. Neither parent could protect their children, and men could not effectively defend their women from the predations of the master in an age when men were unchallenged as protectors and providers. Slave marriages were often between men and women who lived on different farms, since most enslaved people lived on small holdings with small numbers of their peers, especially few who were not blood relatives. It was not uncommon for "abroad husbands" to need a pass to visit their common-law wives and for them to see their wives only a few times per week. This situation created room for infidelity, especially among men.[32]

To make matters horribly worse, women were often raped by their masters, further undermining the attempt to forge a marital bond. Perhaps most devastating was the practice of selling enslaved people away from their families, a further hindrance to familial stability. Historians suggest that slaveholders on the mid-Atlantic seaboard may well have encouraged the production of the maximum number of offspring among slaves to fuel the internal slave trade, particularly after the official end of the trans-Atlantic slave trade. This practice

---

29. Genovese, *Roll, Jordan, Roll*, 452.
30. Edwards, "The Marriage Covenant," 100.
31. Genovese, *Roll, Jordan, Roll*, 452.
32. Patterson, *Rituals of Blood*, 25–44.

motivated masters to treat enslaved men as studs and women as breeders, promoting sexual liaisons whenever possible, regardless of slaves' commitments to common-law spouses.[33] Despite these horrific conditions, slaves formed deep, lasting, and meaningful familial bonds.[34] However in this environment, key aspects of the covenant nature of marriage—its permanence and exclusivity—were massively undermined.

The pattern of family relationships that was arguably established in slavery was reinforced by many of the structural conditions that African Americans subsequently faced. As blacks moved north and west in the Great Migration, they faced virulent racism that trapped them in ghettos, restricted access to quality education, and severely limited job opportunities.[35] African Americans' access to the most important developments that created the white middle class, the New Deal, was deliberately limited by racist Southern Democrats in Congress. As a result, the labor categories in which blacks were most heavily represented, domestic workers and farm laborers, were excluded from social security and unemployment insurance. In addition, the administration of these programs was devolved to local and state officials who excluded blacks from many of the benefits due them.[36] Similar tactics limited blacks' access to the benefits provided by the GI Bill: housing, education, and occupational training.[37] The result of this combination of systemic and *ad hoc* exclusion was that African Americans were vastly disadvantaged economically. The

---

33. Patterson, *Rituals of Blood*, 25–44.

34. Genovese, *Roll, Jordan, Roll*, 450–58.

35. Thomas J. Sugrue, *The Origins of the Urban Crisis: Race and Inequality in Postwar Detroit* (Princeton: Princeton University Press, 1996), 281–59; Kathryn M. Neckerman, *Schools Betrayed: Roots of Failure in Inner-City Education* (Chicago: University of Chicago Press, 2007), 172–84; William J. Wilson, *The Declining Significance of Race: Blacks and Changing American Institutions* (Chicago: University of Chicago Press, 2012), 63–64.

36. Ira Katznelson, *When Affirmative Action Was White: An Untold History of Racial Inequality in Twentieth-Century America* (New York: W. W. Norton, 2005), 25–52.

37. Katznelson, *When Affirmative Action Was White*, 113–42.

pressures of poverty further undermined the stability of African Americans' marriages.

By the middle of the twentieth century, black men often bore a particular burden: earning less than a living wage, they were frequently unable to meet the expectations of wives and children. The disappointment that families felt was combined with the men's sense of failure and perhaps guilt when they were unable to provide for their families.[38] In addition to suffering low wages, black men struggled with high rates of unemployment, which had dogged them for decades and grew worse in the 1960s.[39] Closely associated with these economic pressures were marital conflict, infidelity, and broken families.[40] This was in fact a central claim of the infamous Moynihan Report: that marital instability among working class blacks was closely linked to unemployment among men. Since the 1960s, the employment prospects for poorly educated men have fallen as manufacturing jobs have moved overseas or been automated and the service industry has expanded. Men with less than a college degree have found it increasingly difficult to find a job and to find one that pays well.[41] As is usually the case, these developments have hit black communities the hardest.[42] William Julius Wilson argued in 1987 that poor black men, as a result, become less marriageable.[43]

Low wages and joblessness have not been the only structural issues that have undermined the institution of marriage among the black poor. Black families and communities have been devastated

---

38. Elliot Liebow, *Tally's Corner: A Study of Negro Streetcorner Men* (Lanham: Rowman & Littlefield, 2003), 23–27.

39. Daniel P. Moynihan, *The Negro Family: The Case for National Action* (Washington, DC: US Government Printing Office, 1965), 20–21.

40. Liebow, *Tally's Corner*, 23; Moynihan, *The Negro Family*, 21.

41. Cherlin, "American Marriage," 39; Douglas S. Massey and Robert J. Sampson, "Moynihan Redux: Legacies and Lessons," *The Annals of the American Academy of Political and Social Science* 621, no. 1 (2009): 6–27.

42. William J. Wilson, *When Work Disappears: The World of the New Urban Poor* (New York: Vintage, 1997), 19.

43. William J. Wilson, *The Truly Disadvantaged: The Inner City, the Underclass, and Public Policy* (Chicago: University of Chicago Press, 1987), 145–46.

by the phenomenon of racialized mass incarceration.[44] The prison population in the United States exploded in the last two decades of the twentieth century. Between 1980 and 2000, the number of people incarcerated in prison in the United States rose from 300,000 to over one million.[45] In contrast to this astronomical increase of more than 700,000 prisoners in only twenty years, the prison population grew by only 285,000 in the prior century.[46] It is worth noting that the American incarceration rate far outstrips that of any other developed nation; it is the highest in the world, more extreme than even that in nations such as South Africa, Russia, and Cuba.[47] Not only does the United States imprison men (more than 90 percent of all prisoners are male[48]) at astronomical rates, but the racial disproportion is also egregious.[49] According to the Pew Research Center, blacks were imprisoned at five times the rate of whites as recently as 2016 when the rate of incarceration for blacks was 1,608 per hundred thousand compared to 274 per hundred thousand for whites.[50] These increases in incarceration are largely due to changes in sentencing guidelines that created mandatory minimum sentences and laws that mandated life imprisonment for the third offense, even if the crimes were nonviolent.[51] The prosecution of the War on Drugs and the disproportionate sentencing for drug crimes involving crack

---

44. Bruce Western, *Punishment and Inequality in America* (New York: Russell Sage, 2006), 131–68.

45. Lawrence Bobo and Victor Thompson, "Racialized Mass Incarceration," in *Doing Race: 21 Essays for the 21st Century*, ed. Hazel Rose Markus and Paula M. L. Moya (New York: W. W. Norton, 2010), 324.

46. Bobo and Thompson, "Racialized Mass Incarceration," 326.

47. Christopher Hartney, "US Rates of Incarceration: A Global Perspective," *Research from the National Council on Crime and Delinquency* (November, 2006): 1–8, https://www.nccdglobal.org/sites/default/files/publication_pdf/factsheet-us-incarceration.pdf.

48. Western, *Punishment and Inequality*, 15.

49. Western, *Punishment and Inequality*, 16.

50. John Gramlich, "Gap between Blacks and Whites in Prison Shrinking," Pew Research Center April 30, 2019, http://www.pewresearch.org/fact-tank/2018/01/12/shrinking-gap-between-number-of-blacks-and-whites-in-prison/.

51. Bobo and Thompson, "Racialized Mass Incarceration," 326.

cocaine versus lighter sentences for the use and sale of powdered cocaine contributed to the extreme racial inequity.[52] Incarceration has become the modal experience for young black men with less than a high school diploma: it is more common for a poorly educated young black man to go to prison than it is for him to attend college, belong to a union, or join the armed forces. One third of all men in this category will be incarcerated at some point over the course of their lives. Furthermore, the experience changes the trajectory of a man's life, reducing his chances of graduating from college or holding a stable job. It also reduces his earning power.[53]

One result of disproportionate incarceration is an imbalanced sex ratio in poor black neighborhoods as men have become scarce. Furthermore, the men who are available are seen as less marriageable because they often have a criminal record and therefore less earning power than comparable men.[54] The labor market challenges that black men face, the problem of mass incarceration, and the legal limitations on marriage and family life under slavery are all structural barriers that have affected poor blacks' experience of the covenant of marriage.

The issues affecting the black family that have been discussed so far have largely arisen from how society has been structured and have either affected blacks uniquely or affected them disproportionately. However, there have been some structural changes that have impacted American society at large. One important factor has also produced significant cultural changes, transforming attitudes toward marriage. The entry of large numbers of women into the labor force has changed the relationship between husbands and wives significantly. As women have acquired greater economic independence, they have been less prone to remain in unhappy marriages and more likely to seek divorce.[55] They have also experienced less pressure to enter into marriage and have done so later in life than was true

---

52. Bobo and Thompson, "Racialized Mass Incarceration," 332–36.
53. Western, *Punishment and Inequality*, 11–33.
54. Western, *Punishment and Inequality*, 131–68.
55. The liberalization of divorce laws has also clearly played an important role in this development.

during the heyday of companionate marriage in the 1950s.[56] This situation represents a significant shift in attitudes toward marriage. The result has been a substantial retreat from marriage, especially among less prosperous Americans, a trend that has also contributed to the declining marriage rates among blacks.

Technological and social developments have also had an important impact on marriage across all demographic groups in the United States. Since the middle of the twentieth century, birth control techniques have become accessible to unmarried couples and are, in general, more readily available and more effective. In addition, abortion on demand has become the law of the land. These two developments have contributed to the decoupling of sex from childbearing and marriage, which in turn has promoted lower marriage rates and an increase in out-of-wedlock childbearing, particularly among the less affluent in society. According to Andrew Cherlin, a leading scholar of family life, the very culture of marriage has shifted. Roles for husbands and wives are more likely to be negotiated, and spouses tend to be oriented toward self-fulfillment rather than self-giving love. For many, marriage has become a capstone experience which crowns economic achievement and the testing of a partnership through cohabitation.[57] These trends have hit the black community hard and have further undermined participation in the covenant of marriage.

The State of the Black Family

The changes in American marriage patterns discussed here have affected blacks more than any other demographic group. In the forty-year span between 1970 and 2010, the percent of black women between the ages of forty and forty-four who were married fell from 61 percent to just 37 percent.[58] Since 2005, roughly seven out of every

---

56. Cherlin, "American Marriage," 39–40.

57. Cherlin, "American Marriage," 40; Kathryn Edin and Maria Kefalas, *Promises I Can Keep: Why Poor Women Put Motherhood before Marriage* (Berkeley: University of California Press, 2019), 199–201.

58. Maria Canian and Ron Haskins, "Changes in Family Composition: Implications for Income, Poverty and Public Policy," *The Annals of the American Academy of Political and Social Science* 654 (2014): 33.

ten births among black women have been to unwed mothers; the figure was 72 percent in 2010 and 69.4 percent in 2017.[59] Closely related to this high rate of out-of-wedlock births is a large increase in female-headed households. In 2018, only 40 percent of black children lived with both parents, compared to 75 percent of white children.[60]

The consequences of failed families are dire for women and children. Although blacks experience much higher rates of poverty[61] than whites do, white households headed by single mothers in 1970 were twice as likely to be poor as black and Hispanic married couples. They were also five times more likely to be poor than white married couples.[62] These statistics illustrate the high levels of economic disadvantage associated with father-absent households. The situation in black father-absent households is even more dire since these households experience higher poverty rates than those headed by white women.[63] By 2011, 46 percent of all families headed by a single black woman were poor, compared to only 12 percent of those headed by a black married couple.[64] According to Harvard sociologist Robert Sampson and his colleague Douglas Massey, in 2000 over 50 percent of children in father-absent households were poor, and half of these were extremely poor.[65] Research has shown that children suffer from

---

59. Cancian and Haskins, "Changes in Family Composition," 36; National Center for Health Statistics, "Births to Unmarried Women by Age, Race, and Hispanic Origin of Mother: 2017," ProQuest Statistical Abstract of the US Online Edition (2019). Retrieved from https://statabs-proquest-com.ezp-prod1.hul.harvard.edu/sa/docview.html?table-no=90&acc-no=C7095-1.2&year=2019&z=129E48671EE92631DC92152F3F14AB16926EE9BE.

60. Author's calculations from US Census Bureau, "Table CH 2 Living Arrangements of White Children under 18 Years Old 1960 to Present" and "Table CH 3 Living Arrangements of Black Children under 18 Years Old 1960 to Present," 2018, https://www.census.gov/data/tables/time-series/demo/families/children.html.

61. Cancian and Haskins use the "official poverty rate" to define poverty as families with an income below the federal poverty level. This is a widely accepted measure. See Cancian and Haskins, "Changes in Family Composition."

62. Cancian and Haskins, "Changes in Family Composition," 39.

63. Cancian and Haskins, "Changes in Family Composition," 39.

64. Cancian and Haskins, "Changes in Family Composition," 36.

65. Massey and Sampson, "Moynihan Redux," 6–12.

reduced levels of economic resources in single-parent households compared to those living with married parents, even when transfer payments and taxes are taken into account. The same is true of children living in cohabiting households.[66]

The shortage of economic resources and limitations on parental attention in single-parent households have lasting negative effects on the next generation. Children raised in single-parent households perform less well on standardized tests and have lower grades in school. These children also suffer more behavioral and psychological problems. And these deficits persist into adulthood. According to a review of the literature by Paul Amato, "Compared with children who grow up in stable, two parent families, children born outside marriage reach adulthood with less education, earn less income, have lower occupational status, are more likely to be idle (that is, not employed and not in school), are more likely to have a nonmarital birth (among daughters), have more troubled marriages, experience higher rates of divorce, and report more symptoms of depression."[67] These effects are more keenly felt in the black community where fewer children are being raised in households with two married parents.[68]

However, it is not only children who suffer; single adults forego positive effects that have been found to be associated with marriage. Married men report less depression than their unmarried peers, and married women report fewer problems with alcohol.[69] Marriage is associated with substantially higher wages for men; one study concludes that marriage apparently contributes in a causal fashion to

---

66. Adam Thomas and Isabel Sawhill, "For Love and Money? The Impact of Family Structure on Family Income," *The Future of Children* 15, no. 2 (2005): 57.

67. Paul Amato, "The Impact of Family Formation Change on the Cognitive, Social, and Emotional Well-Being of the Next Generation," *The Future of Children* 15, no. 2 (2005): 75–96.

68. US Census Bureau, "Living Arrangements of Black Children," "Living Arrangements of White Children," 2018.

69. Allan V. Horwitz, Helene R. White, and Sandra Howell-White, "Becoming Married and Mental Health: A Longitudinal Study of a Cohort of Young Adults," *Journal of Marriage and Family* 58 (1996): 895–907.

those higher wages.[70] Both men and women are likely to live longer if married, even when selection effects are taken into account. Married men are less likely to engage in risky behavior and more likely to live healthier lifestyles.[71] All these benefits of the marriage covenant are enjoyed by fewer blacks as a result of their low marriage rates.

As we have seen, numerous enduring, complex factors have led African Americans to either retreat from marriage or violate the marriage covenant after entering it. Egregious laws under slavery undermined the institution from the arrival of Africans in the United States. Persistent racial discrimination created economic barriers that trapped African Americans disproportionately in poverty and fostered familial tensions that undermined a key covenant characteristic of marriage: fidelity. In more recent times, disproportionate rates of incarceration among blacks have reached epidemic proportions, further hindering the formation of marriages among blacks and exacerbating an imbalanced sex ratio that favors men and encourages sexual infidelity.

The general decoupling of sex from marriage and childbearing in American society has also served as a disincentive to marriage among blacks, as well as among all racial and ethnic groups. The decline of the marriage covenant has hurt men and women, but most of all it has hurt children, leaving them to be raised by single mothers, which is unfortunately the situation of the majority of black children. In fact, it appears that the decline of covenantal marriage has hurt the black community more than any other in America. All of this raises the issue of how these trends might be reversed.

---

70. Kate Antonovics and Robert Town, "Are All the Good Men Married?: Uncovering the Sources of the Marital Wage Premium," *American Economic Review* 94 (2004): 317–21.

71. Stephanie A. Bond Huie, Robert A. Hummer, and Richard G. Rogers, "Individual and Contextual Risks of Death among Race and Ethnic Groups in the United States," *Journal of Health and Social Behavior* 43 (2002): 359–81.

The Way Forward

Problems of such an enduring and complicated nature are not easily or swiftly resolved. However, there are some steps that as the nation we can take to begin to address the challenges confronting the black family. There are a number of social policies that are likely to create more favorable conditions for black marriages and reduce out-of-wedlock births. At the time of this writing, the political climate is extremely polarized, a situation that appears likely to endure and which makes enacting any policy remedies extremely difficult. However, there is a growing consensus among conservatives and liberals around one issue of paramount importance to blacks and of great relevance to the issue of the covenant of marriage: mass incarceration.[72] While some steps have already been taken to address the problem at the federal level, the vast majority of prisoners are held in state institutions, which requires a state by state approach to the problem. Laws that drove mass incarceration, such as mandatory minimum sentences (in particular for drug related offenses) and three-strike laws can be reversed with bipartisan support. Alternative sentencing for nonviolent offenses would begin to slowly right the ship of the carceral state. Such approaches would have a meaningful impact given that 60 percent of those held in prison are nonviolent offenders.[73] According to the premier scholar of mass incarceration, Bruce Western, "Only 11 percent of young black inmates are married, compared to 25 percent of those who are not incarcerated. In short, marriage rates among male prisoners in their twenties are only around half as high as in the free population."[74] Western finds that incarceration is associated with reduced marriage rates among black men. He argues that it also stymies the formation of deep and lasting attachments between husbands and wives when married men are imprisoned. Therefore success in reducing incarceration rates

---

72. Barry Krisberg, "How Do You Eat an Elephant? Reducing Mass Incarceration in California One Small Bite at a Time," *The Annals of the American Academy of Political and Social Science* 664 (2016): 136–37.

73. David Dagan and Stephen Telles, "Locked In? Conservative Reform and the Future of Mass Incarceration," *The Annals of the American Academy of Political and Social Science* 651 (2014): 272.

74. Western, *Punishment and Inequality*, 137.

among black men has real potential for improving black family life, especially among the poor, and for fostering loyalty and affection, hallmarks of the covenant of marriage.

Other public policy interventions that should be on the agenda to rebuild the black family include initiatives to improve the earning power of black men so that they are more attractive as partners in marriage.[75] A study of fragile families found that a substantial rise in men's income would have a positive effect on marriage, even if only a small one.[76] These initiatives ought to include job training programs that address both soft skills and occupational skills for growth industries and that provide referrals to appropriate jobs.[77] Improved educational opportunities for black boys are an important part of the agenda as well. Higher educational levels among black girls have also been shown to be associated with higher marriage rates, so states and communities should try to improve educational opportunities for them as well.[78]

While much of what could be done lies in the power of governmental agencies, one course for significant action is of particular importance to the black church. Research has shown an association between beliefs regarding marriage and church attendance: both black and white women who attended church regularly were more likely to disapprove of premarital sex, though the relationship was stronger among whites.[79] As argued earlier, the availability of opportunities for sexual activity has been linked to infidelity, and is arguably related to marriage rates.[80] Therefore, changing attitudes toward extramarital sex may have a positive effect on the stability and

---

75. Wilson, *The Truly Disadvantaged*, 151.

76. Marcia Carlson, Sara McLanahan, and Paula England, "Union Formation in Fragile Families," *Demography* 41, no. 2 (2004): 237–61.

77. Lawrence Katz, "The Economy, Work and Welfare Panel," for a Symposium Celebrating the Career of William Julius Wilson at Harvard University, September 11–13, 2019.

78. Carlson, McLanahan, and England, "Union Formation in Fragile Families," 237–61.

79. Patterson, *Rituals of Blood*, 127.

80. Banks, *Is Marriage for White People?*, 55; Treas and Giesen, "Sexual Infidelity," 59.

formation of marriages among blacks. Other research supports this possibility: Wilcox and Wolfinger found that not only were attitudes different among women who were frequent churchgoers, but their marriage rates were higher and out-of-wedlock births lower. Again, the effects were stronger among whites than among black women.[81] They also suggest that teaching on the subject of premarital sex is provided less often in the black church. This indicates that more attention to this topic in the church setting may begin to alleviate the problem. Higher rates of religiosity among black women are a factor that weighs in favor of this approach.[82] Discussing extramarital sex, however, must be done sensitively because of large numbers of unwed mothers in many churches.

However, the black church has substantial limitations in its ability to reach two important demographic groups: black men and black millennials. Black men have much lower rates of church involvement than black women. In addition, consistent with the trend among millennials, there are falling rates of participation in organized religion among black youth.[83] Pastors and other church leaders need to develop new strategies to reach black men and young African Americans, particularly because relatively few enter the covenant of marriage. In addition, the failure of the church to evangelize and retain the poorest members of society adds to the problem. Given that those in the lowest income groups are most likely to be unmarried, efforts to increase church participation rates among the poor is another potential strategy for increasing marriage rates, one with

---

81. William Bradford Wilcox and Nicholas H. Wolfinger, *Soul Mates: Religion, Sex, Love, and Marriage among African Americans and Latinos* (New York: Oxford University Press, 2016), 91, 121.

82. Neha Sahgal and Greg Smith, "A Religious Portrait of African-Americans," Pew Research Center, January 30, 2009, https://www.pewforum.org/2009/01/30/a-religious-portrait-of-african-americans/.

83. Sahgal and Smith, "A Religious Portrait"; Pew Research Center, "America's Changing Religious Landscape," May 12, 2015, https://www.pewforum.org/2015/05/12/americas-changing-religious-landscape/.

particular relevance for blacks who are overrepresented in this low-income group.[84]

In sum, structural disadvantages and cultural patterns have, over many decades, led to a fewer black people participating in the covenant of marriage, which has hurt large numbers of black children. These patterns have spread to all racial and ethnic groups and are increasingly common at all economic levels. Sociologists like Isabell Sawhill recognize that this situation has created a downward spiral in which the disadvantages of one generation lead to lower levels of well-being in the next.[85] However, this problem is not irremediable. With the right social policy levers and church-based action, it is possible to begin the long, slow process of shifting marriage patterns in the black community and in the United States more generally.

---

84. Ross Douthat, "Do Churches Fail the Poor?" *New York Times*, May 16, 2015, SR11; https://www.nytimes.com/2015/05/17/opinion/sunday/ross-douthat-do-churches-fail-the-poor.html.

85. Isabel V. Sawhill, *Generation Unbound: Drifting into Sex and Parenthood without Marriage* (Washington, DC: Brookings Institution, 2014), 65–83.

9

LITTLE BLACK LIVES MATTER: THE NATIONAL COVENANT AND THE RIGHT TO BE BORN

Alveda C. King with Evan Musgraves

One cannot address the sin of racism in the United States without addressing the issue of abortion, specifically the ways in which abortion has affected the black community. Unfortunately, those who talk most about the presence of racism in American society often ignore the gruesome reality of abortion. For example, movements such as Black Lives Matter or the Women's March not only ignore abortion but actively promote "a woman's right to choose."[1]

What these groups fail to recognize is that one result of racism has been the disproportionate targeting of black babies for abortion. The prevalence of abortion in the black community is no accident. Margaret Sanger, the founder of Planned Parenthood, viewed abortion as part of a larger plan to use birth control as a eugenic tool to decrease the number of "unfit" members of society. African Americans

---

1. For example, the Women's March includes access to abortion as part of their agenda for 2019: "We believe all people should have access to safe, legal, affordable, comprehensive reproductive healthcare, including birth control and abortion." See *Women's March Agenda 2019*, https://www.scribd.com/document/397727839/The-Women-s-March-2019-Women-s-Agenda#from_embed.

were one group, among many others, that she deemed "unfit."[2] Sanger demonstrates that when abortion is compounded with the sin of racism, the result is a most heinous form of genocidal eugenics. Racially based abortion must be considered among America's greatest and most grievous wrongs—a repudiation of the national covenant. To combat this evil in American culture, pro-life citizens must be able to challenge the underlying racist and eugenic logic behind abortion while encouraging fellow Americans to adopt policies that are consistent with our founding ideals that all people have the right to *life*, liberty, and the pursuit of happiness.

How Did We Get Here?

To understand the injustice—the sin—of abortion, it is necessary to place the rise of abortion's acceptability in its proper historical context. Margaret Sanger, the leading voice in pushing for the harmless-sounding "family planning," was shaped by the related movements of social Darwinism and eugenics. Historically, these two movements were intertwined with racism and progressivism. Social Darwinism, eugenics, racism, and progressivism all come together in Sanger and her advocacy for birth control and abortion. While Sanger used the language of feminism to justify abortion, one of her main motivations for increasing access to birth control and abortion was the elimination of the unfit—and blacks most notable among that group of undesirables.

The term *eugenics* was coined by Francis Galton in 1883; it "derives from the Greek word for 'well born' and describes the movement to improve human heredity by the social control of human breeding."[3] Galton linked eugenics to Darwinism by arguing that eugenics sped up the natural process of evolution: weeding out the weak and unfit.

---

2. For an example of Sanger's use of "unfit," see Margaret Sanger, "Birth Control and Racial Betterment," *Birth Control Review* (February 1919), https://www.nyu.edu/projects/sanger/webedition/app/documents/show.php?sangerDoc=143449.xml.

3. Thomas C. Leonard, *Illiberal Reformers: Race, Eugenics and American Economics in the Progressive Era* (Princeton: Princeton University Press, 2016), 110.

Galton argued that "what nature does blindly, slowly and ruthlessly, man may do providently, quickly and kindly."[4] In order to steer the human race toward a healthier genetic pool, proponents of eugenics had to determine who was fit and who was unfit. Most eugenicists and the race scientists who supported them "ranked groups from best to worst ... [and] invariably located African Americans at the bottom of the pyramids of humanity."[5] Race scientists accomplished this ranking by "recast[ing] spiritual or moral failure as biological inferiority and offer[ing] scientific legitimacy to established hierarchies of race, gender, class, and intellect."[6] A prominent eugenics scholar in the early twentieth century, Karl Pearson, warned that the weakening of the white race through the reproduction of the unfit was "the gravest problem which lies before the Caucasian races."[7] Margaret Sanger, and subsequent advocates of abortion, picked up on these themes and promoted birth control, abortion, and even infanticide as useful tools in helping eugenicists achieve their goals.

Margaret Sanger and Planned Parenthood

Margaret Sanger founded the American Birth Control League in 1921; it was later renamed Planned Parenthood Federation of America in 1942. Planned Parenthood would become America's largest abortion provider. Sanger promoted birth control, and by extension abortion, "to prevent the birth of diseased or defective children."[8] One of Sanger's most popular works, *Woman and the New Race*, was published by Eugenics Publishing of New York in 1920 with a contribution from noted eugenicist Havelock Ellis.[9]

Sanger was a "negative eugenicist"—someone who wished to limit the growth of "unfit" populations, but who did not promote the growth

---

4. Francis Galton, quoted in Leonard, *Illiberal Reformers*, 110.
5. Leonard, *Illiberal Reformers*, 119.
6. Leonard, *Illiberal Reformers*, xii.
7. Karl Pearson quoted in Jane Carey, "The Racial Imperatives of Sex: Birth Control and Eugenics in Britain, the United States and Australia in the Interwar Years," *Women's History Review* 21, no. 5 (November 2012): 737.
8. Carey, "Racial Imperatives of Sex," 734.
9. Carey, "Racial Imperatives of Sex," 739.

of "fit" or "desirable" populations.[10] Negative eugenicists were primarily concerned with limiting population growth. Positive eugenicists desired limiting the growth of undesirable populations *and* encouraging the growth of desirable populations. Initially, birth control and abortion were seen as impediments to the cause of positive eugenics because these methods could limit the growth of fit populations. Yet in time, thanks in large part to the efforts of Sanger, most eugenicists would come to support birth control and abortion as useful tools in the eugenics arsenal.[11]

In "Birth Control and Racial Betterment," Sanger succinctly laid out her theory of the usefulness of birth control, including abortion, for eugenic purposes. Sanger began by arguing that both advocates for birth control and eugenicists "are seeking to assist the race toward the elimination of the unfit."[12] Pregnancies should be prevented or terminated "when either mother or father suffers from such diseases as tuberculosis, gonorrhea, syphilis, cancer, epilepsy, insanity, drunkenness, and mental disorders."[13] Eugenicists want to keep the unfit from reproducing while encouraging the fit to bear as many children as possible. Sanger agreed with eugenicists that the reproduction of the unfit must be stopped, but departing from eugenicists, she argued that "all reproduction" should be stopped "when there is not economic means of providing proper care for those who are born in health."[14] Part of her reasoning was that the world was overpopulated and did not need more children, an argument still used today by some abortion proponents.

Most of Sanger's public efforts were directed toward increasing the prevalence and acceptability of birth control. But abortion, and even infanticide, still occupied a place in her eugenic thinking. Publicly, she assured women that birth control was totally effective for preventing pregnancy. But toward the end of her career, she admitted that birth control was not 100 percent effective and that abortion

---

10. Gerald V. O'Brien, "Margaret Sanger and the Nazis: How Many Degrees of Separation?" *Social Work* 58, no. 2 (July 2013): 286.

11. Carey, "Racial Imperatives of Sex," 740–41.

12. Sanger, "Birth Control and Racial Betterment."

13. Sanger quoted in Cary, "Racial Imperatives of Sex," 740.

14. Sanger, "Birth Control and Racial Betterment."

was a necessary backup.[15] In *My Fight for Birth Control*, Sanger's callousness toward infants, born and unborn, was on full display. In recounting how she came to her pro-contraception and pro-abortion views, Sanger described seeing a baby with eczema born to a large family being thrown by the father into the snow, left to die. Sanger then said, "I remember having keen sympathy with that man!... Desperate for want of sleep and quiet, his nerves overcame him, and out of the door and into the snow the nuisance went!"[16] Sanger justified abortion and infanticide by arguing that these two acts were basically self-defense against a greater crime, the "violence" and "slow murder" of "involuntary motherhood."[17]

Many defenders of Sanger and Planned Parenthood try to distinguish her eugenic views from her feminist views. One Planned Parenthood pamphlet designed to refute pro-life opposition to Sanger states that she "believed that reproductive decisions should be made on an individual and not a social or cultural basis"—as did those who advocated eugenics.[18] Sanger, however, saw eugenics, birth control, and reproductive freedom as intertwined. At the end of "Birth Control and Racial Betterment," Sanger, in words oddly reminiscent of Matthew 7:24–27, proclaimed, "Eugenics without Birth Control seems to us a house [built] upon the sands.... Only upon a free, self-determining motherhood can rest any unshakable structure of racial betterment."[19]

In "Birth Control and Racial Betterment," Sanger used race to refer primarily to the human race as a whole. But this does not mean Sanger believed in the absolute equality of all races. In fact, there

---

15. Anne Barbeau Gardiner, "Cruel Crusader: How Margaret Sanger Planned Parenthood by Abortion and Infanticide," *Touchstone* (January/February 2007): 44.

16. Margaret Sanger, *My Fight for Birth Control* (London: Faber and Faber, 1931), 17–18.

17. Gardiner, "Cruel Crusader," 46.

18. Planned Parenthood Federation of America, "Opposition Claims about Margaret Sanger," October 2016, https://www.plannedparenthood.org/uploads/filer_public/37/fd/37fdc7b6-de5f-4d22-8c05-9568268e92d8/sanger_opposition_claims_fact_sheet_2016.pdf.

19. Sanger, "Birth Control and Racial Betterment."

is evidence to suggest that Sanger targeted the African American community, specifically poor African Americans, for her birth control project. For example in 1939, Sanger started the Negro Project, the aim of which was to promote her birth control ideology in poor black communities in the South. Part of her public relations strategy for promoting this project was to "hire three or four colored ministers, preferably with social-service backgrounds, and with engaging personalities. The most successful educational approach to the Negro is through a religious appeal. We don't want word to go out that we want to exterminate the Negro population."[20]

In her promotion of birth control, Margaret Sanger spoke to the Ku Klux Klan. In recounting this event, Sanger explained, "I accepted an invitation to talk to the women's branch of the Ku Klux Klan.... I saw through the door dim figures parading with banners and illuminated crosses.... I was escorted to the platform, was introduced, and began to speak.... In the end, through simple illustrations I believed that I had accomplished my purpose."[21] Evidence of Sanger's racial prejudice can also be found in her approach toward immigrants. Sanger argued that forced sterilization for immigrants was the appropriate "remedy" for the burden these immigrants place upon society.[22]

Defenders of Sanger argue that even if she was racist in her personal views, her goal was not the elimination of the black community. If these defenders are correct about Sanger, there is still little doubt that the Negro Project reflected the racist views of those who began and continued its work. The Margaret Sanger Papers Project notes that "the Negro Project was, from the start, largely indifferent to the needs of the black community and constructed in terms and with

---

20. Margaret Sanger to Dr. C. J. Gamble, December 10, 1939, Smith College Libraries, https://libex.smith.edu/omeka/items/show/495.

21. *Margaret Sanger: An Autobiography* (New York: W. W. Norton, 1938), 367.

22. Margaret Sanger, "The Function of Sterilization," *Birth Control Review* (November 1921): 9. See also Daniela Dell'Orco, "From Women's Rights to the Eugenics of Race: Margaret Sanger and the Birth Control Movement in the US, 1912–1927," *Storia nordamericana* 5, no. 2 (1988): 23–49.

perceptions that today smack of racism."[23] Sanger and those who worked closely with her to begin the Negro Project described African Americans as "the great problem of the South" with "the greatest economic, health and social problems," and who "still breed carelessly and disastrously."[24] Sanger believed birth control and abortion to be useful tools for eliminating the unfit, believed African Americans to be a "great problem," and created an entire project targeting this community in the South. Racial prejudice combined with the ability to eliminate unfit populations was a recipe for disaster for the African American community in the United States. This recipe continues to have tragic consequences even in our own day.

Continuing Effects of the Eugenicist Roots of Abortion

At the most fundamental level, humans of every color are one race. We all share common DNA.[25] This fact has not kept individuals and communities from discriminating against people using the superficial tool of skin color. Racism is the belief that all members of each race possess characteristics or abilities specific to that race, especially so as to distinguish it as inferior or superior to another race or races. In the United States, racism, particularly by whites against blacks, has created profound racial tension and conflict in virtually all aspects of American society. These divisions among human beings due to skin color, visible physical attributes, and certain cultural differences continue to have an impact on these communities today, especially with regard to abortion and the black community.

---

23. Margaret Sanger Papers Project, "Birth Control or Race Control? Sanger and the Negro Project," *The Newsletter* 28 (November 2001), https://www.nyu.edu/projects/sanger/articles/bc_or_race_control.php.

24. Margaret Sanger, Mary Woodward Reinhardt, Florence Rose, "Birth Control and the Negro," 1939, quoted in Esther Katz, "Sanger Project Celebrates Black History Month," Margaret Sanger Papers Project, (blog) February 19, 2018, https://sangerpapers.wordpress.com/2016/02/19/sanger-project-celebrates-black-history-month/.

25. See, for example, the work of S. Joshua Swamidass, who makes a compelling scientific argument that all human beings share a common ancestor, Adam and Eve, in *The Genealogical Adam and Eve: The Surprising Science of Universal Ancestry* (Downers Grove, IL: IVP Academic, 2019).

The eugenic legacy of abortion can be seen in the prevalence of abortion in the black community. Given the history outlined above, it is no accident that the abortion rate among African Americans is higher than among any other racial or ethnic group. Take New York City, for example. More black babies are aborted than born in our nation's largest city.[26] Notably, one of Margaret Sanger's first birth control clinics opened in Harlem in 1930.[27] According to data gathered in 2015 and posted on the Centers for Disease Control and Prevention (CDC) website, the abortion rate (defined as the number of abortions per 1,000 women aged 15–44) for non-Hispanic white women in the United States was 6.8 while the rate for African American women was 25.1.[28] The pro-choice Guttmacher Institute cites research conducted from 2008–2014 and published in the *American Journal of Public Health* that records a 27.1 abortion rate among African American women compared to 10 for white women and 18.1 among Hispanic women.[29] In 2015 among African American women, there were 390 abortions per 1,000 live births. In other words, for every 1,000 babies born alive, there were another 390 aborted. Compare that to the 11 abortions per 1,000 live births among non-Hispanic white women.[30] In the South, where Sanger implemented her Negro Project, the statistics are even more striking. In Georgia, African Americans are approximately 32 percent of the population, but African American

---

26. Bureau of Vital Statistics, New York City Department of Health and Mental Hygiene, "Summary of Vital Statistics 2012, The City of New York, Pregnancy Outcomes," 6; https://cdn.cnsnews.com/documents/Pregnancy%20Outcomes%20%20NYC%20Health%202012.pdf.

27. Clarence Thomas, "Abortion and Eugenics," *First Things*, May 28, 2019, https://www.firstthings.com/web-exclusives/2019/05/abortion-and-eugenics.

28. Tara C. Jatlaoui, Maegan E. Boutot, Michele G. Mandel et al., "Abortion Surveillance—United States, 2015," *Surveillance Summaries* 67, no. 13 (November 23, 2018): 1–45, Centers for Disease Control and Prevention, https://www.cdc.gov/mmwr/volumes/67/ss/ss6713a1.htm.

29. "Abortion Rates by Race and Ethnicity," Guttmacher Institute (October 19, 2017), source R. K. Jones and J. Jerman, "Population Group Abortion Rates and Lifetime Incidence of Abortion: United States, 2008–2014," *American Journal of Public Health* (2017), https://www.guttmacher.org/infographic/2017/abortion-rates-race-and-ethnicity.

30. Jatlaoui, Boutot et al., "Abortion Surveillance—United States, 2015."

women account for 64.4 percent of all abortions.[31] Such radical racial disparities would normally cause activists to investigate the roots of the difference and seek a remedy. Yet most activists ignore these statistics and continue promoting abortion.

One of the largest obstacles to addressing these disparities is a refusal to acknowledge the violence of abortion. This willful ignorance persists in movements that call attention to other violence against black Americans. In 2013, in response to several police shootings of young African American men and women, the Black Lives Matter (BLM) movement emerged. BLM is an international activist movement that campaigns against violence and systemic racism toward black people. The irony is that while the mantra of BLM seems compassionate on the surface, seeking justice for the downtrodden, its leaders deny a broader truth: If black lives truly matter, then black babies in the womb matter. When confronted with this concept, BLM continues to remain strangely silent, ignoring the abortion deaths of millions of babies in the womb. As they continue denying the humanity of their little brothers and sisters in the womb, their silence is both deafening and deadly. One pro-choice activist and BLM supporter recently argued that "Reproductive health [i.e. the ability to have an abortion] is intrinsically linked to … the Black Lives Matter movement." According to this activist, "the lives of women—and especially black women—do not matter" to pro-life advocates.[32] She says nothing of the little black lives (half of them little women) in the womb.

While abortion has eugenic roots with lasting consequences, this "procedure" has, in the words of Supreme Court Justice Clarence Thomas, "potential for eugenic manipulation" in the future.[33] In the past and continuing today, abortion has been used as a means of

---

31. Arthur Goldberg, "Abortion's Devastating Impact Upon Black Americans," *The Public Discourse*, February 11, 2019, https://www.thepublicdiscourse.com/2019/02/48594/.

32. Hannah Levintova, "Here's the Worst Appropriation of #BlackLives Matter We've Seen Yet," *Mother Jones*, January 13, 2016, https://www.motherjones.com/politics/2016/01/tone-deaf-missouri-lawmaker-sponsors-all-lives-matter-act-limit-abortions/.

33. Thomas, "Abortion and Eugenics."

eliminating unwanted groups of people. With the advent of new reproductive technologies, abortion can now be used "to target specific children with unwanted characteristics."[34] In other words, abortion can be used as a tool to ensure parents get the specific child they want, down to eye and hair color. The continuing eugenic potential of abortion can be seen even now in a nation such as Iceland. What Sanger hoped to accomplish with the "unfit" population in the United States, Iceland has done with human beings with Down syndrome. Through the use of abortion, nearly one hundred percent of children with Down syndrome are aborted in utero.[35] Iceland shows in microcosm how abortion is a horrifyingly efficient tool for eliminating an undesirable people group. If this could happen to those with Down syndrome, we should not be surprised if it happens to an unwanted racial group. In fact, it is already happening.

Where Do We Go from Here?

The scourge of abortion is an affront to the national covenant, especially as articulated in the Declaration of Independence, which declares that all people have the right to *"life,* liberty, and the pursuit of happiness." If the promises enshrined in the Declaration of Independence are to be realized, they must extend to all human beings, regardless of race or stage of development. To confront the sin of abortion in American life, pro-life Americans must confront the eugenic logic behind abortion and call other Americans to live in a way that is consistent with our founding documents.

Sanger and other eugenicists cannot be acquitted as simply "products of their time." While eugenics was a popular movement in the time of Sanger, there were dissenting voices, many of them evangelical Christians, raising the alarm over these evil views and practices. Although many liberal Christians such as Harry Emerson Fosdick and Shailer Mathews promoted eugenics and birth control from the

---

34. Thomas, "Abortion and Eugenics."

35. Julian Quinones and Arijeta Lajka, "'What kind of society do you want to live in?': Inside the country where down syndrome is disappearing," *CBS News on Assignment,* August 14, 2017, https://www.cbsnews.com/news/down-syndrome-iceland/.

pulpit, evangelical Christians opposed eugenics because of its roots in evolutionary theory and social Darwinism.[36] William Jennings Bryan, the famous populist and three-time presidential candidate, was one such person who raised concerns about this way of thinking. Bryan's involvement in the Scopes Monkey Trial is typically derided as that of a fundamentalist opposed to evolution. In fact, Bryan's concerns ran much deeper. He was more concerned about social Darwinism. In the words of one historian, Bryan saw "the end of sympathy, compassion, and charity" in social Darwinism.[37]

Bryan sounded the alarm that social Darwinism would "eliminate love," leading society to be callous toward the poor, vulnerable, and suffering.[38] He perceptively noted that social Darwinism "dwarfs the moral nature of those who become obsessed with it." Bryan then turned his sights to eugenics: "Darwin speaks with approval of the savage custom of eliminating the weak so that only the strong will survive.... How inhuman such a doctrine as this!"[39] Bryan noted the great irony that refusing to recognize the humanity and dignity of the weak and vulnerable was itself inhuman. In another prophetic passage, Bryan wrote that Darwinism was "transforming the industrial world into a slaughter-house."[40] While Bryan and these evangelical Christians did not address abortion directly in their opposition to eugenics, they attacked the root ideology that would make abortion plausible. These opponents of social Darwinism and eugenics recognized that trying to improve the lives of the strong by eliminating the weak would end in bloodshed. With the legalization and proliferation of abortion in America, Bryan and his evangelical allies have been proved right.

Just as Bryan stood up against social Darwinism in his day, it is incumbent upon Christians to stand up to the offspring of social

---

36. Christine Rosen, *Preaching Eugenics: Religious Leaders and the American Eugenics Movement* (Oxford: Oxford University Press, 2004), 18, 66–67.

37. Jill Lepore, *These Truths: A History of the United States* (New York: W. W. Norton, 2018), 415.

38. William Jennings Bryan, *The Last Message of William Jennings Bryan* (1925; repr., London: Euston Grove, 2009), 38.

39. Bryan, *Last Message*, 39.

40. Bryan, *The Menace of Darwinism* (New York: Fleming H. Revell, 1922), 55.

Darwinism and eugenics—racism and abortion—even if it earns us the scorn of the more elite parts of society. In his day, Bryan clearly and persistently warned of the dangers of social Darwinism and its claims that only the fit deserved to survive. That language may not be used in our day, but the logic still rules many minds, especially in the debate over abortion. We must oppose abortion, and race-based abortion, by addressing the root issue that makes abortion plausible: a failure, or even a refusal, to recognize our common humanity. This is what racism and abortion have in common: the refusal to acknowledge the common humanity of others. Abortion denies the truth that the baby in the womb is a human being, while racism treats those with different superficial characteristics as subhuman.

Pro-life advocates should also follow the lead of figures such as Frederick Douglass and my uncle, the prophetic Martin Luther King, Jr. Unlike so many progressive movements today that condemn America as a fundamentally evil nation, Douglass and King proposed a positive and hopeful vision that inspired Americans to action. Douglass called Americans to recognize the humanity of slaves and appealed to the Constitution, calling it a "glorious liberty document." Instead of condemning the Constitution and Americans as hopelessly racist, Douglass asked his listeners to "take the constitution according to its plain reading." He said he failed to find "a single pro-slavery clause in it." On the contrary, it contains "principles and purposes entirely hostile to the existence of slavery."[41] In the spirit of Douglass, King used the founding documents of the United States of America to call Americans to treat others with dignity and respect: "In a sense we've come to our nation's capital to cash a check. When the architects of our republic wrote the magnificent words of the Constitution and the Declaration of Independence, they were signing a promissory note to which every American was to fall heir. This note was a promise that all men—yes, black men as well as white men—would be guaranteed the unalienable rights of life, liberty, and the pursuit of happiness."[42] What made these men so

---

41. Frederick Douglass, *A Narrative of the Life of Frederick Douglass, a Slave* (1845; repr., New York: Quarto, 2017), 149.

42. Martin Luther King, Jr., "I Have a Dream" in *A Testament of Hope: The Essential Writings and Speeches of Martin Luther King, Jr.*, ed. James M.

effective in advocating for civil rights was their twofold commitment to remind Americans of the humanity of African Americans and to call Americans to live up to the great ideals of America enshrined in the Declaration of Independence and the Constitution—its national covenant. Our witness to the dignity of every human life must have the same uplifting vision that calls Americans to be faithful to the ideals of the United States by respecting the common humanity of people of every race and stage of development.

The current prevalence of abortion in the African American community in the United States is the direct result of two evils: a culture of death that arose from eugenics and a culture of racism that ignores the simple fact that all human beings are united as one race. What Bryan did with social Darwinism and what Douglass and King did with slavery and Jim Crow respectively, pro-life advocates must do with the issue of abortion. We must show, in word and deed, that every life matters—black and white, born and unborn. Political solutions such as the repeal of Roe v. Wade and the appointment of pro-life justices are essential to reducing the number of abortions, but political solutions alone will not root out a culture of discrimination and death. Families, churches, synagogues, and communities must commit to caring for unborn babies and their mothers in such a way that abortion becomes unthinkable—not simply because of the violence abortion inflicts but because we need a culture where every child of every stage and race is loved. The most powerful witness against a culture of discrimination and death is a culture of life and love.

Washington (New York: HarperOne, 1986), 217.

Part 3

THE THEOLOGY AND PRACTICES OF THE COVENANT COMMUNITY

10

RACIAL SUPREMACY AND COVENANTAL RECONCILIATION

Carol M. Swain

During the 2020 presidential campaign, former Vice President Joe Biden told a small group of reporters, "White folks are the reason we have institutionalized racism. There has always been racism in America. White supremacists have always existed, they still exist."[1] Biden was repeating the familiar refrain of social justice warriors on university campuses: racism is now institutional, and its cause is white supremacy. The presidential campaign perpetuated a trend that started with the 2016 election of President Donald J. Trump, when his victory was blamed on white nationalism. But in the meantime the meaning of these terms—*white supremacy* and *white nationalism*—had changed.

In past decades "white supremacist" had referred to persons who felt that having white skin color made them superior to other racial

---

* Some sections of this chapter draw from previous research published in Carol M. Swain, *The New White Nationalism in America: Its Challenge to Integration* (New York: Cambridge University Press, 2002) and *Be the People: A Call to Reclaim America's Faith and Promise* (Nashville: Thomas Nelson, 2011).

1. Quoted in Errin Haines and Juana Summers, "Biden: Racism in US is institutional, 'white man's problem,'" *AP News*, August 28, 2019, https://www.apnews.com/88bd58010e75449eb5748499724df2f2.

and ethnic groups. "White nationalism" was the belief that whites should constitute a dominant and separate group able to determine their own future. But when Trump became the Republican candidate during the run-up to the 2016 election, these labels were hurled indiscriminately at his white supporters. The Left began to claim that all white people are beneficiaries of white privilege, and that Trump supporters were white "supremacists"—no matter what they said they believed about race. Nor did it matter how they earned their money or place in society. If they were white, what they had was undeserved. If they voted for Trump, they must believe that blacks are inferior—despite their protests to the contrary. Whites are the oppressors, and racial minorities—regardless of their social and economic attainments—are perpetual victims.

Much of the national conversation since then has been a divisive back-and-forth, weaponized dialogue that harms our nation and weakens any possibility for racial reconciliation. In this chapter I will discuss racial issues from the perspective of a black woman who believes in God's providence and the prospect of racial reconciliation that comes from forgiveness and the application of New Testament principles toward both friends and (perceived) enemies. In fact, rediscovering the Golden Rule, to do unto others as you would have them do unto you, would go a long way toward bringing understanding to people of goodwill regardless of their race or religious background.

My Story

Dr. Ben Carson, pediatric neurosurgeon and US Secretary of Housing and Urban Development, wrote, "God has opened many doors of opportunity throughout my lifetime, but I believe the greatest of those doors was allowing me to be born in the United States of America."[2] These words sum up my beliefs about America and the good fortune that comes to those who are willing to work hard and avail themselves of opportunities that come their way.

I was born and raised in rural southwestern Virginia in the small hamlet of Chamblissburg, located in Bedford County. By the grace

---

2. Ben Carson, *America the Beautiful: Rediscovering What Made This Nation Great* (San Francisco: Harper Collins, 2012), 180.

of God, I escaped a life of poverty to eventually become a tenured professor at Princeton and Vanderbilt Universities. Along the way, I defied the expectations of many elites that all blacks should hold a similar set of views about the world. To achieve success, I had to overcome material and spiritual poverty, failed marriages, recurrent bouts of depression, and ostracism. But it was through these struggles that I came to see the world in ways that are strikingly different from what is commonly expected of blacks.

Here are some life lessons I learned from my journey. Taken together, they trumped all the disadvantages I faced being born black and poor.

- Everyone has the potential to overcome life's disadvantages.
- Where you start in life does not determine where you end up.
- America is a land of tremendous opportunity.
- Your attitude toward life, and what you believe about reality, are far more important than your race, gender, or social class in determining what you will accomplish.

Because I started to learn these lessons and tried to hold onto them, I did not let being black, female, and born into poverty become stumbling blocks. None of these became a crippling factor for me.

Neither of my parents was college-educated. My father had a third-grade education, my mother got as far as tenth grade, and my stepfather had no education at all. There were no college-educated relatives in our lives to tell us about the outside world.

As the second girl in a family of twelve children, my life was defined by chores and childcare. Perhaps this is why I never had more than three children of my own; after one died in infancy, I never had another.

During the early part of my life, nine of us—both children and adults—lived in a two-room, tar-paper-covered shack with a tin roof. Our bedroom was the kitchen floor. The house was drafty and lacked indoor plumbing. Our heat came from wood burning stoves, and our water came from a spring that looked more like a mud hole than a fresh water supply. We children had to haul the water in buckets up to the shack that was our home.

As a child, I remember hunger, ill-fitting clothes, missed days and weeks of school, and regular fights between my alcoholic mother and stepfather. Eventually my older sister and I ran away as teens to live with a father we didn't know. I became a ninth-grade dropout and later a teenaged wife and mother.

When people ask me how I escaped poverty, I tell them I have always believed in the American dream and the correlation between hard work and results. National, state, and local pride were ingrained in my psyche even though the adults around me were not politically active. I knew I was fortunate to be an American living in the greatest nation in the world. Being a Virginian was a great source of pride for me. I knew all that was good about Virginia, but the negative parts of my state's history were unknown to me. In grade school it was drilled into my head that Virginia was the home of presidents George Washington, Thomas Jefferson, James Madison, James Monroe, William Harrison, John Tyler, Zachary Taylor, and Woodrow Wilson.

Over the years I began to learn that Virginia also had its fair share of negatives. Former Governor and Senator Harry F. Byrd led a massive resistance to integration following the Supreme Court's 1954 decision in *Brown v. Board of Education*.[3] Although the decision was handed down the year I was born, integration did not reach Bedford County until the late 1960s.

The state continues to elect politicians who stun the nation with their insensitivity toward race and callous disregard for the sanctity of human life. Virginia Governor Ralph Northam shocked the world when he spoke in favor of infanticide during a national debate about New York's late-term abortion law. Northam, a pediatric neurosurgeon, told reporters, "The infant would be delivered. The infant would be kept comfortable. The infant would be resuscitated if that's what the mother and the family desired."[4] In the heat of the controversy

---

3. "Massive Resistance," Virginia Museum of History and Culture, n.d., https://www.virginiahistory.org/collections-and-resources/virginia-history-explorer/civil-rights-movement-virginia/massive.

4. Devan Cole, "Virginia Governor Faces Backlash Over Comments Supporting Late-Term Abortion," *CNNPolitics*, January 31, 2019, https://www.cnn.com/2019/01/31/politics/ralph-northam-third-trimester-abortion/index.html.

over the comments about allowing infants to die, a 1984 medical school yearbook surfaced with Northam featured in blackface.[5] As is often the case for members of the political Left, he survived the scandal without being forced to resign.

While I knew from my childhood that race in Virginia was always a problem, I did not know that what has been called America's "original sin"—slavery—started in my own backyard, so to speak.

Slavery and Race in America

American slavery originated in Jamestown, Virginia, in 1619. That is when the first Africans were brought to America aboard an English ship to serve, at first, as indentured servants. But greed quickly superseded morality, so that covenants were broken and biblical principles rejected. Historian Philip Foner provides some of the details:

> The fact that the early Negroes imported into Virginia held the status of indentured servants is shown by the records of some Negroes' receiving the customary "freedom dues" in the form of land at the end of their term of service. Some obtained land after becoming free by importing servants under the "head-right" system, by which they obtained fifty acres for each servant imported. A small number of Negro landowners not only held black servants, but were sufficiently prosperous to pay the transportation costs of white indentured servants, through each of whom they could obtain fifty acres of land. Anthony Johnson, who was imported into Virginia in 1622, accumulated property after he ended his indentured period, and even though he lost all his holdings in a fire, was able by 1651 to import 5 black servants into the colony, for which he was granted 250 acres in Northampton County. About 1650 Benjamin Dole, a Negro, was granted 300 acres of land in Surry County for having imported 6 servants. Another Negro was granted 550 acres after importing 11 people.[6]

---

5. Alan Blinder and Johnathan Martin, "Governor Admits He Was in Racist Yearbook Photo," *New York Times*, February 1, 2019, https://www.nytimes.com/2019/02/01/us/politics/ralph-northam-yearbook-blackface.html.

6. Philip S. Foner, *History of Black Americans: From Africa to the Emergence of the Cotton Kingdom* (Westport, CT: Greenwood Press, 1975), 190.

Descendants of free blacks in America are often the most prosperous today, having gotten their start from indentured servitude and the freedom and assimilation that ensued. Surprisingly, slave masters and Christian missionaries took the lead in educating slaves prior to 1861.[7] Slavers had a variety of motives, some to make slaves more useful and others for humanitarian reasons. Missionaries had evangelistic reasons. According to historian Carter G. Woodson, "Zealous missionaries, believing that the message of divine love came equally to all, taught slaves the English language so they might learn the principles of the Christian religion."[8]

Permanent slavery in America started in 1640 in Virginia, after John Punch and two white indentured servants were caught attempting to flee their servitude. Although the two white runaways were punished with four additional years of servitude, Punch, a black, was declared a permanent slave.[9] In 1662, permanent slavery became the law, but any slave who converted to Christianity and was baptized was set free. That door to freedom closed in 1667, when the General Assembly revoked what had been automatic emancipation for a fellow Christian.

Permanent freedom for most slaves came on January 1, 1863, when President Abraham Lincoln signed the Emancipation Proclamation, which freed slaves living in the states that were fighting for independence.[10] It took ratification of the Thirteenth Amendment in December 1865 for the remaining slaves to see freedom. But in the decades after the Civil War, black codes and vagrancy laws continued to hold many in bondage.[11]

---

7. Carter G. Woodson, *The Education of the Negro Prior to 1861*, 2nd ed. (Washington, DC: Associated Publishers, 1919), 2.

8. Woodson, *Education of the Negro*, 2.

9. Foner, *History of Black Americans*, 191.

10. Douglas T. Miller, "Abraham Lincoln, The Emancipation Proclamation 1863," American History, n.d., http://www.let.rug.nl/usa/presidents/abraham-lincoln/the-emancipation-proclamation-1863.php.

11. Louis R. Harlan, "Review of Theodore Branter Wilson, *The Black Codes of the South*, Southern Historical Publications 6 (University: University of Alabama Press, 1965)," *The American Historical Review* 72, no. 3 (April 1967): 1104–5, https://doi.org/10.1086/ahr/72.3.1104.

Race, Slavery, and the Bible

> And he made from one man every nation of mankind to live on all the face of the earth, having determined allotted periods and the boundaries of their dwelling place[s]. (Acts 17:26 ESV)

Scripture teaches that God created the variety among men and women we see in the world, and the differences we see manifested in skin color and physical attributes. The Hebrew Bible was written in a world where slavery was taken for granted, and race was not a central factor. At every instance where slavery comes under biblical law, its worst effects were mitigated.[12] By the time of the New Testament, it was implied that Christian slave owners would treat their slave as a brother or sister: "no longer as a slave, but more than a slave, a beloved brother" (Phil. 16a NASB). It wasn't long before the early church fathers would regard slavery as unchristian. Augustine said slavery is against God's will and results from sin; John Chrysostom preached that slavery is the fruit of covetousness and savagery and is rebellion against God the Father.[13]

The New Testament teaches a unity that breaks down all racial and class barriers: "There is neither Jew nor Greek, there is neither slave nor free ... for you are all one in Christ Jesus" (Gal. 3:28 ESV). Therefore, slavers in America broke the covenant that Scripture revealed between God and his people in the ways they should treat their fellow human beings: "Whatever you wish that others would do to you, do also to them, for this is the Law and the Prophets" (Matt. 7:12 ESV).

American history shows that even if Americans knew that someday they would stand as equals before God at the judgment, their natural tendencies to oppress and hate based on immutable differences often won out. The prophet Jeremiah warned us about this when he said, "The heart is deceitful above all things, and desperately sick: Who

---

12. For example, Israelites' slaves were to be freed after six years of service (Exod. 21:2), and kidnapping and selling people into slavery was prohibited (Exod. 21:16).

13. Augustine, *City of God*, bk. 19, chap. 15; John Chrysostom, "Homily XXII on Ephesians vi:5–8," *Christian Classics Ethereal Library*, http://www.ccel.org/ccel/schaff/npnf113.iii.iv.xxiii.html.

can understand it?" (Jeremiah 17:9 ESV). It is the darkness of the human heart that incites some to subjugate others. This darkness of the heart turned the indentured servanthood of the first blacks in America into a permanent state of bondage. This has been a pattern across cultures throughout history: whenever there have been visible differences among groups—in skin color, language, or religion—there has always been discrimination. Such bias is part of human nature. It is to be expected from creatures who carry an inherited sin problem in their heart.

Scientific evidence supports the existence of one human race. Scientists studying genetics and mitochondrial DNA have proved that all human beings descend from a common human ancestor who lived in Africa. That ancestor's offspring are responsible for the world's diversity.[14] Evidence from the Human Genome Project supports the one-race, common-ancestor theory. Scientific mappings have demonstrated that all human beings share 99.9 percent of the same DNA.[15] All races of human men and women can mate with each other and invent nonverbal ways of communicating, even when language barriers exist.

Although racism was at the heart of slavery and its justification, it took the work of nineteenth-century eugenicists to cement in the American mind the notion of distinct groupings of people defined as races according to their biological, genetic, and intellectual capacities. Among the eugenicists of this era were Planned Parenthood founder Margaret Sanger, who wrote *The Pivot of Civilization*; Madison Grant, a lawyer, historian, and anthropologist and author of *The Passing of The Great Race*; and Lothrop Stoddard, who

---

14. J. Cameron Thrash et al., "Phylogenomic evidence for a common ancestor of mitochondria and the SAR11 clade," *Scientific Reports* (June 14, 2011), https://www.nature.com/articles/srep00013 (accessed March 18, 2020).

15. Stephen Openheimer, *The Real Eve: Modern Man's Journey out of Africa* (New York: Basic Books, 2004); Mark Schoofs, "The Myth of Race: What DNA Says About Human Ancestry—and Bigotry," *The Village Voice*, pt. 3, excerpted at http://web.mit.edu/racescience/in_media/what_dna_says_about_human/index.html and accessed on October 31, 2010; Human Genome Project Information, accessed October 31, 2010, http://www.ornl.gov/sci/techresources/Human_Genome/project/info.shtml.

wrote *The Rising Tide of Color Against White World Supremacy*.[16] These three authors introduced the world to the idea of compulsory sterilization that devastated ethnic groups for decades and nearly decimated politically powerless groups such as the mentally retarded. Stoddard's work played a role in the shaping and passage of the Immigration Act of 1924, which established nation-of-origin quotas limiting the number of immigrants who could enter the United States from certain countries.[17]

If racism is supported by neither the Bible nor science, it nevertheless feeds on social tendencies. People tend to congregate based upon similarities like race, education, social class, religion, and shared values. This natural inclination produces disparities and discrimination when one group or individual possesses resources superior to other groups, and then uses those resources to favor or disadvantage others. Throughout history, humanity has used skin color to create rankings of racial superiority. Lighter-skinned people typically are designated as superior to those with darker skin.[18]

Economist Glenn Loury has written about the tragic impact of slavery and its lingering impact on the attitudes and behaviors of generations of blacks unable to escape inner-city ghettos. Well-informed people are aware of "the crime, drug addition, family breakdown, unemployment, poor school performance, welfare dependency, and general decay in these communities."[19] Black ghetto dwellers have become pariahs to many in society. Although billions of dollars have been spent in governmental programs, the problems affecting minority communities stubbornly persist. No matter how far removed we

---

16. Margaret Sanger, *The Pivot of Civilization* (New York: Brentano, 1922); Madison Grant, *The Passing of The Great Race; or, The Racial Basis of European History* (New York: Scribner, 1916); Lothrop Stoddard, *The Rising Tide of Color Against White World Supremacy* (New York: Scribner, 1920).

17. Immigration Act of 1924, National Archives, https://www.docsteach.org/documents/document/immigration-act-1924.

18. Thomas Sowell, *Discrimination and Disparities* (New York: Basic Books, 2019).

19. Glenn Loury, "An American Tragedy: The Legacy of Slavery Lingers in Our Cities' Ghettoes," *Brookings*, March 1, 1998, https://www.brookings.edu/articles/an-american-tragedy-the-legacy-of-slavery-lingers-in-our-cities-ghettos/.

are from slavery and the Jim Crow segregation that followed, the positioning of blacks at the bottom of society is all too common. The political Left points to this positioning as evidence of white supremacy and privilege because the average white has more wealth and is more economically advantaged than the average black. Whether or not this dubious connection can be proven, we can all concede that blacks are behind the curve, and they are not thriving as a demographic. But at this stage in American history, I think we need to ask how it will help inner-city blacks to perpetuate this narrative. Should we keep telling them that they cannot thrive because of slavery in centuries past and white privilege today? Will this really help them? Is it even true?

I don't think so. There are plenty of blacks, like me, who have come from dire circumstances and have risen above the circumstances of our birth. One thing missing from the usual narrative is the role of individual autonomy: individuals make choices about how they are going to spend their time and their money. What they believe about the world influences their actions, and if they believe the wrong story, it can limit their opportunities.

Pooja Sawrikar and Ilan Katz are Australian social scientists who make a compelling argument that the existence of racism does not prove pervasive white belief in white supremacy.[20] They argue that we should acknowledge the role of "prejudice" in racism, but not focus exclusively on the element of "power."[21] By focusing on prejudice, "individuals can be better empowered to exercise their own personal power and choice to be vigilant on their racial prejudices, and all racial groups can be better empowered to take responsibility for protecting each of our human rights to racial equality."[22] Rejecting the much-repeated argument that blacks and other racial minorities cannot be racist because they lack power, Sawrikar and Katz make the case that any group can harbor prejudice that is harmful to others.

---

20. Pooja Sawrikar and Ilan Barry Katz, "Only White People Can Be Racist: What Does Power Have to Do with Prejudice?" *Cosmopolitan Civil Societies Journal* 2, no. 1 (2010): 80–95, UTS ePRESS, https://epress.lib.uts.edu.au/journals/index.php/mcs/article/view/1075.

21. Sawrikar and Katz, "Only White People Can Be Racist," 95.

22. Sawrikar and Katz, "Only White People Can Be Racist," 95.

The exclusive focus on white supremacy lets other prejudiced offenders off the hook.

But let us be clear. Any racial group that sees itself as morally superior to another racial group believes in racial supremacy. Even white Americans who loathe other whites, whom they dismiss as white trash because of their views, are engaging in a harmful form of stereotyping that can lead to discrimination and diminished opportunities for those they castigate. The same can be said for blacks such as rapper Snoop Dogg, who in 2018 publicly castigated fellow rapper Kanye West after West expressed support for President Trump.[23]

We cannot move beyond race if we are fixated on the past. But some people keep encouraging the young to constantly look in the rearview mirror for evidence to explain the unequal results we see in the world. They presume that all whites are recipients of undeserved privileges that enable them to benefit from the sins of their ancestors. This is usually untrue, but it provides a convenient excuse for those on the Left.

From this perspective, blacks are absolved from responsibility for self-destructive behaviors because they are victims of historical racism that has crippled them since slavery. Regardless of what is done or said, liberal professors and social justice warriors assure us that blacks cannot be racist against whites because blacks lack the institutional power and positioning to inflict harm. We are assured that it is irrelevant that America has had a black president, two black Supreme Court Justices, two black Secretaries of State, and two black attorneys general as well as black successes in many other spheres of American life.

Our young people are told that racism is everywhere and that European Americans and Western civilization bear most of the responsibility for everything that has gone wrong in the world. On college campuses, students are expected to understand to which category they belong—the oppressor or the oppressed. Sociologist Ted Thornhill teaches a course on "White Racism" at Florida Gulf

---

23. Zamira Rahim, "Snoop Dogg launches expletive-ridden attack on 'racist' Donald Trump and Kanye West," *Independent*, September 20, 2018, https://www.independent.co.uk/arts-entertainment/music/news/snoop-dogg-donald-trum-kanye-west-racist-f-word-sirius-xm-interview-a8546011.html.

Coast University, where he uses racism to explain different outcomes in the "labor market and workplace, education, and even in access to clean water." Race matters, he insists, "in health care, the criminal justice system, and even everyday retail and dining experiences."[24] Here is a paragraph from his syllabus:

> In this course, we will interrogate the concept of race; examine the racist ideologies, laws, policies, and practices that have operated for hundreds of years to maintain white racial domination over those racialized as nonwhite; and discuss ways to challenge white racism and white supremacy toward promoting an anti-racist society where whiteness is not tied to greater life chances.[25]

A student who takes a course like this is probably more likely to join Antifa or Black Lives Matter than they are to do something constructive with their lives. If they are from a minority group, they will be told in this classroom that their own effort cannot help them get ahead, and that non-whites face a system designed to keep them down.

Students will also be instructed that politics is fundamentally about protest and should aim at Marxist utopianism under the guise of today's "socialism," where it is presumed (falsely) that equality can be socially engineered. Meanwhile, whites are left ridden with guilt. Blacks and other minorities often leave such classes filled with anger and a sense of entitlement for what others have worked to attain. I have seen this firsthand during my twenty-eight years of teaching on university campuses. This identity politics approach to American politics and university culture is not only destructive to the human spirit, but it also kills any hope for forgiveness and reconciliation. Whites are silenced, and moral superiority is imputed to racial, ethnic, and religious minorities.

---

24. Ted Thornhill, "Why I Teach a Course Called 'White Racism,'" *The Conversation*, February 1, 2018, https://theconversation.com/why-i-teach-a-course-called-white-racism-90093.

25. Ted Thornhill, "Why I Teach a Course Called 'White Racism.'"

What Does Scripture Say about Race?

Both the Old and New Testaments promote the ideas of a common Creator and human solidarity—ideals that are inconsistent with notions of racial superiority, prejudice, and hatred. Genesis 1:27, for instance, provides an account of creation in which all humans are depicted as descending from a single human ancestor, Adam (Hebrew for "man" or "humanity"), who is created "in the image of God." Similarly, in Acts 17:26 the apostle Paul declares the peoples of all nations to be descended from "one man," hence united genealogically.

The exodus story of the Israelites' four-hundred-year bondage and redemption offered powerful hope to enslaved blacks in America. It fueled their agitation for freedom from their cruel masters. They understood, long before many whites, that the Bible condemns the slave trade: "Whoever steals a man and sells him, and anyone found in possession of him, shall be put to death" (Exod. 21:16 ESV).

Black slaves also rejected the interpretation of the biblical curses on Ham and the Gibeonites that some white slave owners used to justify their ownership of slaves.[26] They realized what later Bible scholars argued, that in the text Ham himself was not cursed (only his son Canaan) and that skin color is never mentioned in either story (Gen. 9:20–27; Josh. 9:1–27). Slaves then, and their descendants ever since, used the same Bible to argue the universal redemptive power of Christ: "There is neither Jew nor Greek, there is neither slave nor free, there is neither male nor female, for you are all one in Christ Jesus" (Gal. 3:28 ESV).

While Christian principles about universal humanity and brotherhood have inspired reform movements of great benefit to humanity, Christians have responded to these principles more by their violation than observance. Christianity's checkered history on race has given its opponents much fodder for ridiculing America's majority religion. We just mentioned America's misuse of the curse against the sons of Ham in Genesis. Later, the Ku Klux Klan repurposed Christianity's most potent symbol—the cross—for its own racist purposes. Klan gatherings typically lit crosses of fire while singing Christian hymns such as "Amazing Grace," "The Old Rugged Cross,"

---

26. See the next section for an explanation of these racist interpretations.

and "Onward Christian Soldiers." Today another racist movement known as Christian Identity distorts Scripture by teaching that Caucasians are God's "chosen people" and that Anglo-Saxons are "true Israelites." Of course, Scripture taken out of context can be used to support almost any theology.[27]

To defend slavery and the subordination of blacks, Christian racists have sometimes cited Colossians 4:1: "Masters, treat your bondservants justly and fairly, knowing that you also have a Master in heaven" (ESV). They also use Ephesians 6:5, where Paul urges servants to be obedient "to your human masters with fear and trembling" (CSB). Racists never explain that slavery as practiced in the ancient world in which Paul lived was not based on race (slaves could be of any race), and that the New Testament proclaims a religion that transcends racial categories.

To this day, a world that transcends racial and ethnic categories has not emerged. Until the return of the Messiah, it is doubtful that we will ever see the eradication of racial barriers and tensions. Meanwhile, racism and ethnic violence are rearing their ugly heads at unprecedented levels worldwide. We know from the histories of other multiracial, multiethnic societies of the horrors that can occur when racism is given free rein. In *The Disuniting of America*, Arthur Schlesinger, Jr. writes, "Within nation-states, nationalism takes the form of ethnicity or tribalism. In country after country across the third world—India, Burma, Sri Lanka, Indonesia, Iraq, Ethiopia, Nigeria, Angola, Trinidad, Guyana—ethnic groups struggle for power and, in desperate cases, for survival. The ethnic upsurge in America, far from being unique, partakes of the global fever." Schlesinger argues, "The cult of ethnicity exaggerates differences, intensifies resentments and antagonisms, and drives awful wedges between races and nationalities."[28]

Unfortunately, today in America we see a proliferation of racial resentments. If we are to cool the flames of those resentments, we

---

27. For a recent reading of how the Bible has been used and abused on slavery, civil rights, abortion, and homosexuality, see Jim Hill and Rand Cheadle, *The Bible Tells Me So: Uses and Abuses of Holy Scripture* (New York: Bantam, 1996).

28. Arthur Schlesinger, Jr., *The Disuniting of America* (Knoxville: Whittle Direct, 1991), 48.

must question our recent identity politics and look back to the ideals that united us in past centuries. A proper sense of nationhood, stripped of racism and identity politics, can help bring us a new unity that we desperately need. We should begin again to think of ourselves as Americans rather than as members of racial or sexual subgroups.

Race and the Fear Factor[29]

The ethnic impulses of blacks, whites, and Hispanics threaten race relations by causing leaders to pursue racial group interests rather than strategies that focus on the well-being of the nation as a whole. Among whites there is a long history of literature that feeds hatred and animosity toward minorities. *The Communist Manifesto*, *Mein Kampf*, and *The Sayings of Chairman Mao* are well-known examples of movement-inspiring literature that has justified and fueled white supremacy.[30]

Among more radical white nationalists, white supremacists, and neo-Nazi groups in America, other books have played a parallel role. Perhaps the most important has been William Pierce's futuristic racial apocalypse, *The Turner Diaries*, published under the pseudonym Andrew Macdonald.[31] The FBI has called this book the "Bible of the racist right."[32] Many Americans first heard of *The Turner Diaries* when they learned that Timothy McVeigh, the Oklahoma City bomber, had read this work and might have been inspired by it.[33]

---

29. Paragraphs from this section draw heavily from pages 37–41 of Carol M. Swain, *The New White Nationalism in America: Its Challenge to Integration* (New York: Cambridge University Press, 2002).

30. Karl Marx and Friedrich Engels, *The Communist Manifesto* (New York: Signet Classics, 1998); Adolf Hitler, *Mein Kampf*, trans. Ralph Manheim (Boston: Mariner, 1998); Mao Tse-Tung, *Quotations from Chairman Mao Tse-tung* (China: China Books and Periodicals, 1990).

31. Andrew Macdonald, *The Turner Diaries*, 2nd ed. (1978; Hillsboro, WV: National Vanguard, 1980).

32. Robert L. Snow, *The Militia Threat: Terrorists Among Us* (New York: Plenum, 1999), 95.

33. "'Turner Diaries' Introduced in McVeigh Trial," CNN Interactive, April 28, 1997, http://edition.cnn.com/US/9704/28/okc/.

William Pierce, a former university physics professor and head of the influential white supremacist group the National Alliance, published *The Turner Diaries* in 1978. The novel describes in graphic detail a race war in which white patriots in California, collectively known as the Organization, launch a successful attack against the Zionist Occupied Government (ZOG) in Washington for its crimes against white Americans. Members of the Organization assassinate federal officials, law enforcement personnel, and politicians. They slaughter Jews, nonwhite minorities, and race traitors, and then launch a nuclear attack upon the state of Israel with the nuclear arsenal assembled by ZOG. The book's conclusion offers Pierce's view of the necessity of violence: "There is no way to win the struggle in which we [whites] are engaged without shedding torrents—veritable rivers—of blood."[34]

Yet whites are not the only ones preaching racial superiority or advocating violence. Minister Louis Farrakhan's Nation of Islam and the New Black Panther Party have produced Black Nationalist speakers who preach racial hatred of white people. In 1993, Khalid Abdul Muhammad gave an infamous speech at Kean University in which he lambasted Jews and spoke of killing white South Africans who refused to leave the country: "We kill the women. We kill the babies. We kill the blind. We kill the cripples. We kill them all.... When you get through killing them all, go to the graveyard and kill them again because they didn't die hard enough."[35]

The Nation of Islam suspended Muhammad for his speech. However in 2010, Malik Zulu Shabazz, a member of the New Black Panthers Party, echoed Louis Farrakhan's theme of killing white people. Shabazz, who calls himself King Shamir, has spewed racist expletives filled with venom. "I hate white people, all of them. Every last iota of a [white man], I hate him.... You want freedom? You are

---

34. Andrew Macdonald, *Turner Diaries*, 79.

35. Khalid Abdul Muhammad, "Lecture to Kean College, in Union, New Jersey, November 29, 1993," YouTube video, https://www.youtube.com/watch?v=Nlo31CTtmdo.

going to have to kill some [whites]. You are going to have to kill some of their babies."³⁶

In attempting to put a positive spin on the flip side of white racism, political scientists Darren W. Davis and Ronald E. Brown have argued that black nationalism "stresses the importance of a connection to African origins and identity, pride in being black, a desire for blacks to control their own communities, and sometimes a desire to establish a black nation in Africa or some part of the United States."³⁷

Latinos have jumped onto the racist bandwagon by forming their own hate groups and supremacist ideas. The most prominent of these is MEChA, which stands for Movimiento Estudiantil Chicano de Aztlan. The preamble to MEChA's Constitution states that "Chicano and Chicana students of Aztlan must take upon themselves the responsibilities to promote Chicanismo within the community, politicizing our Raza with an emphasis on indigenous consciousness to continue the struggle for the self-determination of the Chicano people for the purpose of liberating Aztlan."³⁸

In May 2007, authorities in California arrested members of Latino gangs and charged them with engaging in a "violent campaign to drive blacks out of the unincorporated Florence-Firestone neighborhood that allegedly resulted in 20 homicides over several years."³⁹ Rutgers University professor of law Tanya Hernandez has written that "murder was a manifestation of an increasing common trend: instances of Latino aggression toward African Americans in multiracial

---

36. Malik Zulu Shabazz, aired on The Glenn Beck Show, "Black Panthers Respond to 'Kill Cracker Babies' Comment" (expletives deleted), The Glenn Beck Radio Clips, July 9, 2010, http://www.glennbeck.com/content/articles/article/198/42766/.

37. Darren W. Davis and Ronald E. Brown, "The Antipathy of Black Nationalism: Behavioral and Attitudinal Implications of an African American Ideology," *American Journal of Political Science* 46, no. 2 (April 2002): 241.

38. Movimiento Estudiantil Chicano de Aztlan (MEChA) Constitution, March 30, 2003, http://clubs.arizona.edu/~mecha/pages/PDFs/NationalConstitution.pdf.

39. Scott Glover, "Huge Sweeps Target Latino Gangs That Allegedly Attacked Blacks," *Los Angeles Times*, L.A. Now, May 21, 2009, http://latimesblogs.latimes.com/lanow/2009/05/huge-gang-sweeps-targets-latino-gangs-that-allegedly-targeted-blacks.html.

neighborhoods."[40] Hernandez points out that "racism and anti-Black racism in particular is a pervasive and historically entrenched reality of life in Latin America and the Caribbean.... The legacy of the slave period in Latin America and the Caribbean is similar to that of the United States. Lighter skin and European features increase one's chances of socioeconomic opportunity, while darker skin and African features severely limit mobility."[41]

Nicolas Vaca, author of *The Presumed Alliance*, observed that in the 1960s, "relations between Blacks and Latinos were viewed through rose-colored glasses. It was the 'brothers under the skin,' 'a house divided will fall,' Latinos and Blacks united against the 'white oppressor' that swept differences under the rug."[42] Blacks and Latinos now fight over affirmative action, housing, jobs, and political power. According to Vaca, the emotions behind the shared discrimination in the civil rights era of the 1950s and 1960s blinded minority leaders to "the frictions that existed or could exist in the future between coalesced minorities."[43]

No racial group can claim a monopoly on decency. Fear is the catalyst that pushes ordinary citizens to embrace extremist causes when they believe they can reshape society.[44] As I explained in my 2002 book *The New White Nationalism in America*, "A combination of factors can drive seemingly ordinary and reasonable people toward extremism. One such factor is fear for personal safety and security. If people believe their life or property is genuinely threatened, they may seek to eliminate that threat as expeditiously as possible. White

---

40. Tanya K. Hernandez, "Latino Anti-Black Violence in Los Angeles: Not 'Made in the USA,'" *Harvard Journal of African American Public Policy* 13 (Summer 2007): 37.

41. Hernandez, "Latino Anti-Black Violence," 38.

42. Nicolas Vaca, *The Presumed Alliance: The Unspoken Conflict Between Latinos and Blacks and What It Means for America* (New York: Rayo 2004), ix.

43. Vaca, *Presumed Alliance*, ix.

44. Eric Hoffer, *The True Believer: Thoughts on the Nature of Mass Movements* (New York: Harper & Row, 1951).

racial leaders prey upon this fear in whites by focusing on crime statistics that paint African Americans as criminals."[45]

Fear, however, does not always drive people toward extremism; fear can also motivate people toward acts of courage. These acts can include the courage to debate unpopular issues, the courage to tell the truth and stand up to extremist views, and the courage to search for responsible answers to the complex issues all Americans face. Far too many political leaders lack the courage to confront racial demagogues who exploit the silence of cowardice to perpetuate racism.

Few leaders, either political or religious, are willing to talk about the new racism where whites are being assailed for their "whiteness"—presumed to be racist because of the color of their skin. Yet many who make these accusations ironically claim the mantle of Martin Luther King, Jr. who hoped for the day when his children would "one day live in a nation where they will not be judged by the color of their skin but by the content of their character."[46]

The New Racism

We see this new racism on college campuses and in major institutions in America whose leaders use language and behavior that would make them pariahs if their targets were non-whites. Here are a few examples from the academic world:

> [W]hite people begging us for food feels like justice. It feels like Afro-Futurism after America falls. It feels like a Black Nationalist wet dream. It has the feels [sic] I rarely feel, a hunger for historical vengeance satisfied so well I rub my belly. (Nicholas Powers, professor of literature, SUNY[47])

---

45. Carol Swain, *The New White Nationalism in America* (New York: Cambridge University Press, 2002), 128–29.

46. Martin Luther King, Jr., "I Have a Dream," Address Delivered at the March on Washington for Jobs and Freedom, August 28, 1963. The Martin Luther King, Jr. Research and Education Institute, https://kinginstitute.stanford.edu/king-papers/documents/i-have-dream-address-delivered-march-washington-jobs-and-freedom.

47. Nicholas Powers, "Seeing Poor White People Makes Me Happy," *racebaitr*, June 11, 2009, http://archive.vn/2cRrM#selection-1095.55-1095.255.

> I am a white people [sic], for God's sake, but can we keep them—us—us out of my neighborhood? I just went to Harlem Shake on 124 and Lenox for a Classic burger to go, that would be my dinner, and the place is overrun by little Caucasian assholes who know their parents will approve of anything they do.... I hereby resign from my race. (James Livingston, historian, Rutgers University[48])

> I will always call on my Black women students first. Other POC [people of color] get second tier priority. WW [white women] come next. And, if I have to, white men. (Stephanie McKellop, graduate instructor, University of Pennsylvania[49])

Outside of academia, there is a double standard for public speech that allowed *New York Times* editor Sarah Jeong to survive racist remarks she put on Twitter in 2018. Her tweets, which used the hashtag #CancelWhitePeople, targeted white people.

> Oh man, it's kind of sick how much joy I get out of being cruel to old white men.

> Are white people genetically predisposed to burn faster in the sun, thus logically being only fit to live underground like groveling goblins.

> white people [are] marking up the internet with their opinions like dogs pissing on fire hydrants.[50]

---

48. Quoted in Emma Whitford, "White Professor Accused of Antiwhite Racism," *Inside Higher Ed*, August 23, 2019, https://www.insidehighered.com/news/2018/08/23/professor-accused-antiwhite-racism-others-say-its-free-speech.

49. Stephanie McKellop, quoted in Geoffrey Miller, "U. Penn history teacher explains what 'social justice' really means in university classes," Twitter, October 20, 2017, https://twitter.com/primalpoly/status/921408382916890629.

50. Sarah Jeong, "NY Times stands by 'racist tweets' reporter," *BBC News*, 2 August 2018, https://www.bbc.com/news/world-us-canada-45052534.

In contrast, white employees of *The New York Times* who have criticized racial or ethnic minorities or used politically incorrect language, for example, Quinn Norton and Jonathan Weisman, have either been terminated for old tweets or demoted.[51]

Attacks on white people come at a time when blue-collar American whites are experiencing new and profound social problems. Princeton economists Anne Case and Angus Deaton have documented rising mortality rates among these whites from preventable causes such as drug abuse, alcoholism, and suicide. Case and Deaton refer to these as "deaths of despair" that come from a pervasive sense of hopelessness.[52] Sociologist Charles Murray has shown that the black and white underclasses in America are remarkably similar in social dysfunction.[53] If we want our nation to reconnect with our covenantal God, we minorities must not ignore the suffering of other groups. We must do our part. We should insist that the discrimination we have suffered does not justify turning a blind eye to discrimination against white Americans. If we decry racism toward blacks, we must also denounce racism toward whites as another example of sinful prejudice.

In other words, we can play a role in turning the corner in our national covenant. It does not mean ignoring the past. We must not ignore the fact that white Americans made decisions more than four hundred years ago that continue to hurt our nation. Nor should we forget that instead of asking for national forgiveness, American leaders often defended what was indefensible. Our long history of racial conflict might indeed have been divine judgment.

But judgment can be lifted if we obey covenant principles. Obedience will require blacks and whites to stop looking in the rearview mirror.

---

51. Paul Farhi, "New York Times demotes editor after Twitter controversy as paper takes fire from left, right, and within," *The Washington Post*, August 13, 2019, https://www.washingtonpost.com/lifestyle/style/new-york-times-demotes-editor-after-twitter-controversy-as-paper-takes-fire-from-left-right-and-within/2019/08/13/d0cb58fa-bde4-11e9-a5c6-1e74f7ec4a93_story.html.

52. Anne Case and Angus Deaton, *Deaths of Despair and the Future of Capitalism* (Princeton: Princeton University Press, 2020).

53. Charles Murray, *Coming Apart: The State of White America, 1960–2010* (New York: Crown, 2012).

We should acknowledge that today's Americans are a different generation from those responsible for the sins of long ago. We must also begin focusing on the hard realities we see in inner-city communities, where social pathologies are not helped by making excuses. We should admit that the billions of dollars spent on affirmative action and other social programs intended to help minorities have failed—because the programs never truly allowed for self-sufficiency. Government programs designed to help the poor have often hurt them by rewarding behaviors that prevent people from getting on their feet.

Today those responsible for these failed government programs try to shift the blame by accusing others of white racism and white supremacy. Yet the accusations only make matters worse by stoking the fires of greed, jealousy, and racial hatred. What is needed for racial reconciliation is a change of attitude. Minorities who have been taught (and find it convenient) to blame others for their inability to get ahead need to realize that the blame game will not help them. They need to see that what they believe about the world will determine how hard they work and whether or not they accomplish their goals. Those who believe in Christ should look to principles of wisdom found in Proverbs and the Psalms, where they will find power to accomplish things they never imagined for themselves.

All Americans, whether we are religious or not, have a shared duty to speak up whenever we see discrimination against any race or gender, including whites. If we show concern for those outside our group, we can move our society an inch or a foot toward reconciliation where fewer people regard others outside their group as individuals to be hated.

11

BLACK CHURCHES AND THE NATIONAL COVENANT

Derryck Green

God acts in human history. In his sovereignty, he engages not only with individuals but also with nations. When God made a personal covenant with Abraham, he promised to make Abraham into a great nation that would be a blessing to other nations (Gen. 12:3; 17:5–6). While the covenant he made with Israel was unique, God said he would reward other nations for just behavior and judge them for injustice. For example, he punished Egypt for its treatment of the Israelites. He sent Jonah to warn Nineveh "because its wickedness has come up before me" (Jonah 1:2).

America too has been guilty of wickedness. One of its most grievous was enslavement of Africans. It can be argued plausibly that our nation's continued racial conflicts since the abolition of slavery in 1865 are part of God's judgment on our nation. At the same time, it should be acknowledged that the civil rights movement of the 1960s was a sincere attempt to address the legal and moral problem of racial injustice in America. In many ways the movement was a success. It forced the country to acknowledge its failures and to enact legislation that granted American blacks political and economic access to American society. It should also be noted that the civil rights movement was the result of the long history of black churches pursuing biblical justice. I will argue in this chapter that just as God used black churches to achieve racial neutrality and integration during the 1960s, he will use black churches again to renew our civil compact with one another and to renew our national covenant. But in order for these things to happen, the theology of black churches must change. Let me explain by first outlining my interpretation of America's national covenant and then arguing why black churches need to change their approach.

* * *

America's national covenant was suggested in the opening words of the Declaration of Independence: "We hold these truths to be self-evident, that all men are created equal, that they are endowed by their Creator with certain unalienable Rights, that among these are Life, Liberty and the pursuit of Happiness." I can think of no other national founding document that regards the rights to life and the pursuit of human flourishing as the foundation for self-determination. Even more strikingly, the signatories declared that these rights come from God, not a government of human beings. In other words, American rights are from the God who enters into covenant with those nations that acknowledge him.

By its own definition, this audacious statement of freedom should have included blacks. After all, the Declaration specifies that "all men" are equal. So, from their very beginning, the States were in violation of their own covenant because they denied the equality of blacks. The justification for this contradiction—the denial of equality—was predicated on the refusal to acknowledge the humanity of blacks. Blacks were treated as subhuman rather than human. Worse, most blacks in America were seen as property—"things" that could be owned—rather than as persons of equal worth and dignity. But if the fullness of black humanity could be denied, then covenantal fidelity was impossible.

Eventually, rights and privileges for freed slaves were protected in three amendments to the Constitution. The Thirteenth Amendment outlawed slavery. The Fourteenth Amendment granted citizenship and equal protection, and prohibited states from enforcing laws that undermined the privileges and rights protected by the Constitution. The Fifteenth Amendment granted blacks the right to vote.

But the national covenant was compromised once again. Several states passed laws that prevented blacks from enjoying the constitutional rights and privileges that were theirs by virtue of being Americans. This violation of the national covenant was the result of the Supreme Court's ruling that the Civil Rights Act of 1875 was unconstitutional. This opinion crippled the federal government's ability to reconstruct Southern society by undermining sections of the Thirteenth and Fourteenth Amendments. Power reverted to the Democrat-controlled southern states (their "states' rights"), which started a new era of oppression for blacks living in the American South under Jim Crow segregation.[1]

Clearly, the national covenant wasn't being defended by those entrusted with its preservation. Nor was it being extended to its rightful heirs. The Declaration had rooted the nation's covenant in God, implying that he was the source of its citizens' liberty and pursuit of prosperity. Then the Constitution broadened this covenant by detailing the rights and liberties belonging to the people of this new nation:

> We the people of the United States, in order to form a more perfect Union, establish Justice, insure domestic Tranquility, provide for the common defense, promote the general welfare, and secure the blessings of liberty to ourselves and our posterity, do ordain and establish the Constitution of the United States of America.[2]

But from the beginning "we the people" excluded blacks. Black theologian J. Deotis Roberts laments,

> Even though the platitudes were written into the principal documents of this republic, there is a real question as to whether the Founding Fathers had in mind the "image of God" in black skin. The history of this country would indicate that in law, custom, and theology, blacks were excluded from the minds of

---

1. C. Vann Woodward, *The Strange Career of Jim Crow*, 2nd ed. (New York: Oxford University Press, 1966).

2. The authors and signers of both the Declaration of Independence and the US Constitution were overwhelmingly Christians who believed in the God of the Bible.

those who penned the liberation documents upon which this nation was based.[3]

After nearly a century of Jim Crow, the black church decided to challenge this failure to fulfill the national covenant. The civil rights movement of the 1960s was, in many senses, a revival—a Spirit-led awakening to redeem the national covenant. Not only did it help repair the covenant between the government and its citizens, but it also sought to restore the covenant between God and the American nation. Through this movement, the black church helped other parts of the American church repent of the racial sins they had committed and justified in God's name. This movement was not only about civil rights but also moral imperatives. It called the nation to account for its performance of the covenant, in response to prophetic calls from the black churches. God spoke through his prophets. And this time the nation listened.

This listening was no small thing. Christians were compelled to revise their understanding of the *imago Dei*—the image of God in every human being. Most Christians thought they had understood the image of God in their neighbors. But now many realized that if they did not approve of full rights and privileges for blacks in American society, their understanding of the *imago Dei* was impaired.

To be sure, the civil rights movement was not accepted by all Americans. It was resisted in many quarters. But it also triggered the beginning of the end of systemic racial injustice, and the beginning of racial and cultural reconciliation.

But in the decades since the 1960s, we have witnessed a new approach to black religion that has deviated from orthodox Christianity.[4]

---

3. J. Deotis Roberts, *A Black Political Theology* (Philadelphia: Westminster, 1974), 100.

4. James H. Cone, *Black Theology and Black Power* (New York: Seabury, 1969); Cone, *God of the Oppressed* (Maryknoll, NY: Orbis, 1975); Cone, *For My People: Black Theology and the Black Church* (Maryknoll, NY: Orbis, 1984); Cone, *A Black Theology of Liberation* (Maryknoll, NY: Orbis, 1986); Cone, *Martin & Malcolm & America: A Dream or a Nightmare* (Maryknoll, NY: Orbis, 1991); Cone, *Risks of Faith: The Emergence of a Black Theology of Liberation, 1968–1998* (Boston: Beacon, 1999); Alistair Kee, *The Rise and Demise of Black Theology* (Burlington, VT: Ashgate, 2006).

It uses a narrow theological style that seeks racial self-definition and self-empowerment. It is committed to self-determination and cultural uplift, both of which are commendable. But its aggressive demand for social and economic equality differs from the approach taken by the religious leaders of the civil rights movement. The difference is in both content and application, and it comes with great consequence. The nonviolent civil rights movement, born in black churches and infused with black religion, advocated racial neutrality that gives no significance to race. It simply sought moral and political equality.

But this new Black Power movement rejects nonviolence, racial neutrality, and racial integration.[5] It deliberately stresses racial distinction, racial pride, and racial separatism. Where the civil rights movement sought an identity that *transcended* racial oppression, this movement seeks an identity that *depends* on racial oppression. Theologically, it is fed by black liberation theology, sometimes called radical black theology.[6] This theology has evolved over the decades since its introduction.[7] Though radical black theology has had more influence in academia than the pulpit, its racial impact on black

---

5. Stokely Carmichael, "Black Power Address at UC Berkeley," October 29, 1966, https://www.americanrhetoric.com/speeches/stokelycarmichaelblackpower.html; Stokely Carmichael and Charles V. Hamilton, *Back Power: The Politics of Liberation in America* (London: Penguin, 1967).

6. James H. Cone is widely considered the father of radical black theology, specifically black liberation theology. There are significant methodological and theological flaws within Cone's innovative framework. Cone argued that the black experience is the starting point of radical black theology, which contradicts the more traditional understanding of Christianity's universality. Additionally, Cone suggested that any traditional Christian teaching that does not have black liberation in view should be rejected. See Anthony B. Bradley, *Liberating Black Theology: The Bible and The Black Experience in America* (Wheaton, IL: Crossway, 2010); and J. Deotis Roberts, *Liberation and Reconciliation: A Black Theology*, 2nd ed. (Louisville: Westminster John Knox, 2005).

7. National Committee of Negro Churchmen, "'Black Power'—Statement by the National Committee of Negro Churchmen," The Archives of the Episcopal Church DMS/PECUSA. Accessed March 9, 2020, https://episcopalarchives.org/church-awakens/files/original/65f9d1d9a7fbb097a43284ec4b8f3d8e.pdf; Gayraud S. Wilmore and James H. Cone, "Black Theology—Statement by the National Committee of Black Churchmen, June 13, 1969," *Black Theology Statement: A Documentary History, 1966–1979* (New York: Orbis, 1979), 100–102;

churches has been enormous. Its residue is a preoccupation with racial identity that is characteristic of an increasing number of black churches.[8] The result is a shortsighted preoccupation with black racial pride and identity that has damaged black religion, black culture, the national covenant, and racial reconciliation.

* * *

In recent years, far too many black people (including black Christians) have chosen to define themselves racially, and typically in relation to white oppression and anti-black racism. They want to connect with Africa in ways that are psychologically comforting but extremely superficial. They criticize and shame other blacks who reject black groupthink. They try to humiliate blacks who reject the narrative of omnipotent and omnipresent white racism.

It is clear that for those who support this prevailing narrative of omnipresent anti-black racism, being black is not merely a racial identity but an ideology, a worldview. If the question were merely one of race, and race did not define every bit of one's personhood, one black person could object to this aspect or that aspect of the narrative and not be excluded from the social world of those who hold the narrative. But challenging or rejecting the narrative—that race negatively affects every part of who we are and that every part of us has been victimized by white racism—leads to exclusion. Those who hold to this prevailing narrative do not brook disagreement. They condemn any black individuality or understanding that differs with theirs. They consider the notion that blackness-is-not-all-of-who-we-are to be heresy, and damnable heresy at that.

Gayraud S. Wilmore, *Black Religion and Black Radicalism: An Interpretation of the Religious History of African Americans* (Maryknoll, NY: Orbis, 1998).

8. One example is Trinity United Church of Christ, which was previously led by Rev. Dr. Jeremiah A. Wright, Jr. and was the church home of former President Barack H. Obama and his family. On its website, Trinity explicitly states that it is, "a congregation which is Unashamedly Black and Unapologetically Christian." Pastor Emeritus Wright has repeatedly acknowledged the influence and importance of black liberation theology in his ministry. "The History of Trinity," Trinity United Church of Christ, n.d., https://trinitychicago.org/the-history-of-trinity/.

Unfortunately in the late 1960s, black clergymen adopted this new narrative in an effort to keep pace with radical black activists.[9] Even more unfortunately, their successors have continued to hold and teach this narrative. It is now what could be called black orthodoxy both within and outside the black churches.

This black orthodoxy has been documented by Jason E. Shelton and Michael O. Emerson in their recent study of racial differences that guide the religious practices and faith of black and white Protestants. Shelton and Emerson found "profound faith-based similarities and entrenched differences" that affect religious convictions and practices, political stances, and possibilities for racial reconciliation within the church.[10] They show the ways in which racial group membership takes precedence over individual denominational affiliations within Protestantism. Though identity politics affects both black and white Protestants, Shelton and Emerson argue that it takes a greater toll on black Protestants than on white Protestants.[11]

Shelton and Emerson define America's race problem as racial inequality in quality-of-life indicators.[12] They conclude from surveys that most blacks think that these socioeconomic discrepancies between blacks and whites are primarily the result of racial discrimination.[13] For this reason they call blacks "structuralists" because they put principal emphasis on the contribution of social factors on socioeconomic success. Conversely, whites tend to be more individualistic, focusing on personal responsibility, merit, work ethic, and intelligence.[14] Emerson and Shelton point out that structuralists think that the "American social 'system'—or the way that our society's

---

9. Ron Christie, *Acting White: The Curious History of a Racial Slur* (New York: Thomas Dunne, 2010). Christie argues that this division goes back to slavery, articulated in the "house slave"/"field slave" dichotomy, and led to blacks being criticized for "acting white."

10. Jason Shelton and Michael O. Emerson, *Blacks and Whites in Christian America: How Racial Discrimination Shapes Religious Convictions* (New York: New York University Press, 2012), ix.

11. Shelton and Emerson, *Blacks and Whites*, 161, 180.

12. Shelton and Emerson, *Blacks and Whites*, 172.

13. Shelton and Emerson, *Blacks and Whites*, 172–73.

14. Shelton and Emerson, *Blacks and Whites*, 173.

institutions, patterns of relationships, and dynamics of status are organized—provides some people with an advantage while placing others at a disadvantage."[15] These dynamics work in such a way that "determinants lying outside of family they were born into ... greatly influence whether they will 'make it' in life."[16]

Shelton and Emerson suggest that this difference in perception of the root cause of the race problem—either structural or individual—is missed by most social scientists.[17] Black Protestants see racial inequality as a structurally systemic problem,[18] whereas white Protestants see racial inequality as more of an individual issue related to motivation or values.[19]

Perhaps the most surprising take-away from Shelton and Emerson's data is how pervasive this structural view is among blacks. For most in this demographic, it seems more important to embrace and be defined by their racial identity than by their Christian identity. This is true for both Protestants and non-Protestants in the American black community. This means that racial group membership, not religion or political party, provides the framework that most blacks use to interpret what they see in the social world.[20] Thus denominational affiliations and religious identities are more consequential for white Protestants than for black Protestants.[21] In consequence, we can say that it is racial group membership rather than denominational or theological affiliation that shapes blacks' commitments to identity politics.[22] As Shelton and Emerson put it, beliefs rooted in identity politics "strongly influence the manner in which black Protestants

---

15. Shelton and Emerson, *Blacks and Whites*, 173.
16. Shelton and Emerson, *Blacks and Whites*, 173.
17. Shelton and Emerson, *Blacks and Whites*, 172.
18. For blacks, structural problems require structural interventions/solutions. This is why blacks overwhelmingly support governmental policies to address inequality with little or no thought to how this intervention potentially exacerbates the "structural" problem(s) desired to be solved.
19. Shelton and Emerson, *Blacks and Whites*, 174.
20. Shelton and Emerson, *Blacks and Whites*, 180.
21. Shelton and Emerson, *Blacks and Whites*, 180.
22. Shelton and Emerson, *Blacks and Whites*, 180.

go about their religious faith."[23] The same cannot be said for whites.[24] Shelton and Emerson note that whites show far more diversity on this phenomenon than blacks: "Differences in commitments to identity politics are wider and deeper among white mainline Protestants and white evangelicals than they are among black Protestants and black non-Protestants."[25]

At one level, these findings should not be a surprise. Blacks routinely demonstrate political fidelity to one political party and have done so for more than fifty years: above 90 percent during 2008 and 2012 presidential elections; 89 percent in the 2016 presidential election. But what is new is this recognition of the dominance of—and commitment to—racial identity over religious identity. Also (somewhat) new is the exclusion that takes place when individual blacks dissent from black identity politics. They are told by fellow blacks that they are no longer "black."[26] The marginalized black is expelled from racial group membership—even if it is Christian blacks expelling another black Christian. Identity politics trumps Christian identity.

The upshot of Shelton and Emerson's flawed[27] but important book is that American black Christians tend to subordinate Christian identity to a racial identity. This subordination needs to be challenged by black Christians and black churches. The one framework that should displace all others is the identity of being a new creation

---

23. Shelton and Emerson, *Blacks and Whites*, 196.

24. Shelton and Emerson, *Blacks and Whites*, 159–60, 179–80.

25. Shelton and Emerson, *Blacks and Whites*, 160.

26. It is difficult to deny what many blacks have said, and continue to say, about Clarence Thomas, Ben Carson, John McWhorter, Shelby Steele, Condoleezza Rice, and others like myself. All of these thinkers have been charged with race betrayal (called "Uncle Tom"), not being "black" (as commonly defined and approved); labeled a "coon;" or worse. The accusers define black identity by who is included and excluded. The latter are no longer afforded racial protection dependent on racial group membership or the benefit of the doubt. See Peter M. Robinson, "Under the Skin: Shelby Steele on Race in America," *Hoover Digest* 3 (July 30, 2001), www.hoover.org/research/under-skin-shelby-steele-race-america.

27. The authors' tacit support for structuralism suggests that blacks are not autonomous moral agents capable of transcending social limitations. They also imply support for the romantic goal of racial socioeconomic parity, which is utopian and unattainable, dooming to despair all who aspire to it.

in Christ. This new identity, which includes brotherhood with Christ in the family of God, should supersede all other identifiers and man-made divisions.

Of course, this displacement is easier said than done. It is difficult for all Christians to live this out. And no Christian or church has done so perfectly. But if blacks cannot, or are unwilling, to overcome the idolatry of race in the body of Christ, moral redemption and reconciliation will not happen. Maintaining racial divisions based on an identity of oppression and victimization preserves the kind of acrimony the peace of Christ seeks to overcome. This is why blacks should embrace a firm, unadulterated Christian identity as opposed to a racial one.

Don't get me wrong. I am not saying that celebrating one's racial identity is a bad thing. It can be a good thing when it is not turned into one's core identity. But when it eliminates and replaces more important issues such as black well-being, black individuality, and Christian identity, it becomes recognizably troublesome. Shelby Steele writes that this replacement comes at a cost.

> [T]he price paid ... is to suppress individuals with the mark of race just as certainly as segregation did, by relentlessly telling them that their racial identity is the most important thing about them, that it opens to them an opportunism in society that is not available to them as individuals. Black politics [and identity] since the sixties, ha[ve] been based on this hidden incentive to repress individuality so as to highlight the profitable collective identity. The greatest threat to [racial gatekeepers] is a society in which individuality of blacks supersedes their racial identity in importance.[28]

Steele insists that racial identity is far less secure than identity based on individual achievement.

> Doesn't race enhance individuality? I think it does but only when individuality is nurtured and developed apart from race. The race-holder ... feels inadequate or insecure and then seeks reassurance through race. When, instead, a sense of self arises

---

28. Shelby Steele, *A Dream Deferred: The Second Betrayal of Black Freedom in America* (New York: HarperCollins, 1998), 61.

from individual achievement and self-realization. When self-esteem is established apart from race, then racial identity can only enhance because it is no longer needed for any other purpose.[29]

* * *

I have argued that the black church-led civil rights movement of the 1960s tried to minimize race in response to white racists who used race to establish human identity. For them, race was superficial. Equality was far deeper, rooted in the *imago Dei*. It was because of this anthropology—preached from black pulpits and shown on American TV screens—that the civil rights movement convinced America of its moral obligation to desegregate American society. Eventually it won the war. Blacks came to enjoy the social and economic opportunity of the American dream. They started to enjoy the same rights as white Americans, and to experience equality before the law.

The Black Power movement, propelled in part by radical black theology, rejected these claims. Though black militants publicly defended the idea that blacks and whites are equal, they emphasized black oppression and white supremacy. They insisted that equality would never be attained without material redistribution. Even after the gains of the civil rights movement, they demanded financial reparations for the past history of slavery and segregation. Blacks, they suggested, were still victims. Their liberation would come from divine orchestration—but through the human means of material redistribution from whites to blacks. This would be white penance but without absolution. Blacks would achieve justice through white atonement, which would be necessary for true "equality." For these early militants and too many black Christian leaders today, blacks are still victims of white supremacy. They seek consolation in racial solidarity, nostalgic veneration for Africa,[30] and a racialized ideology

---

29. Shelby Steele, *The Content of Our Character: A New Vision of Race in America* (New York: HarperCollins, 1990), 29.

30. The hyperventilation, undue celebration, and black reverence for the Marvel movie "Black Panther" is a testament to this misplaced veneration of Africa, represented as Wakanda in the film. Moreover, the silliness of this one-dimensional effort to boost black self-esteem is found not only in the fact that

dependent on white guilt. Being black is simultaneously a source of pride and chip of insecurity on the shoulder of blacks in America.

If race has replaced religion for black identity, can a Christian identity emerge for blacks that will help them seek reconciliation? On its face, the question seems silly. After all, for centuries in America, black churches kept the souls of black Americans and inspired the country as a whole. The black church is still highly revered as the "invisible institution" that ministered to the spiritual need of slaves, was the center of black social and religious life, and until the end of the civil rights era, was the epicenter of the last great moral movement of our country.[31] Blacks continue to be the most religious demographic group in America,[32] and are more likely than other groups in America to believe that the Bible is the word of God and that it should be understood literally.[33] Black millennials are more religious than other millennials.[34]

Wakanda is a fictionalized place on the eastern coast of Africa where black slaves most certainly didn't originate, but it was created by white men: Stan Lee and Jack Kirby. Thus, even the idolization of a fictional homeland for racial pride was dependent not upon black accomplishment or history but white creativity.

31. A. H. Pinn and A. B. Pinn, *Introduction to Black Church History* (Minneapolis: Fortress, 2002), 1–2. The "invisible institution" refers to the time when slaves held secret religious meetings where they developed a form of Christian faith, worship style, and experience that spoke directly to their needs and concerns of being enslaved and how to be free. These meetings were illegal and punished severely if discovered.

32. Frank Newport, "Religion and Party ID Strongly Linked Among Whites, Not Blacks," *Gallup*, July 1, 2011, http://www.gallup.com/poll/148361/religion-party-strongly-linked-among-whites-not-blacks.aspx.

33. Jeff Diamant, "Blacks More Likely than Others in US to Read the Bible Regularly, See It as God's Word," *Pew Research Center*, May 7, 2018, http://www.pewresearch.org/fact-tank/2018/05/07/blacks-more-likely-than-others-in-u-s-to-read-the-bible-regularly-see-it-as-gods-word/.

34. Jeff Diamant and Besheer Mohamed, "Black Millennials Are More Religious than Other Millennials," *Pew Research Center*, July 20, 2018, http://www.pewresearch.org/fact-tank/2018/07/20/black-millennials-are-more-religious-than-other-millennials/.

Nevertheless, being black has become more important for blacks than being Christian. According to one poll,[35] blacks are the great anomaly in their embrace of religion and politics. While most Americans lean Left politically as they lose religion,[36] blacks are "the most religious of the four race and ethnic groups [in America]"[37] but reliably vote for the party of the Left.[38] A later poll (2014) confirmed this pattern.[39] This vindicates what Emerson and Shelton found in their analysis of blacks' religious and political identities—the former has little to no influence on the latter.[40]

Another sad phenomenon—the collapse of the black family—might be traced to this same troubling pattern, the replacement of religious for racial identity. Despite the self-professed Christian religiosity of blacks, many of the social dysfunctions affecting black communities stem from a broken moral system. These dysfunctions reflect a poor foundation in applied Christian faith. When this failure of Christian morality is combined with separatism, the explicit desire to exempt themselves from the social standards expected from their multiracial counterparts, the results are lower standards of morality and higher levels of entitlement predicated on a cultural identity of victimhood. Oddly, there is much the same assent to Christian faith

---

35. Newport, "Religion and Party ID."

36. It is my experience that those who self-identify with the Left, who have given up traditional religious practices and beliefs, adopt politics as a substitute religion—accompanied by recognizable doctrines, dogmas, and behavior that resemble a distorted form of spirituality.

37. Newport, "Religion and Party ID."

38. "Washington Post-Kaiser Family Foundation Poll of Black Women in America," October 6 to November 2, 2011, http://www.washingtonpost.com/wp-srv/special/nation/black-women-in-america/. A subset to this reality is that black women are responsible for blacks being the most religious group in the country.

39. Frank Newport, "Religion Remains a Strong Marker of Political Identity in US," *Gallup*, July 28, 2014, http://www.gallup.com/poll/174134/religion-remains-strong-marker-political-identity.aspx.

40. This isn't to necessarily suggest that blacks must become more Right leaning politically. However, considering the decrease in traditional religiosity and its corresponding value system among those on the political Left, it is to suggest that either blacks are attempting to synthesize a religious value system that is generally at odds with a political value system or that the political value system has taken priority.

as there was sixty years ago, but missing in action are the Christian religiosity, Christian identity formation, and Christian discipleship of sixty years ago.

Without a thick Christian culture that shapes morality, self-sabotaging behaviors have been destigmatized and excused. Black churches no longer teach their members how to overcome acts of discrimination and feelings of resentment by following biblical admonitions such as, "You shall not hate your brother in your heart" (Lev. 19:17 NKJV), or "Do not seek revenge or bear a grudge against anyone among your people, but love your neighbor as yourself. I am the LORD" (Lev. 19:18 NIV), or "In your anger do not sin; Do not let the sun go down while you are angry" (Eph. 4:26 NIV), or "Get rid of all bitterness, rage, anger, harsh words, and slander, as well as all types of evil behavior. Instead, be kind to each other, tenderhearted, forgiving one another, just as God through Christ has forgiven you" (Eph. 4:31–32 NLT), and so on. Instead, too many black churches follow failed secular agendas that claim to promote racial and "social justice."

Because racial and social justice messages are familiar in black churches, white churches, even if they have blacks and other racial minorities among their members, feel impotent and confused when engaging racial issues. When churches and Christian organizations try to address the enduring consequences of racial discrimination (if they engage this topic at all), the starting point is usually the premise that blacks are forever victims of white, anti-black racism.[41] These churches and organizations then reproduce secular processes of trying to find ways to achieve "racial justice" for "nonwhite minorities."[42] The obligation is always on white people, in this context white Christians, to curtail their disposition and behavior to "end" racial discrimination.

---

41. This starting point is found both in predominantly black churches and predominantly white churches.

42. Arguably, Christians should not seek any form of compartmentalized justice, such as "racial justice," "social justice," or "economic justice." For these usually involve coercion that benefits one favored group at the expense of a less-favorable group. Biblical justice and righteousness as described in Lev. 19:15; Deut. 16:20; Ps. 106:3; Isa. 61:8; Amos 5:24; and Micah 6:8 are neither segmented nor coerced. Biblical justice is not supposed to be segmented or partial but should be reflected in the totality of one's life.

Usually there are few honest examples proving racial discrimination. But they seek the elusive "racial justice" with no obligation, expectation, or participation required of black Christians that would truly demonstrate equality in the brotherhood of Christ. In these discussions black Christians are not seen as co-laborers in Jesus Christ; in fact, because these discussions exempt black Christians from responsibility, they reinforce inequality. This inequality suggests that white Christians still think blacks are not capable moral agents to be partnered with to overcome sins of separation and racial discrimination. Thus, the process of reconciliation cannot begin, even within churches and regardless of their ethnic makeup. Even in the multiethnic body of Jesus Christ, we are still not equal.[43]

In these fruitless attempts, it is always the presumption of white guilt/black innocence and the demand that whites must absolve themselves from the original sin of racism. This presumption simply imitates the way that secular political programs such as Black Lives Matter approach racial issues. They combine virtue-signaling with a look-busy-while-doing-nothing self-righteousness that keeps the "conversation" going interminably. The conversation will never end because it is presupposed that the only guilt is white guilt and the only victims are blacks. Even if today's whites are not guilty of enslavement or segregation, they must forever atone for the sins of their fathers.[44] This ongoing liturgy would be condemned if it were not stoked by fear and resentment. White Christians genuflect in front of blacks in a ritual act of confession, admitting their white, guilt-by-association sins (racial privilege and "supremacy") even if

---

43. It bears saying and thus repeating, blacks have too often attempted to secure human dignity through what has become the virtue of powerlessness. Because blacks have consistently embraced powerless, there's neither external urgency nor obligation to be taken seriously because there's no internal urgency or desire to take us seriously. This is why whether in the church or outside of it, blacks aren't considered capable or coequal in pursuit of reconciliation and racial "justice," respectively.

44. Jemar Tisby, *The Color of Compromise: The Truth about the American Church's Complicity in Racism* (Grand Rapids: Zondervan, 2019). Tisby makes similar claims in his book, arguing that whites today are guilty of preserving systemic racism. To achieve justice, white Christians must submit to some form of church-based restitution.

they have never personally committed these sins.[45] The next step in the liturgy is for whites to express self-loathing through obligatory sacramental acts of contrition, followed by attempts to seek dispensation, which whites instinctively know they will never receive because they intuitively sense that blacks will never grant it.

Sadly, this means that without a change in black consciousness, there will be no reconciliation for blacks and whites in America. The church body will remain broken. Blacks will maintain their racial ideology of victimization while feeling inadequate and angry, and whites will enjoy a measure of self-validation for having attempted acts of propitiation. Those acts will free them from feeling guilty and being accused of racism.

Despite the fact that all this will be done in the name of Jesus, there will be no resolution. Churches will have imitated the world's way of reparation rather than using their own theologies of redemption and atonement. They will have sacralized the secular. The churches will continue to suffer self-inflicted wounds as a result of plagiarizing false profiteers and baptizing their secular programs with tainted water. Black Christians will still be victims, and white Christians will still be racial oppressors.

Yet books continue to be published that perpetuate these self-defeating myths. In *America's Original Sin: Racism, White Privilege, and the Bridge to a New America*, progressive evangelical Jim Wallis argues that white racism is still pervasive in America.[46] Wallis argues that white Americans (and by extension, white Christians) are obligated to seek contrition for being vessels and conduits of racism.[47] He says that white Christians should listen to their "black and brown brothers and sisters" when they tell their stories of racial injustice

---

45. In December 2015, InterVarsity, an evangelical, interdenominational campus ministry, not only invited a representative of Black Lives Matter to give a keynote address to its 2015 Urbana Student Missions Conference, but it also encouraged attendees to support the black "social justice" group, despite the group's overtly secular political platform that conflicts with Christianity.

46. Jim Wallis, *America's Original Sin: Racism, White Privilege, and the Bridge to a New America* (Grand Rapids: Brazos, 2016).

47. Wallis presupposes white guilt without proper evidence while simultaneously exempting himself from being implicated.

because their pain-filled experiences are important. White Christians must accept the prevailing paradigm of black victimization/white oppression. This shut up-and-listen approach, characterized by white subordination and racial genuflection, is supposed to initiate the process of racial justice and reconciliation.

Wallis laments churches that have "baptized us into our racial divisions" rather than teaching and modeling that our baptism, and the Lord's Supper, unite us in a way that transcends all earthly limitations.[48] Wallis is right about churches christening racial discord but not for the reasons he suggests. American churches have baptized Christians into current racial divisions precisely because the church has eagerly followed the world's unsuccessful template of trying to engineer superficial "racial justice" on false pretenses and self-righteousness, none of which is found in the gospel of Christ or biblical justice.

Drew G. I. Hart is a black Anabaptist college professor and former preacher who promotes the narrative of black helplessness and white guilt. In *Trouble I've Seen: Changing the Way the Church Views Racism*, there is little that cannot be heard from secular social justice activists on campuses around the country.[49] Hart demands that white Christians apologize for their whiteness and privilege, and endorses separatism by excusing black misbehavior as a consequence of racism. Hart makes his argument using in the language and mindset reflective of black liberation theologian James Cone and secular contemporary racial activist Ta-Nehisi Coates.[50] Like Jim Wallis, Hart excludes black moral obligation and agency in his quest to mitigate what he defines as the Christian perpetuation of white supremacy.

Hart's approach is similar to that of Jemar Tisby, a black Christian in the Reformed movement (PCA), who once sought to increase the visibility and viability of Reformed theology among black Americans

---

48. Wallis, *America's Original Sin*, 8, 106.

49. Drew G. I. Hart, *Trouble I've Seen: Changing the Way the Church Views Racism* (Harrisonburg, VA: Harold, 2016).

50. Ta-Nehisi Coates, *Between the World and Me* (New York: Spiegel and Grau, 2015); Coates, "The Case for Reparations," *The Atlantic*, June 22, 2014, https://www.theatlantic.com/magazine/archive/2014/06/the-case-for-reparations/361631/.

through his Reformed African American Network (RAAN). Tisby recently founded The Witness: A Black Christian Collective, designed to "serve black people." He explained his transition from a theological mission to what appears to be racial identity politics:

> The Witness has returned to its original mission to serve black people. The move from 'African American' to 'black' acknowledges this endeavor is international scope. The Witness is for the entire African diaspora.[51]

Though Tisby claims the Collective is "attempting to articulate an approach to faith as black Christians in the current context,"[52] the website's content is more concerned with celebrating racial identity than reinforcing Christian identity or discipleship.

God forbid that a Christian black reject racial victimhood and the church's adoption of a secular gospel. Other black Christians will shame and try to silence the black brother or sister who strays from the plantation. Christian whites will be afraid to welcome or comfort this black brother who "strayed" for fear of being perceived of aiding and abetting racism.

But these occasional blacks who have the courage to reject the dominant narrative are on to something. These dissenters realize that so-called Black Power has led to black disempowerment and has persuaded blacks to become victims of their own narrative. According to this story, they can never be free from white dominance. Consequently, many are afraid to build their identity on their own achievements.

These black dissenters recognize that black churches have become *churches of blackness*. Radical black theology has produced a *theology of blackness* and a religious faith that shows only the faintest resemblance to historic Christian faith. Moreover, black dissenters have found that this new faith in blackness is impotent. It has no power to uplift or edify human dignity. In contrast, there is infinite power in the gospel of Jesus Christ.

---

51. Jemar Tisby, "The Journey from RAAN to 'The Witness: A Black Christian Collective,'" *The Witness*, October 31, 2017, https://thewitnessbcc.com/raan-witness-black-christian-collective/.

52. Tisby, "The Journey from RAAN."

Only when blacks reject the false gospel of race and embrace the gospel of Jesus will they find the grace and *power* they seek. They must end their incessant preoccupation with being black. Or, at the very least, black identity must be *subordinated* to Christian identity. At best, black racial identity must cease to mean anything close to its current, post-civil-rights configuration. At present, black faith, culture, churches, and identity depend on this misleading configuration. But if blacks crucify "the flesh with its passions and desires" (Gal. 5:24 NIV) and resurrect themselves anew in Jesus Christ by the power of the Holy Spirit, blacks and their churches can experience redemption and reformation—and reconciliation besides.

How would this change affect their relations with whites? Much in every way. They will come to see that extending freedom and equality to others means doing to others what they would have done to themselves.[53] Jesus' Golden Rule does not mean doing to people *what they have done to you* in the past under some mistaken belief of entitlement or retribution. Nor does it mean refusing to act in favor of other people because they have not yet done something to be reciprocated. What Jesus' commandment requires is that we have a moral obligation to treat others—even those who have mistreated us—as we would like to be treated. There are no guarantees of appreciation or reciprocity. But this is a groundbreaking, counterintuitive, subversive, and proactive moral way of freedom and righteousness. It demands that we not return tit for tat, imitating the way we have been treated. Nor should we be passive because our previous acts of goodwill were ignored. Instead we should focus on the gift, donating to another free person rather than doing only what helps us.[54]

To follow the Golden Rule means that we take on what we have demanded from others, the *imago Dei*. The image of God in every other person should be the foundational way we think of others and their dignity. It will set us free. Rather than being bound by past hurts, we can transcend them by the power of the Spirit and live into the new person Jesus is making us. We can cast aside the slights

---

53. Tod Lindberg, *The Political Teachings of Jesus* (New York: HarperCollins, 2007), 3.

54. Lindberg, *Political Teachings*, 2–3.

and traumas of the past and look on others as if we were looking at ourselves. This is as close to empathy as we can get.

For black Christians, the implication is clear. Blacks must cast aside—*forgive*—all past and historical racial slights, real or imagined. We must forgive the physical and emotional traumas that are preventing us from treating our white neighbors as we would like to be treated. This is what the Bible calls love.[55]

For black Christians and predominantly black churches, the implications are clear. Racial reconciliation cannot be contingent on blacks being compensated for historical sins of racism and oppression by those who didn't commit them. Innocent white Christians cannot be made to pay a debt that they did not incur.[56] Nor should they be made to feel guilty for everything thought by blacks to be discriminatory. Blacks should not think that outcomes of inequality are the result of deliberate racism that mandates some form of socioeconomic payout.[57] There is no proof that differing socioeconomic outcomes are primarily or only the result of racism.[58] And the demand for reparations, besides the fact that it is counter-productive, is morally wrong. It is extortion.

---

55. The empathetic ability to see oneself in others is not just for blacks, but of course for whites as well. But our focus needs to be on blacks taking the initiative to chart new, reparative relationships with white brothers and sisters in Christ. This will begin the process of healing and reconciliation.

56. In *Color of Compromise,* the thrust of Tisby's argument is that systemic racism has adapted to the times, making it less obvious than it once was but still a very real presence that continues to threaten black lives. White Christians are not absolved for their complicity in the continuance of white supremacy and racial sins, and therefore must continue in deferential penitence to blacks indefinitely. This must happen if racial justice in the American church is to be achieved.

57. Tisby's *Color of Compromise* justifies some form of reparations be given to descendants of slaves as a necessary response to right the wrongs of multiple centuries of racial injustice.

58. Heather MacDonald, *The Diversity Delusion: How Race and Gender Pandering Corrupt the University and Undermine Our Culture* (New York: St Martin's, 2018); MacDonald, *The War on Cops: How the New Attack on Law and Order Makes Everyone Less Safe* (New York, Encounter, 2016).

Please do not mistake my argument. I am not denying racism, past nor present. Blacks have been systematically targeted, attacked, hurt, and damaged. Slavery and segregation, while not unique to America, were evil. They were sins against the national covenant, and these sins have been massive impediments to the peace and unity which most blacks and whites seek. The residual of white racial chauvinism, though legally outlawed, continues to guide far too many hearts and minds. Some black anger and resentment are therefore understandable; some are not. But it doesn't matter. Jesus was very clear that the obligation of his followers is to upend the normal cycle of reciprocating anger, antipathy, and hostility. As his disciples, black folks in the churches must initiate reconciliation, and that begins with forgiveness. This approach is dramatically different from intimidation, manipulation, and compulsion. The reconciliation that Jesus commends proceeds with humility, faith, courage, love, and grace. It is a difficult and painful process. If it were easy or obvious, blacks would have initiated this long ago.

Of course, whites who are guilty of racial discrimination, or racial anger and resentment, are not exempt from their own obligation to repent. But forgiveness is not dependent on the repentance of those we forgive. As Jesus was suffering and dying on the cross, he asked God to forgive those who mocked, tortured, and murdered him.

Christian blacks are not incapable of this, if they seek the power of the Holy Spirit. In fact, for black Christians to set aside their racial pride and past hurts, and current frustrations, and to initiate the process of forgiveness and racial reconciliation in the church is *black empowerment*. To take the first painful, humble step of forgiving past grievances, even while acknowledging pain and anger, and admitting our own self-doubt and sins is to live and lead in freedom. It is freedom from hatred and resentment that defeats the "powers and principalities" of this age. This liberty is at the heart of Christian self-determination and renewed life in Christ.

Now is the time to reject the practices of protest and grievance, holding white brothers and sisters in Christ accountable for acts of cruelty perpetrated by their ancestors. It is time to forgive and to approach the altar of God together, reconciled and edifying one another. It is time to recapture a Christian black anthropology firmly rooted in dignity and equality.⁵⁹ Blessed are the peacemakers, for they will be called sons and daughters of God.

History is our witness that black churches have developed exemplary Christians who have taken their faith seriously. Black churches once were great reservoirs of hope, sanctuaries that were guiding lights in very dark times. Blacks knew whom to serve and why. They knew they were black, and they knew their condition and treatment were due to the hearts and minds of their fellow citizens having been corrupted by the sin of racial discrimination. Blacks knew they were victims, but they did not use that knowledge as a cornerstone of their identity. They identified first as Christians and second as blacks.

Blacks should imitate the example of their fathers in refusing to retreat to victimhood. They should fortify themselves in Jesus Christ, rejecting the discipleship of race and embracing the discipleship of Christ. If they do so, they will redeem their reputation as the most religious demographic in the country and turn it into something tangible and believable. Blacks will be not only religious but truly Christian. They will restore integrity to the invisible institution, making black churches once again a visible ark of Christian identity and discipleship. They will then become our nation's preeminent example of reconciliation, leaders for the rest of the country to follow. Just as black churches led the nation out of an age of racial separation, they can lead the nation into an age of racial reconciliation. But they will do so only if they claim their primary identity as Christians rather than blacks.⁶⁰

---

59. Self-determination and dignity were among several self-defining concepts that civil rights activists and Black Power activists wanted to achieve. However, Black Power rhetoric emptied these concepts of the responsibility that comes with freedom and access to mainstream America.

60. The strategy I favor parts ways with a number of Christian blacks who suggest that racial discrimination remains the comprehensive obstacle to reconciliation. See Eric Mason, *Woke Church: An Urgent Call for Christians in America to Confront Racism and Injustice* (Chicago: Moody, 2018).

12

The Hispanic Church and the National Covenant

Osvaldo Padilla

What is the relationship between the Hispanic church in the United States[1] and the national covenant, as the latter has been described in the introduction and other chapters of this book? The question is simple, but difficult to answer in concrete form. I will approach it by reflection on how the Hispanic church in the United States can help in the healing of the American national covenant and hence contribute to the end of exile being experienced by this nation. Let me begin by considering a musical piece that is very popular with Latin Americans in the United States.[2]

---

1. By "Hispanic" I am referring to those churches—both Protestant and Roman Catholic—who use Spanish as their language of worship and/or who explicitly view themselves as Hispanics, even if their language of worship is English.

2. There is debate on how one should refer to Latin Americans in the United States in keeping with a sociolinguistics approach that privileges synchronic rather than diachronic understanding of semantics, I will employ the term being used on the ground at the moment: *Latino* for masculine and *Latina* for feminine; or simply *Latino/a* for both. For the plural I will use *Latinos*. To refer to the church, I will use the term *Hispanic*.

Margins and Bridges

The world-famous, late Cuban-American singer Celia Cruz interpreted a piece called "*Pasaporte Latinoamericano*" (Latin American Passport). The song is meaningful to Latinos because it describes movingly our reality in a new land. The lyrics begin: "I left in a dark night from my beloved land, one hand forward and one hand backward. Except for many dreams, I carried nothing else. And I arrived alone in this land, where I am a stranger, land of the hamburger and of the hot dog. People talk different, the sun doesn't feel the same way." After this opening, the mood of the music changes. New melodies suggest new possibilities, but hint also of caution. She continues: "The rules of the game I don't know so well; it may be that at the start the same thing happened to you. Don't look where I come from, I am Latina, that is all, sharing in a strange land my nationality" (my translation). The song continues speaking of both the marginal existence of Latinos in this nation as well as the joyful experience of sharing with so many different Hispanic nationalities in this new land. The point is that our existence on the borders, on the edges of society, can be a fulfilling one—but only if we live in interpenetrating community.

This piece encapsulates the experience of many Latinos. On the one hand, many of us exist in a place of *marginality*. From the perspective of the dominant culture, the word *margin* carries unwelcome connotations. To live at the margins means to exist as "the other," to be meaningless, to live in undesirable places, at the edge of the map. Marginality is viewed like a wilderness where nothing good grows; in fact, where death is. Contrary to the supposedly lush existence of the dominant center, marginal existence is portrayed as a desert where bleached bones and a merciless hot wind prevail.

On the other hand, and from a different perspective, the margins can be viewed not as borderlands at the edge of the map but as places of *crossings* and *meetings*. If our map is not a flat sheet of paper but a globe, then the margins may not at all be abandoned borders almost falling off the page but actually *bridges*. What from one perspective is an abandoned margin, from another perspective is a place where people from different origins can meet as they cross. Theologian Edwin Aponte puts it like this: "Social margins as cultural and social borderlands are the places where many cultures meet, not just in a geographic sense or political boundaries, but rather as a fluid place of consciousness, indeed of alternative consciousness. The meetings of cultures may also produce the *transformation* of cultures."[3]

From Margins to Oases

Many Latinos have found that life in the margins is actually different from the way it is often represented by the dominant majority. For them the margins have become an oasis, in large part because of the riches of the different Hispanic cultures that meet there. Many of us Latinos wonder if we can help other "marginal" people turn their margins into exotic, lush places. Even more, can our marginality be a bridge where different races can meet? Perhaps this might help in the healing of the broken national covenant.

A number of Latino/a theologians from both the Catholic and Protestant traditions have also been suggesting that one of the core missions of the Hispanic church in the United States is to serve as a bridge between the different cultures in this country. In 2007 the Academy of Catholic Hispanic Theologians of the United States (ACHTUS) titled its annual colloquium: "Building a Latino/a Ecumenical Theology." Participants in the colloquium were both Roman Catholics and Protestants. One of the goals of the meeting was to reflect on how a united Hispanic church might help in the healing of the spiritual and social situation of the nation. They observed that racism was considered to be one of the nation's most serious maladies. The colloquium produced an important book for theologians (and others) who desire to engage in the relationship between Hispanic church ecumenism and the most serious problems facing our culture in the United States.[4]

---

3. Edwin David Aponte, "Views from the Margins: Constructing a History of Latina/o Protestantism," in *Hispanic Christian Thought at the Dawn of the 21st Century*, ed. Alvin Padilla, Roberto Goizueta, and Eldin Villaf Añe (Nashville: Abingdon, 2005), 85–94, at 89. Emphasis added.

4. *Building Bridges, Doing Justice: Constructing a Latino/a Ecumenical Theology*, ed. Orlando Espín (Maryknoll, NY: Orbis, 2009).

One of the core beliefs of the meeting participants, well expressed in the introduction to the volume (penned by Orlando Espín), is that ecumenism is not only a matter of agreements (or disagreements!) on doctrinal *topoi*. To be sure, without robust discussion on core doctrines like God, Holy Scripture, salvation, and so forth, the conversation cannot get off the ground. Nevertheless, the ecumenical conversation must go *beyond* the doctrinal to the concrete, including the ethical impact of a united church on its native soil, in this case the United States. Espín continues by explaining that this must be so because our core doctrinal beliefs do not exist in the abstract; rather, they are beliefs to be *believed* by humans in their respective cultures. Thus, ecumenism must have an ethical component that reaches all the way down to the daily existence of human cultures. Short of this, ecumenism falls short of being *Christian*.

Why so? Helpfully, Espín grounds this view of ecumenism in Christology, particularly the incarnation. For in taking on flesh Jesus became part of a specific Jewish culture. The God of Christianity does not remain far off in some ethereal location without interacting with his creation. Rather, in Christ he was incarnate, thus providing the Christian model of what ecumenism should look like. If ecumenism is grounded in Christology, it must have as one of its tasks to work out the relationship of doctrine—and therefore the church—to actual human lives and cultures. Espín states:

> Ecumenical conversations *also* have to be about real people, real lives, and, most emphatically, about the cultural (and other) contexts that make real people human, that allow them to hear and respond to the gospel, and that mold and influence every doctrine, every biblical interpretation, every ethical claim, and every faith experience.[5]

One of the questions that these Latino/a theologians asked, therefore, was how a Hispanic ecumenism could help *concretely* in the spiritual health of the nation.

---

5. Espín, "Constructing a Conversation," in *Building Bridges*, 6. Emphasis original.

Family and Borderland

This question was taken up by Robert Goizueta in the same volume. He suggests that in order to construct bridges with the current culture so as to help its healing, it may be helpful to build on two concepts: *Pueblo de Dios* (People of God)[6] and "Borderland Ecclesiology."[7] The first concept is meant to communicate the Hispanic understanding of a people as a family, a *familia*. That is, an important paradigm for the self-understanding of Hispanic churches is the concept of the family, although one must be careful in not romanticizing how this works at the concrete level (families have their disagreements!). The united Hispanic church, with its self-understanding of family, can model for the rest of the culture just what it means to be family.[8] Goizueta himself does not develop this concept at length, but I briefly illustrate it at the end of this chapter by suggesting that racial variety is not antithetical to being one family.

The second concept is that of "Borderland Ecclesiology." Again returning to Christology, Goizueta observes that the majority of Jesus' earthly ministry took place in Galilee, not Jerusalem.[9] Goizueta notes that this location was, from the perspective of Jerusalem, a borderland: God was working outside the so-called privileged places of the nation! Likewise, the Hispanic church must embrace its borderland location as a place of opportunity, where God is moving. Latinos

---

6. It is difficult to carry over into English the nuance of the Spanish word *pueblo*. "People" misses the nuance of family, unity, and solidarity (and sense of poverty?) that the word *pueblo* conveys in Spanish. The Latin *populus* when used of the Roman people may be adequate.

7. Roberto S. Goizueta, "*Corpus Verum*," in *Building Bridges*, 145–46.

8. It should be noted that the concept of the church as a family has New Testament roots, especially visible in the metaphor of the household (*oikos*) as found in the Pastoral Epistles. See especially Roger Gehring, *House Church and Mission: The Importance of Household Structures in Early Christianity* (Grand Rapids: Baker Academic, 2009).

9. Of course, this model privileges the Synoptic Gospels. In the gospel of John, much of Jesus' earthly ministry takes place in Judaea and its vicinity, including Jerusalem.

therefore "have a responsibility to bequeath not only to our adopted country but, especially to our church, a church born on the border."[10]

We may think of a Hispanic ecclesiology in the United States that sees as part of its vocation a modeling of its plurality of races under the lordship of Jesus Christ. We could move this concept forward by applying it especially to the broken racial relations between African Americans and Anglo Americans. In short, I would like to suggest that the Hispanic church has a *bridging* vocation, humbly attempting to model the possibility—indeed the richness—of a multiethnic society. How is this possible?

A Matter of Providence

In order to move forward it is necessary, I suggest, to view the multiracial reality of the Hispanic church in this nation *theologically*. Here I would like to invoke the theological concept of *providence*. This is not a word that we use often today. Yet there is a sense in which all Christians believe in providence, at least in a minimalist way: God is ultimately in control of all that transpires in the world. Yet I want to use a thicker version of providence by employing a particularly Reformed understanding of the concept.

In his *Institutes of the Christian Religion*, John Calvin speaks of providence as that work of God which goes beyond his creation. Many people believe that God created the universe; but a robust Christian faith also believes that "he sustains, nourishes, and cares for, everything he has made, even to the last sparrow."[11] God's providence is based on his power, by which he is able to rule every detail. As omnipotent, "he so regulates all things that nothing takes place without his deliberation."[12] Yet Calvin warns that God's providence is not some naked, blind power; rather, God rules the world with

---

10. Goizueta, "*Corpus Verum*," 163.

11. John Calvin, *Institutes of the Christian Religion*, I.16.1. I use the text *Calvin: Institutes of the Christian Religion*, 2 vols., ed. John T. McNeill, trans. Ford Lewis Battles (Philadelphia: Westminster, 1960), which is based on the 1559 Latin text.

12. Calvin, *Institutes*, I.16.3.

exquisite goodness and grace.[13] Because of God's providence, Christians can rest on the truth that God will only allow that which is for the good and salvation of his people.[14] This is to be remembered in particular when dealing with other humans, who at times may seem to have ultimate say over us: "As far as men are concerned, whether they are good or evil, the heart of the Christian will know that their plans, wills, efforts, and abilities are under God's hand; that it is within his choice to bend them whither he pleases and to constrain them whenever he pleases."[15] In this respect, Calvin reminds us that in fact God uses humans as intermediate causes to bring about his will. God even uses the deeds of evil people for his purposes, without himself being guilty of sin.[16]

The Dutch theologian Herman Bavinck, following the Reformed tradition of Zwingli, Calvin, and Polanus, speaks of God's work of providence in the following way: "All things are grounded in God's ordinances. Heaven and earth, light and darkness, day and night, summer and winter, seedtime and harvest, are ordered, both in their unity and in their diversity, by God, who is 'wonderful in counsel, and excellent in wisdom.'"[17] Bavinck helpfully applies God's providence to the movements and boundaries of peoples, citing Acts 17:26 (see below).[18] Furthermore, Bavinck bases the diversity of creation—including humanity—on God's providence: "God's good pleasure alone explains all being and all diversity of being."[19]

Karl Barth's discussion of providence in his *Church Dogmatics*, particularly III.3 1–55, is also helpful. Barth's effort in this section, as indeed in all of the *Church Dogmatics*, is to bring a Christological foundation to every biblical doctrine. Thus, he clarifies and insists that we must see a difference between providence and predestina-

---

13. It is striking how often in his chapter on providence Calvin speaks of God's care, goodness, fatherly love, etc.

14. Calvin, *Institutes*, I.17.6.

15. Calvin, *Institutes*, I.17.6.

16. Calvin, *Institutes*, I.18.1–4.

17. Herman Bavinck, *Reformed Dogmatics. Volume Two: God and Creation*, trans. John Vriend (Grand Rapids: Baker Academic, 2004), 375.

18. Bavinck, *Reformed Dogmatics*, 375.

19. Bavinck, *Reformed Dogmatics*, 376.

tion. The former is the servant of the latter. Since God's "original" will, his election of grace, is to become incarnate in Jesus Christ in order to rescue humanity, providence must be viewed as a doctrine having to do with creaturely reality, not God's ontology, which is the case with election.[20] That is, since for Barth God has chosen not to be God without at the same time electing Jesus Christ as the archetypal human, election has to do with who he is. The creation of the world, under which the doctrine of providence finds its place, is the *theater* where God's elect, Jesus Christ, does his work.[21]

Barth gives the following "definition" to providence: "In the belief in providence the creature understands the Creator as the One who has associated Himself with it in faithfulness and constancy as this sovereign and living Lord, to precede, accompany and follow it, preserving, co-operating and overruling, in all that it does and all that happens to it."[22] Christian belief in providence does not emerge from observation, thinking, or feeling. Rather, it is believed only on the basis of the Word of God.[23] Furthermore, belief in providence is belief in the Lord God of the Bible, not a philosophy of history as such.[24] Lastly, belief in providence is belief in the God and Father of the Lord Jesus Christ, not a God in the abstract. With all of this in mind, Barth provides an explanation of the goal of providence within God's covenant of grace: "As God co-ordinates and integrates the history of the creature [providence] with that of His covenant of grace, so that it may co-operate in this history, the creature is not only a means but also an object of the divine action. As God works through creation, He works on it and for it."[25] Thus, God's providence is not devoid of his love, as if he were using humans as no more than marionettes to accomplish his salvific purposes. No, those very humans, who always rebel against God, are themselves the object of his love.

---

20. Karl Barth, *Church Dogmatics* (London: T & T Clark, 2010), III.3: 1–13.
21. See also Barth, *Church Dogmatics* III.1: 17–21, 93–227.
22. Barth, *Church Dogmatics* III.3: 14.
23. Barth, *Church Dogmatics* III.3: 14–17.
24. Barth, *Church Dogmatics*, III.3: 17–25.
25. Barth, *Church Dogmatics*, III.3: 47.

Variety as Gift

I want now to suggest that the multiplicity of ethnicities that makes up Latin American reality is an example of God's providence. Ultimately, the varied mixture of races of the continent is not accidental or merely the will of conquistadors. Nor, I suggest, is the movement of many from Hispanic countries to the United States. Ultimately, our varied ethnicity is an example of God's providence, which ultimate goal is the knowledge of the Lord Jesus Christ.

When the Spaniards came to the new world in 1492, first establishing themselves in the island of Hispaniola (my own country), their goal was at best a mixed one. To be sure, Isabella and Ferdinand, having made the Iberian Peninsula Catholic, wanted to continue the expansion of Catholicism to other lands. In a sense, therefore, their sending of Columbus had a missionary dimension to it. Sadly, however, the type of Christianity they sponsored was a militant one which would win converts by the cross and, when necessary, by the sword.[26] Furthermore, although attempts had been made to reform the clergy in Spain, mostly external conformity was accomplished. The carnality, lust, and greed of many clergy had not been uprooted. Furthermore, there was a significant lack of theological education for the clergy who initially set foot in the new world.[27] Thus, the clergy who came in the first two trips were also driven by a great desire for wealth and power. This resulted in the theft, forced labor, slavery, and incarceration of the Taíno Indians of the Dominican Republic, which indignities killed them: "While the number of inhabitants on the island before the arrival of the Spaniards is unclear, what is clear is that, by 1509, there were only around sixty-two thousand (a

---

26. I am here indebted to the work of Ondina González and Justo González, *Christianity in Latin America: A History* (Cambridge: Cambridge University Press, 2008), 12–27. For reference work on Latin America and Christianity, the reader is directed to the *Cambridge Encyclopedia of Latin American and the Caribbean*, ed. Simon Collier et al. (Cambridge: Cambridge University Press, 1985). For readers with Spanish and Portuguese, Latin America church history resources can be found under CEHILA (Comisión para el Estudio de la Historia de la Iglesia en América Latina y el Caribe): http://www.cehila.org.

27. See helpfully John Lynch, *New Worlds: A Religious History of Latin America* (New Haven: Yale University Press, 2012), 1–6.

decline of just under 95 percent on the high end and to 69 percent on the low end). By 1540, there were a few hundred Indians left on the island."[28] A similar pattern could be observed, although at times less lethal, in the rest of Latin America. To be sure, there were godly and courageous men who stood against this annihilation—men like Bartolomé de Las Casas and Antonio de Montesinos, who stood and preached against the colonizers and for the Indians.[29]

With the natives dying, Africans, especially from the west of the continent, were brought as slaves to Latin America, particularly the Caribbean and Brazil.[30] The ultimate result was a mixture of races. Children born from Spaniards and natives were called *mestizos*. Children from Spaniards and Africans were called *mulattos*. The mixing has continued. So in many parts of Latin America today, you will find Europeans, Indians, black Africans, *mestizos, mulattos*, and other combinations! New races have been born as a result of the brutal Spanish (and other European) colonization.

Here is where the theological concept of God's providence provides a lens for this new reality. We noted how Herman Bavinck included Acts 17:24–28 as a biblical text to employ God's providence as the grounds for variety. This Scripture indeed speaks of God ordering the dwelling places of humans: "And he made from one man every nation of mankind to live on all the face of the earth, having determined allotted periods and the boundaries of their dwelling places" (Acts 17:26 ESV). The statement here suggests that God so superintended the movements of humans that they ultimately dwell where it pleases him. The goal of this ordering is a gracious one, as the next verse indicates: "That they should seek God, and perhaps feel their way toward him and find him" (17:27 ESV).[31] The ultimate purpose of this supervision, therefore, is one of reconciliation between God and humanity. We may also think of the beautiful text from Genesis

---

28. González, *Christianity in Latin America*, 29–30.

29. For similar men and women, see *Fathers of the Church in Latin America*, ed. Silvia Scatena, Jon Sobrino, and Luiz Carlos Susin (London: SCM, 2009).

30. See González, *Christianity in Latin America*, 36–38.

31. For further explanation of this text including its connection to the Old Testament, see Osvaldo Padilla, *The Acts of the Apostles: Interpretation, History and Theology* (Downers Grove, IL: InterVarsity, 2016), 177–88.

50:20, where Joseph surely expresses God's voice in his conclusion: "You intended to harm me, but God intended it for good, to accomplish what is now being done, the saving of many lives" (NIV).

The Latin American experience is fundamentally *varied*. True, there are groups of Europeans or Africans or natives who have not mixed very much. However, as a whole, we can think of a spectrum in Latin America with the majority being *mestizos* and the minority being non-mixed. This mixing has been multiplied with these already mixed and diverse ethnicities emigrating to the United States, where there is even more diversity! Now a Chilean can marry a Dominican; or an Argentinean marries a Cuban. Again, Latin American existence in native countries and now in the United States is irreducibly multicultural. And we have found that this is good! We have found that, although it is far from being free of conflict, this multicultural existence is beautiful and complex and rich—and we are the better for it. We have found that this extensive multi-ethnicity can be *normal* and nothing to be afraid of. It is simply the reality that we live. The Spaniards' desire for exploitation has actually been used by God to produce a new, rich mixture of races, a *mestizaje* which simply is. This is the result of God's gracious providence.

My vision is that those in the United States who are afraid of, or hostile to, many different cultures living beside them may see that this is not alien to humanity: neither is it abnormal or bad or subhuman or un-American. I believe that Hispanics can and should model this crossing, this bridging of races for our country. Let me be clear. I am not suggesting that different races *have* to mix in intermarriage if we are to overcome the broken national covenant. My point is that there is a beautiful existence where being black or white or *mestizo* or a mixture of all three and more which does not need to be viewed as abnormal or less than optimal.

The Hispanic church in the United States of course reflects our racial variety. And as Latino Christians, I believe we have a bridging vocation before us. We must model for the North American church the riches of a multicolored church. Could it be that God would use this reality as one of the ways of healing the broken covenant? This reality is a significant part of the work of Hispanic ecclesiology, for there are dimensions of racial reconciliation that can only be experienced by those who are "in Christ." For those who, whatever church they belong to, follow the Christ of the Holy Scriptures, let me unpack this statement with two further underlying principles.

First, *the Christian vision for humanity is one of radical equality.* This vision began with Jesus Christ himself when he relativized even family relations: "Who are my mother and my brothers?... Here are my mother and my brothers! For whoever does the will of God, he is my brother and sister and mother" (Mark 3:33–35 ESV). The apostle Paul extends it: "There is neither Jew nor Greek, there is neither slave nor free, there is no male and female, for you are all one in Christ Jesus" (Gal. 3:28 ESV). And the Apocalypse closes it: "by your blood you ransomed people for God from every tribe and language and people and nation" (Rev. 5:9 ESV). The basic vision of Christianity for the world is one of multiformity of races worshiping God and therefore existing with each other in love. The vision is more than the French *liberté, égalité, fraternité*; it is more than the American Declaration of Independence where "the Creator," to be sure, is invoked. The Creator of the Declaration is the God of the Enlightenment—not the biblical God per se—although, to be sure, many of our founding fathers were genuine Christians. In the Christian vision, God is the one who has taken on humanity through Jewish flesh, which as such means that he is for the rest of the world, a light to the nations. Yet not only did he take on flesh for the nations but he was also crucified and raised for the sins of all the nations. The Christian vision is radically Christological: God was made flesh for all humanity. *God* is the foundation of racial reconciliation. And where God is present, there is hope.

But second, *ecclesial work through the bridging of the Hispanic church can be powerful because it is based on the power of the Holy Spirit.* The Spirit empowers us to overcome differences. I have experienced this overcoming in the little Hispanic church in South Florida where I congregated as a young Christian. We were all from different parts of Latin America now in the United States. We could and often annoyed each other; we often failed. But because we had been baptized into Christ by the Holy Spirit, by God's pure grace, we kept striving and trying to love each other as brothers and sisters and as those whom Christ forgave.

Conclusion

Racism is, at root, a spiritual malady. It is a heart disease that is radically contrary to the heart of God. Sociologically, racism is in part an attempt to reduce racial variety. For this reason it is opposed to God's purposes for providence. It is *God* who has created a varied world. Thus, racism is a type of *uncreation*, an attempt to return to the formless void and chaos which God overcame by his Spirit.

But just as the Spirit overcame chaos from the creation, there is hope today from that same Spirit. The same Spirit who hovered over the dark waters is the one who can bring about racial reconciliation. I have suggested that the Hispanic community—generally but especially as a community of faith in Jesus Christ—can have a bridging vocation to help heal the racial brokenness that exists in our country. If by God's grace we could show that our exiled marginality has actually become for us an end of exile, perhaps others may see that our multiethnic existence is not a condition of poverty, but an embarrassment of riches.

I close by relating the following experience. As is the case in many theological institutions preparing future ministers, so in the institution I teach there is a required cross-cultural component to the curriculum. We require our students to spend some time in a different country or a different culture to observe and learn. One of my African American students, keen to learn about the Latino culture in the US, asked if he could complete his requirement in the Hispanic church where I converted many years ago. And so after some arrangements, my student went to the heart of South Florida and spent two weeks in a little Hispanic church: a little church with nationalities ranging from Caribbean (including Haitian) to Central and South American and North American. Upon his return, the student and I had a long conversation. This student had lived his entire life in a region of the United States where there is very little racial variety. Not surprisingly, it was this rich variety that had the greatest effect on him. In particular, he was surprised at how *normal* this existence was. He was beginning to realize that ethnic variety *living together* was very possible.

I do not recount this vignette to project some sort of triumphalism for the Hispanic church: had my friend stayed in the church longer, he would have seen the many warts and challenges of the community! But I do believe that this anecdote can enliven and give hope to churches in our nation, and so to the nation as a whole. God can take a people born out of the malice and greed of others and recreate in Jesus Christ something beautiful. Our nation has a horrendous history of murdering and enslaving that, in part, constitutes the broken covenant. But God's loving providence (a tautology I realize, for God is love) can heal all things. The Hispanic church in the United States has the responsibility of modeling this healing, even as we ourselves have a long way to go.

13

Race and School Choice

Robert L. Woodson, Sr.

The essence of America's national covenant, expressed in the Declaration of Independence, is the commitment to equal opportunity and justice for all. One dimension of the national covenant in which a nation under God commits itself to his standards is its generational covenant, in which parents commit themselves to pass those standards on to the next generation. This commitment is expressed in Deuteronomy 11:18–19: "You shall put these words of mine in your heart and soul.... Teach them to your children" (NRSV). The mission of my five-decade career has been to empower parents to educate their children in ways that honor those standards.

Time and again, as I sought solutions to even the most entrenched and devastating problems of low-income communities, one maxim was proven true time and again. Substantive and sustainable solutions cannot be developed at the desks of distant academics and policy "experts," but by committed men and women who have a firsthand experience of the problems they address, live within the same geographic and "cultural zip codes" as the people they serve, are available on a 24/7 basis, and are personally committed for the long-term. As I listened to testimonies of the victories these committed people have won throughout the years, I understood one more time-honored principle: For nearly all who succeed, the source of their dogged pursuit of their callings was their faith. It has been through the work of these grassroots neighborhood healers that I have repeatedly witnessed the fulfillment of our national covenant.

In this quest, one crucial arena is education, where the life trajectories and future prospects of future generations can be set. Tragically, it is in this arena where opportunities for children of different races, ethnicities, and income levels have sharply differed. As our nation's history has unfolded, very different ideas have emerged about how to close the gaps among children of different races and incomes.

The Civil Rights Movement and Busing Black Students

I was first introduced to different agendas when I worked in the civil rights movement in the 1960s. The most prominent spokespersons of the movement focused on desegregation of schools to address inequities in education. They demanded mandated busing of black students to white schools.

In contrast, I believed that the solution was to strengthen and better equip the inferior schools within black neighborhoods, especially those where students were being left behind academically. I felt this would not only improve black students' education but also strengthen the community and enable parents to be more involved with their children's schools. In West Chester, Pennsylvania, nearly one thousand parents and concerned residents demonstrated in support of this view. Nevertheless, the proponents of busing students succeeded, and their demands were met.

When high school students were later surveyed, it was discovered that blacks comprised 80 percent of those who were taking the "general course" of studies—a curriculum that was not academic, business, or even vocational, but only a virtual dumping ground. Conversely, black students made up only seven percent of those who were in the academic (college-bound) course. In essence, those students were being re-segregated.

Meanwhile, because the system was sending black children on buses to schools far away from home, their parents were frustrated because they didn't have cars and couldn't easily get to school PTA meetings or conferences with teachers or counselors. It was clear to me that while we had won the battle regarding school segregation in the county, we had lost the war because of shortsighted and counter-productive ideas of how integration should be implemented. The lesson learned from this experience was that regardless of the intent or source of a proposed solution, its value must be determined by the impact on the lives of people it is intended to help.

Vouchers and School Choice

The issue of school choice has been bantered about in a tug-of-war between liberal pro-teachers-union politicians and anti-union conservative activists. Lost in this ideological and political combat has been the interest of low-income minority parents seeking a better education for their children. Although the issue of school choice has been framed as Left versus Right, with the former in opposition and the latter being supportive, the desire of the originators of the school-choice movement—low-income black parents in Milwaukee—has been obscured and ignored.

It should be kept in mind that the movement for educational options such as school choice and vouchers was initiated in the late 1980s by a black Democratic state legislator in Milwaukee, Polly Williams. She had the support of a black educator, Howard Fuller, who would later become the superintendent for the city's school system. Superintendent Fuller worked to improve the public schools while never denying his support for vouchers. In 1989, I helped arrange for parents, students, and community residents to attend the hearing on vouchers, and as the fate of Williams's initiative hung in the balance, a Democratic legislator who had not supported vouchers voted for them, saying she could not in good conscience side against so many people in the community.

Echoing the Milwaukee parents' stand on school choice thirty years ago, in 2018 the outcome of the Florida gubernatorial election was determined by nearly one hundred thousand black women who voted in support of the Republican candidate who had supported school choice and a program enabling low-income students to attend private schools. The "school-choice moms" voted to protect their ability to choose where their child goes to school.

Today's polarized political debate regarding our children's education must be defused and replaced with a cooperative effort to provide all students with a pathway to success. In addition to empowering parents through vouchers, an effort must be made to improve public schools so that they can be competitive with private and charter schools.

In our nation's most disadvantaged communities, even the engagement of parents may not be enough to help their children access educational opportunities. Many lack the practical capacity to help. For example, they may not have a computer or the skills needed to navigate online applications. Educational opportunities must be accompanied by capacity-building support, or they will be unreachable for those who are most in need.

Providing opportunities that will optimize future prospects for all of our nation's children—and ensuring that they can take advantage of those opportunities—should be among our priorities. It will take much more than an either-or, win-or-lose polarized debate on school choice to meet this challenge.

School Violence

Tragically in many urban schools today, one of the primary deterrents that keep students from getting the full benefit of their classes is fear of violence. Twenty years ago, the Woodson Center launched a Violence-Free Zone (VFZ) initiative to address this critical situation. The VFZ program has since expanded to more than thirty schools in five states. This program is based on a model that is led by a local community organization, supported by representatives of the school and law enforcement, and, most importantly, involves teens and young adults from the neighborhoods who have redirected their lives and now serve as peer mentors.

Studies based on police data have documented the dramatic success of this initiative. In some of the cities' most dangerous schools, violence, truancy, and disruptive incidents sharply declined while academic success rose. In some cases, even crime rates in the adjacent neighborhoods fell.

The program was created in 1997 to address a crisis of violence between warring factions in the Benning Terrace Public Housing complex in Washington, DC. Benning Terrace was a notorious killing field where there had been fifty-three murders in two years within the five-square-block complex.[1] Police were afraid to enter the complex, residents were afraid to use the streets, and the playgrounds were empty.

All of this changed when the National Center for Neighborhood Enterprise (now the Woodson Center) was contacted by a local grassroots organization, the Alliance of Concerned Men, who asked for help. The Center focused on setting up leadership "crews" in rival gangs. The men of the Alliance knew firsthand the conditions the gang members lived in, since they had faced the same challenges. And because they had a long-term commitment to these young men and were available 24/7, they earned their trust. The crew leaders agreed to come together at our offices. After an hours-long meeting, remarkably, they agreed to a peace pact. Shooting in the neighborhood ceased immediately, and there was not a single crew-related murder for twelve years. The truce made headlines around the country, and authorities—including the Metropolitan Police Department and the D.C. Housing Authority receiver—did what they could to support the newly established peace.[2]

Gang members who had once destroyed and divided their community joined together as the Concerned Brothers of Benning Terrace. They rolled up their sleeves and went to work, removing graffiti, landscaping, and serving as peer mentors.

The model of the VFZ initiative has been influential. It has been embraced by public school systems throughout the country and implemented successfully in some of the most dangerous schools of Milwaukee, Dallas, Atlanta, and Baltimore. The young adults who have been enlisted as youth advisors to be present in the halls, cafeterias, and detention rooms of schools are known, respected, and trusted by the students, and are included within their social media networks. When alerted of an impending altercation or act of violence,

---

1. Marcia Greene, "Long-Troubled D.C. Neighborhood Hopes Peace Will Prosper," *The Washington Post*, April 21, 1997, A01, https://www.washingtonpost.com/wp-srv/local/daily/april/21/truce.htm.

2. Marcia Greene, "Long-Troubled D.C. Neighborhood Hopes Peace Will Prosper."

these mentors have been able to intervene proactively and defuse the situation. The VFZ initiative has operated in Milwaukee Public Schools for fourteen years and is credited with helping to produce a twenty-five year low in violent incidents.[3]

The youth advisors' access to students' communications is a vital component of violence reduction in both urban and suburban schools. In 2004, the US Department of Education and the Secret Service published a report reviewing thirty-seven school shootings and school attacks from 1970 to 2000 to determine if there was a common element in the shooters' profiles.[4] There wasn't. But the study did reveal one element that was found in nearly all of the shootings: The killers had told someone in their social network what they were going to do. This information was unavailable to authorities, who are not tuned into the wavelength of the youths' communication system, known on the street as "the buzz." The VFZ youth advisors fill this information gap. They provide a conduit for student input in schools in the multicultural, affluent suburban community of Montgomery County, Maryland, as well as in the inner-city schools of Baltimore.

The success of the Violence-Free Zone initiative is evidence that a key solution to the crisis of youth violence can be found among those who are suffering from the problem and that the young can play a critical role in their own protection. Recognizing the unique capacity that exists within the population suffering from the problem should be a key element of our nation's strategy to effectively address the tragedy of school shootings and youth violence.

The crisis we face cannot be solved by a strategy that focuses only on more police and fewer guns. We must recognize and use the transforming capacity that exists within the afflicted neighborhoods themselves.

---

3. "Woodson Center Violence-Free Zone," YouTube video, February 27, 2018, https://www.youtube.com/watch?v=DQqQWJSPEPk.

4. Bryan Vossekuil, Robert A. Fein, et al., "The Final Report and Findings of the *Safe School Initiative*: Implications for the Prevention of School Attacks in the United States" (Washington, DC: United States Secret Service and United States Department of Education, 2004), https://www2.ed.gov/admins/lead/safety/preventingattacksreport.pdf.

Neighborhood-Based Innovation to Meet the Challenge

Charter schools and state-of-the-art personalized educational instruction using current technological advances provide vital opportunities that are critical for the future prospects of many children in our nation's rural and urban low-income and impoverished communities. But they reach only a few. This is not by design but by default. Because of social and financial disadvantages, most families in these communities can neither recognize nor take advantage of these opportunities.

But the Woodson Center has found ways to double and even triple participation in these new technologies. On the basis of forty years of on-site work in low-income communities throughout the country, Community Academy initiatives have achieved these remarkable results. Let me explain.

Background: The 30 Percent and 70 Percent Populations in Disadvantaged Communities

The majority of children in our nation's inner-city neighborhoods are growing up in single-parent homes, increasing the likelihood that they will drop out of school or become involved in destructive and self-destructive behavior. Yet in spite of these odds and disadvantages, there is a portion of parents in those communities (say, 30 percent) who manage to raise children who graduate from high school and avoid negative behavior. These parents are engaged in their children's education and work to help them access opportunities for a better future. They are more likely to be aware of available educational programs and to have the confidence and wherewithal to help their children navigate through the application process. They are also likely to monitor their children's progress and guide them to take personal responsibility to make optimal use of their opportunities.

Sadly, the remaining 70 percent of the parents in those communities have succumbed to the many challenges that confront them and have developed debilitating attitudes. The presence of opportunity alone is insufficient for children in the 70 percent to respond. Without the guidance, encouragement, and involvement of their parents, they are beyond the reach of innovative educational initiatives and even conventional organizations such as the YMCA or Boys and Girls Clubs. There must also be some catalytic agent that can reach their parents and help them change their attitudes in order to mobilize them.

These catalysts for transformation can be found among the parents in the 30 percent. These are the indigenous leaders who serve as role models, mentors, and no-nonsense coaches to the parents in the 70 percent. The mission of the Woodson Center has been to identify and strengthen the leaders who live within the communities suffering from these problems. These are the leaders who have already committed themselves to forging solutions. They have a firsthand understanding of the problems they address, are typically available on a 24/7 basis, and have earned the trust of the people they serve. They are the ones to whom the 70 percent turn in times of crisis.

The Woodson Center has established a nationwide network of these community antibodies and has documented a range of their successful efforts to improve the academic achievement and prospects for the future of the children in their neighborhoods. The task at hand is to formalize, strengthen, and bring resources to these effective grassroots initiatives. To maximize the impact of educational opportunities for children in low-income communities, the Woodson Center has proposed the creation of three tiers of "Community Academies."

Community Academies:
After-School, Five-Day Residential, and Boarding Schools

These tiers were developed after doing careful analysis of the problems. We had to study and identify carefully the characteristics of those who are to be served.

With regard to poverty, this meant recognizing that not all poverty is rooted in the same cause and that the solutions for each type of poverty must be designed with the cause in mind. When we focused on education, we came to realize that within the same disadvantaged neighborhoods, there were different groups with different levels of readiness to take advantage of opportunities. This is why our help had to take three different forms.

1. *After-School Community Academies* are informal gatherings where parents and children of the 30 percent and the 70 percent come together in a home or church in the neighborhood. Parents receive personal guidance from peer mentors on addressing their own challenges and providing support for their children's school progress and success. Children receive homework help and mentoring on various subjects. The gatherings are also a hub for community information exchange and a source of basic study supplies and computer access. Participants attend these sessions at their own pace and have an option to have after-school snacks or dinners together. Each after-school "academy" is uniquely designed to meet the needs of its specific community. Some of these neighborhood initiatives are listed below under "Models of Success."

2. *Community Academy Weekday Residential Schools.* For students whose home environments do not promote educational activities and whose communities present obstacles to academic achievement, the Community Academies take the form of Weekday Residential Schools where youths focus on their research and homework and share productively and positively with peers, teachers, and mentors about their projects and goals. The weekends offer times for the students to share progress with their parents, who become part of their journey to success.

3. *Community Academy Boarding Schools.* For young people whose physical and emotional well-being is jeopardized in their home environments, the opportunity to attend a full-time boarding school, staffed by members of their community whom they know and trust, provides the best chance for academic achievement and a successful future.

Robert L. Woodson, Sr.

Models of Success

College, Here We Come

An early example of the model of parent-to-parent mentoring was created through a spontaneous response to a need in the Kenilworth Parkside public housing project in north east Washington in the early 1980s. A woman named Kimi Gray had emerged as an indigenous leader in that neighborhood. Although Kimi was the single parent of five children by age nineteen, she managed to earn a degree and guide each of her children to complete high school and attend college. The neighbors were aware of her success and came to Kimi to ask how she had accomplished all of this. Was there a way she could help them to do the same? After-school homework and tutoring sessions began in one of the housing units and multiplied in several others. In time, the first four of the students in the program went on to college. When they returned to Kenilworth, these students said they were embarrassed to invite their college friends to the development. With her hallmark energy and no-nonsense expectations, Kimi turned that problem into a challenge. A community-wide revitalization initiative was launched—including building repairs, economic opportunity, and tackling issues of drugs and crime. Meanwhile, the educational element of Kenilworth's initiative expanded to a "College Here We Come" program that provided contributions to tuition costs (raised through bake sales and raffles) and a hope chest with supplies, a suitcase, and a one-way ticket to campus. Within twenty years, nearly one thousand young men and women at Kenilworth went on to higher education.

Over the last forty years, the Woodson Center has strengthened and supported a wide range of similar educational initiatives launched by neighborhood leaders throughout the country.

Spontaneous Outreach—Values Education

In Pennsylvania, one of the first community antibodies I encountered was Mercedes Greer, a hairdresser and a font of wisdom and advice for all in the neighborhood. Greer invited twenty teenaged girls from an adjacent housing project every Saturday night for dinner and discussion. The girls became an "extended family" who broadened their horizons through bus trips outside the city. Of that first group of twenty teens, only one became pregnant in the course of two years. With Greer's support and encouragement, eventually hundreds of girls from that low-income neighborhood attended college and went on to hold administrative and professional positions.

In Milwaukee, Cordelia Taylor created a group home called Family House where the elderly could be treated with dignity and respect. Yet in the afternoons, the home became a haven for a much younger cohort. Teenaged girls, attracted to the safe and warm environment, gathered on the porch to do their homework. Taylor invited them in and began Teen Talk sessions where they could share about their issues of concern and receive guidance. The outreach soon grew to include peer counseling, field trips, visits to museums, outings to restaurants (where the teens received etiquette tips), and movie dates followed by discussion groups. All of this contributed to greater self-esteem and a larger vision for their future. Teen Talk has since reached and added value to the lives of more than two hundred young ladies.

Arts and Culture Outreach

Other educational initiatives launched within low-income areas have focused on the arts. The Northeast Performing Arts Group (NEPAG) group was created in 1979 by a little woman with a giant vision. Rita Jackson was committed to use the performing and visual arts as an alternative to street life to teach critical lessons of self-discipline, commitment, and team motivation. Since its founding, NEPAG has trained over seven thousand youths and helped more than four hundred enroll in college.

In violence-plagued DC, the Urban Nation HIP HOP (Hope, Integrity, Power—Helping Our People) was founded by musician Rickey Payton, Sr. and Dr. Sheila Johnson Newman to channel underserved youths' creative and artistic energies to promote excellence in all facets of their lives. In addition to performances in jazz, contemporary, inspirational, folk, and classical music, Urban Nation emphasizes education, academic excellence, community service, and intercultural appreciation.

Although these educational and preparatory programs vary in their nature, all have some common qualities such as emerging from the communities suffering from problems and being embraced and trusted by the individuals they serve. Above all, they were created not by outsiders but by insiders—people from within the community in response to their neighbors' needs. Participants arrived at their doorstep, in some cases even before the program took shape. This repeated pattern shows that people in these neighborhoods want something better and are eager to get it. These programs typically continue for decades with more people joining every year. They do not go away when funding from a grant is no longer available.

A Model of Success: The Rosenwald Schools

In 1912, an initiative begun by Sears president Julius Rosenwald, a Jewish immigrant from Germany, had an impact that went far beyond the benefits that the company's retail practices had for black Americans. A collaborative project created by Rosenwald and Booker T. Washington, founder of the Tuskegee Institute (where Rosenwald was a trustee), was to change the course of black education in the South.[5] Within two decades, throughout the rural South, nearly five thousand state-of-the-art schools were built.

Designed by Tuskegee architects to enhance the educational environment, the schools typically incorporated banks of windows to allow maximum lighting in an era where electricity was not available.[6] Plans specified that the buildings were to be positioned so that the sunlight would enter from the left, so students' hands would not cast shadows on their work. Most schools included a meeting room that served as a gathering place for community meetings and events. By 1928, one-third of the South's rural black schoolchildren and teach-

---

5. Kate Kelly, "The Rosenwald Schools: Schools for African-Americans in the Rural South," America Comes Alive!, https://americacomesalive.com/2014/09/30/rosenwald-schools/.

6. Witold Rybczynski, "Remembering the Rosenwald Schools: How Julius Rosenwald and Booker T. Washington created a thriving schoolhouse construction program for African Americans in the rural South," *Architect*, September 16, 2015, https://www.architectmagazine.com/design/culture/remembering-the-rosenwald-schools_o.

ers were served by Rosenwald schools. Among the schools' notable alumni are poet Maya Angelou and Rep. John Lewis.

Importantly, in the words of one Rosenwald Fund official, the initiative created "not merely a series of schoolhouses, but a community enterprise in cooperation between citizens and officials, white and colored."[7] Rosenwald funding required the white school boards to agree to operate the facilities. The funding came as a matching grant. "The Rosenwald Fund contributed $4.3 million to construct the schools," and rural black communities raised more than $4.7 million from churches, organizations, and individuals.[8] Community investments included cash, labor, lumber, materials, and land as a site for a school—as well as nickels and dimes from "box parties" where women put together box lunches for neighbors to bid on.

The impact of the Rosenwald schools went beyond educational opportunities that transformed the futures of hundreds of thousands of children. An evaluation financed by the Federal Reserve Bank of Chicago, using data on communities that had a Rosenwald school and those that did not, found that the schools had a significant impact on both the children and their communities.[9]

In the 1920s, the gap in educational attainment between black and white males in the South was three years. Blacks had on average a fifth-grade education, compared to eighth grade for whites. By the 1940s, that gap had closed to just six months—in an era when the local government funding for black schools was a fraction of that spent for white schools. This dramatic closing of the educational racial gap largely has been attributed to the Rosenwald schools.[10]

---

7. Lenora Gobert, "The Unfortunate Lost History of the Rosenwald Schools," *Creolegen*, October 13, 2014, http://www.creolegen.org/2014/10/13/the-unfortunate-lost-history-of-rosenwald-schools/.

8. The Herbert S. Ford Memorial Museum, https://web.archive.org/web/20060515144853/http:/ford.claiborneone.org/.

9. Daniel Aaronson and Bhashkar Mazumder, "The Impact of Rosenwald Schools on Black Achievement," *Federal Reserve Bank of Chicago Working Paper*, no. 2009–26 (September 23, 2011), https://papers.ssrn.com/sol3/papers.cfm?abstract_id=1521585.

10. Daniel Aaronson and Bhashkar Mazumder, "The Impact of Rosenwald Schools on Black Achievement."

The impact of the schools had a ripple effect that impacted the trajectories of their students.[11] Researchers Daniel Aaronson and Bhashkar Mazumber summarized as follows:

> We find significant effects on school attendance, literacy, years of schooling, cognitive test scores, and Northern migration. The gains are highest in the most disadvantaged counties, suggesting that schooling treatments have the largest impact among those with limited access to education.[12]

Though a white Northerner, Rosenwald's religious heritage made him feel a kinship with African Americans because, as the philanthropist stated, "The horrors that are due to race prejudice come home to the Jew more forcefully than to others of the white race, on account of the centuries of persecution which they have suffered and still suffer."[13]

Today's social justice warriors can learn from these past and present successes. We all would agree that education is critical to closing the gaps between blacks and whites in this country. The collaborative efforts I have described in this chapter demonstrate ways to overcome barriers of race, ethnicity, and income level to benefit hundreds of thousands of young people. If we are willing to use these and similar efforts, we can go a long way toward fulfilling the national covenant's call to liberty and justice for all.

---

11. Gabrielle Emanuel, "Built a Century Ago, 'Rosenwald Schools' May Still Have Lessons to Teach," *NPR*, October 17, 2015, https://www.npr.org/sections/ed/2015/10/17/436402544/rosenwald-schools-built-a-century-ago-may-still-have-lessons-to-teach.

12. Aaronson and Mazumder, "Impact of Rosenwald Schools," abstract.

13. Quoted in Tom Hanchett, "Saving the South's Rosenwald Schools," *History South*, n.d., https://www.historysouth.org/schoolhistory/.

14

GEOGRAPHY, HISTORY, AND ETERNITY: A THEOLOGICAL STEWARDSHIP

Timothy George

This book focuses on two biblical words, both central to the traditions of Jewish and Christian faith represented by writers in this volume. The two words stand for two great, if contested, concepts: *covenant* and *reconciliation*. I want to introduce a third word, also from the Bible, a word that may serve as a link between covenant and reconciliation: *stewardship*.

In 2018, Beeson Divinity School's beloved friend and mentor Dr. James Earl Massey left this world for a better one. On three occasions, he presented the annual William E. Conger Lectures on Biblical Preaching at Beeson. One of those lecture series became a book which he titled *Stewards of the Story*, based on Paul's statement in 1 Corinthians 4:1, "This is how one should regard us," Paul wrote, "as servants of Christ and stewards of the mysteries of God" (ESV).

Dr. Massey argued that preachers of the gospel are stewards of the mysteries of God, stewards of the story.[1] The Greek word is *oikonomos*. We get "economy" and "economics" from that word. It sounds very similar to another Greek word, *episcopos*, for "overseer" or "bishop."

---

1. James Earl Massey, *Stewards of the Story: The Task of Preaching* (Louisville: Westminster John Knox, 2006), 6.

A steward is a person into whose care and responsibility something greatly valued and precious has been entrusted. Stewards are not owners of that over which they have responsibility and keep watch. They are trustees. Stewardship often refers to something literal or physical such as stewardship of land, material wealth, or the environment. But the word can also be used in a more expansive sense: to be a steward of the story is to receive and pass on intact a series of symbols, myths, and values that give meaning to life and summon us to a faithful witness in the service of faith, hope, and love. While Dr. Massey was speaking particularly to preachers about the task of preaching, stewardship has a wider application with reference to racial reconciliation and the national covenant. I want to say that we have, all of us, a threefold stewardship: a stewardship of geography, a stewardship of history, and a stewardship of eternity. This chapter will use Birmingham, Alabama, as a sort of "test case" for these three stewardships. Nearly every community in the United States has a legacy of racism or racial prejudice. Birmingham, given its history of segregation and its prominence in the civil rights movement, can help point the way forward in addressing past wrongs and moving toward reconciliation.

First, the stewardship of geography. I will take you back to the early 1920s in Birmingham, Alabama, and describe briefly two major rallies that took place. The first occurred on October 21, 1921, in downtown Birmingham in a large public space then called Capitol Park, and now known as Linn Park.

Birmingham had a population of 180,000 people in 1921, and more than 100,000 people attended this rally to hear the recently elected president of the United States, Warren Gamaliel Harding. The year was the fiftieth anniversary of the city of Birmingham. Birmingham is a post–Civil War city, founded in 1871. President Harding was invited to celebrate the Magic City's fiftieth birthday. He came and 100,000 people turned out to listen to him. President Harding chose race as the topic of his address.

Harding said he was going to address the topic of race "whether you like it or not."[2] Race was a surprising topic for the new president

---

2. "Harding Says Negro Must Have Equality in Political Life," *New York Times*, October 21, 1921.

to address. We do not usually associate Warren G. Harding with anything progressive. His campaign theme had been a "return to normalcy." It was this blah, blah republicanism. But on that particular occasion in Birmingham, Harding said something that W. E. B. Du Bois later declared was a braver, clearer utterance on race than Theodore Roosevelt had ever dared to make or than William Taft or William McKinley ever dreamed of. What did he say?

First of all, he argued that race was not merely a "sectional question applicable only to the Southern States but a national question which must be met as such." Harding went on to say that political and economic inequality between whites and blacks "is the problem of democracy everywhere. [I]f we mean the things we say about democracy as the ideal political state ... our democracy is a lie unless you stand for that equality."[3] This was bold for Birmingham (or anywhere) in 1921, even though Harding did not advocate social egalitarianism between the races.

Second, Harding argued for black suffrage. He said that blacks should be allowed to vote if they were fit and that whites should be disallowed to vote if they were not fit. Now, he spoke at Capitol Park in a segregated space. African Americans were separated from the whites by a chain-link fence. When he made statements like that, they erupted in great applause. The whites sat sullenly silent.

Third, in his speech, Harding promoted the anti-lynching law he had recently proposed to Congress. This law was not passed in the 1920s because it was filibustered by Southern Democratic senators. It was even opposed by Franklin Roosevelt in the next decade because he was concerned about the impact the passage of such a bill might have on his reelection contest in 1936. As late as 2005, the United States Senate passed a resolution apologizing for the failure to enact the anti-lynching bill of the 1920s.

There was another rally in Birmingham two years later on September 13, 1923. Samford University is on a road called Lakeshore Drive. Some students say, "Why do we call this Lakeshore Drive? There's no lake." Well, there used to be a lake across the road from where the campus sits today. Across Lakeshore Drive from our campus, you will find Homewood High School. It sits by a big park and

---

3. "Harding Says Negro Must Have Equality."

a nice walking trail meandering along what used to be Edgewood Lake. Early in 1923, the dam broke, and Edgewood Lake became a dry bed. This lakebed had become a very popular place for picnics, for parties, for dances, for political gatherings.

On September 13, 1923, at Edgewood Lake, there was a great rally. It drew not 100,000, but 25,000 people. This rally took place in the evening. This was a meeting of the Robert E. Lee Klan No. 1, the oldest and most influential Ku Klux Klan in Jefferson County, and one of the largest in the South. From all across the region, members of the Klan had come to hold a mass initiation ritual. At nine o'clock the flaming crosses came out. It was then that the inductions of new members took place.[4]

On that night, one of those people who was inducted into the KKK was the teacher of the largest Sunday school class in Birmingham, Alabama. That class met at First Baptist Church which in those days was located in downtown Birmingham. Some 1,000 Sunday school students would regularly come to hear this man teach the Bible. His name was Hugo Black.[5]

Black was from Clay County, Alabama. He was a very ambitious lawyer. That night he was inducted into the KKK. He resigned his Klan membership two years later because he was making plans to run for the United States Senate, and he was concerned that his Klan connection could be a liability. He joined the Klan, he later declared, because it was politically advantageous for him to do so. He resigned from the Klan for the same reason. However, he still sought their support for his election and later spoke at another rally they convened.

Over the years, Hugo Black became known as one of the most liberal justices on the United States Supreme Court. He was a strong advocate for the First Amendment. He was also the justice who, in 1967, swore in a new fellow Supreme Court justice named Thurgood Marshall. This was the same Hugo Black who was a member of the KKK in 1923. We have a stewardship of geography.

---

4. Leah Rawls Atkins, "Remembering Edgewood Lake," *The Homewood Star*, October 29, 2013.

5. Roger K. Newman, *Hugo Black: A Biography*, 2nd ed. (New York: Fordham University Press, 1997), 91–92.

Let me say a brief word about a stewardship of history. Pope John Paul II in his groundbreaking encyclical *Ut Unum Sint* (That They May Be One) introduced the term "reconciliation of memories" to ecumenical discourse. This reconciliation of memories, or purification of memories, acknowledges "the burden of *long-standing misgivings* inherited from the past, and of mutual *misunderstandings* and *prejudices*" and relies upon the grace of God "to *re-examine together their painful past* and the hurt which that past regrettably continues to provoke even today."[6] Why is this important? Because, as William Faulkner said, "The past is never dead. It's not even past."[7] There can be no reconciliation of memory without a prior purification of memory because the consequences of the past still remain. They still make themselves felt, like radioactive nuclear material. You can bury it, you can hide it, but it has an afterlife. It can still do damage for many years to come.

The reconciliation of memories works on that same premise. It requires an act of courage and humility to recognize the wrongs that have been done—especially in the case of church divisions and recriminations that have often been done in the name of Jesus Christ, or in the name of the church of Jesus Christ. The reconciliation of memories makes theological sense only because the mystical body of Christ is extended across time as well as space, and because Jesus Christ has once and for all taken on himself the sins of the whole world (Heb. 10:10; 1 John 2:2).

So we have a stewardship of history. I want to mention two recent reports, both controversial, both concerned with race and covenant, and both aimed at a reconciliation of memory. One is from Princeton University, "The Princeton and Slavery Project."[8] Princeton was founded in 1746. The first nine presidents of Princeton, including Jonathan Edwards, held slaves. Princeton always saw itself–and perhaps still does—as centrally positioned geographically along the

---

6. John Paul II, encyclical letter *Ut unim sint* (May 25, 1995), §2., original emphasis.

7. William Faulkner, *Requiem for a Nun* (1950; repr., New York: Vintage, 2011), 121.

8. Martha A. Sandweiss, director, *The Princeton & Slavery Project*, https://slavery.princeton.edu.

Eastern seaboard drawing from the strengths of the North and the South and the West. In 1851, ten years before the Civil War started, 63 percent of the students at Princeton came from slave states. New Jersey had passed a law in 1804 calling for the gradual abolition of slavery, but this did not happen all at once. It took a long, long time.

Princeton issued this report in 2017 acknowledging these unpleasant facts of history—not so much apologizing or repenting for them as saying they are part of who we were. They have impacted us. Even after the Civil War, these memories were hard to bury. The question arose for schools such as Princeton and Harvard and Yale: What about the alumni from our schools who had fought and died for the Confederacy? How are we going to honor the war dead?

Harvard has a large building called Memorial Hall that honors the alumni veterans who died in war. At Harvard and at Brown, only Union soldiers were named. Those who died in Confederate uniforms were obliterated from memory. At Yale, both Union and Confederate alumni were listed by rank and military affiliation. Princeton, to my knowledge, is the only place where all of the fallen dead were listed in simple alphabetical order without designation of whether they had fought for the North or for the South.

Not long after the Princeton report, The Southern Baptist Theological Seminary in Louisville, Kentucky issued its own report. This report quoted a resolution of the Southern Baptist Convention from 1995 which acknowledged the nature of American slavery and the way that Southern Baptists in particular had failed to support—and in some cases opposed—legitimate initiatives to secure the civil rights of African Americans. The president of the seminary, Dr. R. Albert Mohler, acknowledged that the seminary has "been guilty of a sinful absence of historical curiosity."[9] This report from the seminary in Louisville confessed the role of that particular institution in the syndrome of slavery and its sequel of segregation.

Both the Princeton and the Southern reports have been criticized. What are the criticisms? "Too little, too late." That was from the Left,

---

9. R. Albert Mohler, "Letter from the President," *Report on Slavery and Racism in the History of the Southern Baptist Theological Seminary*, 2, https://sbts-wordpress-uploads.s3.amazonaws.com/sbts/uploads/2018/12/Racism-and-the-Legacy-of-Slavery-Report-v4.pdf.

but there were criticisms from the Right as well. "You cannot apologize for something you did not do. You cannot repent for the dead. You're just trying to reinstitute a form of works righteousness, and you are not depending as you ought to on the grace of God." These reports elicited a number of such criticisms, but others applauded the institutions for coming clean on an obscured and forgotten part of their past. In a larger perspective, a charitable reading of these reports indicated that these two institutions were trying to take a baby step toward the reconciliation of memories.

I have described three stewardships, but I want to mention one more—the one I know least about because I have not experienced very much of it: the stewardship of eternity. Samford University has a seal with three Latin words that define the vision of our university: *Deo, Doctrinae, Aeternitati*, which we render "for God, for learning, forever." Now, that last word does not mean that Samford University is forever. As Robert Frost wisely reminded us,

> *Nature's first green is gold,*
> *Her hardest hue to hold.*
> *Her early leaf's a flower;*
> *But only so an hour.*
> *Then leaf subsides to leaf.*
> *So Eden sank to grief,*
> *So dawn goes down to day.*
> *Nothing gold can stay.*[10]

I have been to Athens. I have seen where Socrates and Aristotle taught, and it is in ruins today. I have walked through the Forum in Rome which was once the nerve center of a great empire. It too is now in ruins, stone upon stone. Nothing gold can stay. Nothing can last for very long. Yet eternity, the Bible says, God has placed in our hearts (Eccl. 3:11). We do have a stewardship of eternity because we cherish the values of a life fit for eternity. Such is a life more kind than clever, one more shaped by compassion than by competition.

---

10. Robert Frost, "Nothing Gold Can Stay," in *The Poetry of Robert Frost: The Complete Poems*, ed. Edward Connery Lathem (New York: Henry Holt, 1979), 222–23.

It is a life fit for faith, a faith that outweighs fears and a hope that gives confidence. If we do not have a stewardship of eternity, we will turn it on ourselves. There is no way out.

I know that this truth can be misappropriated, and it has been. I have read Karl Marx. Religion, he wrote, "is the opiate of the people," and sometimes in history, regrettably, that has been all too true. And yet at the heart of the biblical faith for both Judaism and Christianity is this fact: The Bible teaches that this world does not terminate on itself. God has placed eternity within our hearts or, as Augustine put it in book one of the *Confessions*, "You have made us for yourself, O God, and our hearts are restless until they find their rest in you."[11] Only from the perspective of a stewardship of eternity does it make any sense to care about those children yet waiting to be born, so expendable in our society today. Only with this perspective do we see a connection between the two great evils in our society today: the culture of abortion and the still-festering wound of racism. As Russell Moore has aptly pointed out, "Abortion and racial injustice are not two separate impulses. They are one. Both seek to make invisible the vulnerable neighbor one's group wishes to sacrifice for their own ends. Both use a spectrum of ways to get around the human conscience, which, when functioning, would recoil at smothering a baby on a table or lynching an African-American man."[12]

When I was a student at Harvard Divinity School many years ago, preaching was not taught. They did not think we needed it! But I was the pastor of a small multiracial church in Chelsea, Massachusetts, inner-city Boston. I knew I needed preaching, and my congregation knew and sometimes they told me! Some of us Harvard Divinity School students, mostly the African American students, I have to confess, along with a few of us white guys too, petitioned the dean. We petitioned our dean, Krister Stendahl. We told him that we needed to have preaching, even if it was not a part of the regular curriculum. We recommended that he fly up Dr. Gardner Calvin Taylor, one of

---

11. Augustine, *Confessions*, trans. Henry Chadwick (Oxford: Oxford University Press, 1991), 3.

12. Russell Moore, "What We're Missing in the Ralph Northam Scandal," (blog) *Ethics and Religious Liberty Commission*, February 2, 2019, https://www.russellmoore.com/2019/02/02/what-were-missing-in-the-ralph-northam-scandal?.

the great preachers of our time, to Boston from Brooklyn one day a week. Dr. Taylor pastored Concord Baptist Church.

The dean kindly agreed to do that. So every Wednesday afternoon in Andover Chapel at Harvard Divinity School, Dr. Taylor would hold forth, in his own inimitable way, about preaching, about church, about ministry, but mostly about life. I shall never forget a story he told. He was a young pastor in Louisiana preaching one Sunday night in a rural area just as electricity was being introduced into that part of the country. Suddenly the lights went out. He did not know what to say. An elderly deacon in the congregation cried out, "Preach on, preacher. We can still see Jesus in the dark."

I have thought about that a lot. We can still see Jesus in the dark. The message of the gospel that Gardner Calvin Taylor proclaimed and tried to help us to learn how to proclaim is that even when we cannot see Jesus in the dark, he can see us in the dark. And he promises never to leave us, never to forsake us.

We have a stewardship of geography. We have a stewardship of history, and yes, we also have a stewardship of eternity. God help us to be good stewards of all three.

Epilogue

I Don't Want No Trouble at the River*

Robert Smith, Jr.

I contend the stigmata of Jesus Christ, em*power*ed by the Spirit of God, enable the believer to overcome the stigma of racism. The power works through immediate justification and progressive sanctification.

If you, as an unbeliever, steal my car on Tuesday and get saved on Wednesday, I really believe on Thursday you will return my car and return it with a full tank of gas. Why not return the car on Wednesday after getting saved on Wednesday? On Wednesday one is justified, which is a one-time experience. But time is required for progressive sanctification—an indefinite period represented by the time between Wednesday and Thursday.

John Calvin is right in his conviction that good works do not produce salvation—salvation produces good works. John Newton, the author of "Amazing Grace" and one of the leaders of the evangelical movement in the Church of England, took three voyages as captain of a slave ship after his conversion and did not declare himself

---

*This epilogue is adapted from a sermon delivered at the National Covenant and Racial Reconciliation conference at Samford University, February 12–13, 2019.

against the slave trade until three decades later.[1] But eventually the power of his justification worked through sanctification. In other words, the indicative of justification precedes the imperative heard in sanctification, and the order is not reversible according to Herman Ridderbos.[2] Ridderbos believed that the indicative (who God has made us in Christ) and the imperative (what we are to do as a result of being made in Christ) are not only irreversible in their order, but the imperative always rests on the indicative.

The same applies to the dilemma of race in America. I have not given up hope that there will ever be racial reconciliation. But I believe racial reconciliation can only be accomplished through Jesus Christ. There are many residing in glory who saw so much injustice and heard so much slander—and experienced so much pain—that they gave up all hope for reconciliation between races. But I think that the only way for racial reconciliation to effectively take place is through the gospel of Jesus Christ and its adherents living out the gospel message in their everyday lives regardless of their social location.

I believe the church ought to be a Kodak moment for the future state of eternity so that we can reflect on earth what is already a reality in heaven—"Thy kingdom come, thy will be done on earth as it is already done in heaven." When I was in Little Rock, Arkansas, I discovered there was a street that used to be known as Confederate Boulevard. After the 2015 Charleston church shooting at Emanuel African Methodist Episcopal Church in which nine people were killed by a gunman who had posed with a Confederate flag, the residents asked that the name of the street be changed from Confederate Boulevard to Springer Boulevard in honor of a prominent African American family who served the community since the Civil War.[3] The

---

1. Marcus Rediker, *Slave Ship: A Human History* (New York: Penguin, 2007), 157–86, esp. 184; see also D. Bruce Hindmarsh, *John Newton and the English Evangelical Tradition between the Conversions of Wesley and Wilberforce* (Oxford: Oxford University Press, 1996), xvi–xvii, 18–23.

2. Herman Ridderbos, *Paul: An Outline of His Theology*, trans. J. R. De Witt (Grand Rapids: Eerdmans, 1975), 254–55.

3. Steve Barnes, "Arkansas capital renames street long known as Confederate Boulevard," Reuters, October 20, 2015, https://www.reuters.com/article/us-

Little Rock Board of Directors by an 8–2 vote obliged the residents and changed Confederate Boulevard to Springer Boulevard.

Emmett Till was murdered sixty-five years ago on August 28, 1955. The two men who killed him were acquitted of the crime. The same courthouse where they were acquitted has now become a civil rights museum. There is a move to make it a national park.

Even as we worship here today on February 12, 2019, we recognize it is President Abraham Lincoln's birthday. Daniel Chester French who sculpted the Lincoln Memorial took a cast of Lincoln's hands. A careful look at his left hand will discover it clenched, which suggests power and strength. His right hand is more relaxed, suggesting compassion and peace. These hands signed the Emancipation Proclamation that declared slaves to be free. The signature by these hands did not make the slaves free. However, there is one whose hands bear the stigmata—the scars and wounds. These omnipotent hands submitted to impotence to the point that they could not carry the cross to the crucifixion site. On Friday Christ died. He died in weakness that was strength. He died in compassion. He died in meekness. On Sunday morning the Holy Spirit raised Jesus from the dead (Rom. 8:11). If the Holy Spirit of God can raise Jesus from the dead, then the Spirit of God can enable us to overcome the stigma of racism and change our community into Martin Luther King, Jr.'s Beloved Community. In fact Jesus prayed to the Father that we would be one even as he and his Father are one (John 17:11).

I stand with Manuel L. Scott, Sr. regarding the power of the gospel being represented cross-culturally and cross-communally. He said, "I would not have a gospel that could only be preached on one side of town."[4]

In Numbers 27:12–14, God issues a prohibition to Moses. God tells him he will not lead the Israelites over the Jordan River to take possession of the promised land because he did not honor and glorify

---

arkansas-confederate/arkansas-capital-renames-street-long-known-as-confederate-boulevard-idUSKCN0SF02920151021?feedType=RSS&feedName=domesticNews.

4. Manuel L. Scott, Sr., cited in Jared E. Alcántara, *Crossover Preaching: Intercultural-Improvisational Homiletics in Conversation with Gardner C. Taylor* (Downers Grove, IL: InterVarsity, 2015), 295.

God before the waters of Meribah Kadesh. God essentially said, "You will not lead the people over the Jordan to take possession of the promised land because you did not honor me and glorify me before the waters of Meribah." What a word! Moses must have been shocked to learn he would not lead his people into the promised land as he thought he would.

God did not leave his people leaderless, however. In Numbers 27:15–23, the Lord spoke to Moses and said, "Moses, your successor is right by your side. He's your assistant. He is your aide. He is your minister. He is Yehoshua." In front of all Israel, Eleazar and Moses commissioned Joshua to do what Moses would leave as an uncompleted action. Joshua would now be in control of the twelve tribes of Israel. In Numbers 32, three tribes are identified—the full tribe of Reuben, the full tribe of Gad, and the half tribe of Manasseh. They reach a place of hesitation and say to Moses, "We found our promised land on the east side of the Jordan River. There is lush territory. It is roomy in Bashan of the Gilead area. That's where we want to stay."

Moses became irritated at first because he thought they were trying to renege on their commitment to the unified effort of all twelve tribes taking possession of the promised land. But they said, "No, we just want to set up residence here. We are going to leave our families. We're going to leave our livestock, our animals. We're going to leave the residents here, and we're going with the rest of the nation of Israel across the Jordan River. We'll fight until the inhabitants have been totally defeated, until the nations have been destroyed and we have taken possession of the land. We will fight until we have defeated the Canaanites and Ammonites and the Perizzites, the Hittites, the Hivites, the Girgashites, the Jebusites. We're going to fight until that's over."

When Moses saw how serious they were, he understood they were making a covenant of brotherhood. "We will join our brothers and fight alongside of them until victory is won and only then will we return back to our land on the east side of the Jordan River and find renewal with our families." Moses charged them to keep that promise.

In Joshua 1:2, God preached the eulogy of Moses very briefly: "Moses my servant is dead." It was his expiration date. In Joshua 1:3–5, God said to Joshua, "You will execute what Moses did not live long enough to complete. You therefore and all of Israel go over this

Jordan and take possession of the land I am about to give you. In fact I've already given it to you. No one is going to be able to stand before you all the days of your life. As I was with Moses, so will I be with you."

In Joshua 1:12–18, these two and a half tribes once again renewed their commitment made under Moses' administration. They said, "We're going to do what we told Moses we were going to do. We're going to fight in this land until we have taken it under control, until all the territorial lots and all the territory and inheritance have been assigned to each tribe. Only then will we return back to the land to be with our families. If anyone disobeys your commands, let that individual be killed."

This brings us to chapter 22 of Joshua. It's a wonderful beginning to the settlement of the tribes. These two and a half tribes—now that the territorial lots have been assigned, the battle has been fought, and the victory has been won—were ready to go back home. Joshua gave them a wonderful send-off. He gave them animals and livestock. He said:

> You've been faithful. You have lived up to your covenant of brotherhood. You have fought until victory has been achieved. I'm giving you valuables. I'm giving you equipment. I'm giving you everything that you need so that you can go back home full.
>
> I know that you missed birthdays. Some of you have had children, and you were not there for the birth of your children. You missed funerals. You missed significant days, but you lived up to your covenant of brotherhood. Now go back. Celebrate.

Then a crisis broke out. Word got out that the tribes on the east side of the Jordan River had built an imposing altar at Geliloth near the river. It was such a monumental altar that it could be seen from either side of the river. Trouble was brewing at the river. When the nine and a half tribes on the west side of the river heard that the two and a half tribes had built this imposing altar, they decided to go to war (Josh. 22:11–12). They understood that if one tribe violated God's law, all tribes would have violated his law and would face judgment.

They intended to fight against Reuben, Gad, and the tribe of Manasseh. What a tragedy! If this happened, the half tribe of Manasseh on the west side of the Jordan and the half tribe of Manasseh on the east side of the Jordan would fight each other. Blood brothers would fight each other. Nephews would fight each other. Cousins and uncles would fight each other. This is almost like what took place in Judges 20 when the eleven tribes almost wiped out the tribe of Benjamin by killing twenty-five thousand of them. Brothers fought each other. Again these were brothers and were called "brothers" in Joshua 22:3, 4, 7. The nine and a half tribes intended to make war against their brothers.

Phineas, the son of the reigning priest, Eleazar, made a wise decision. The story is told in Joshua 22:13–20. Phineas had been appointed (apparently by Joshua) to select a person from each of the full tribes on the west side of the river, nine of them, and one from the half tribe of Manasseh. He led this group of men to negotiate with the two and a half tribes about their imposing altar.

When they arrived, Phineas challenged them:

> You have built an altar in an undesignated place. Don't you know that Deuteronomy 12:5–7 says that no altar should be built and set in a place unless the place has been designated by God, and that that place is Shiloh? That's where any altar of sacrifice must be built. And here you are ignoring what God has said and establishing an altar outside of Shiloh. It's an undesignated place.
>
> Don't you care? Don't you understand that you have put us in a position where God's judgment and wrath could fall down on us? Don't you remember back in Numbers 25 where the women of Moab seduced the men and turned them to idols, and God killed 24,000 of them (Num. 25:9)?
>
> And don't you remember at Ai when Achan stole what was devoted to God and to be used in the tabernacle? He stole things and hid them in his tent. And even though God had told Joshua that no one would be able to stand against him all the days of his life, thirty-six men lost their lives at Ai, and the nation lost the battle. Don't you realize that you are setting us up for the judgment of God?
>
> Don't you care? Where is your faithfulness? You've been faithful for seven plus years of this military campaign, and you have almost finished. Now you have come near the Jordan River and built this imposing altar. But you never cleared it with heaven. Now judgment might fall on us!

You're unfaithful. You're ungrateful! Look how God has taken care of your families. You haven't been there, but he's kept your children. He's kept your wives. He's kept your daughters and your sons. He's kept them alive. He's fed them. And this is how you express your gratitude? You are ungrateful wretches!

Trouble was brewing at the river, but Phinehas's challenge started the process of redemption. Toward the end of the chapter in Joshua 22:21–29, the leaders of the two and a half tribes spoke up.

> We know there's only one designated place to build an altar for sacrifice, but we didn't build this altar for sacrifice. We built this altar for a memorial because we know how subject you are to amnesia. We don't want you to write us out of our history. We don't want our children growing up and being told that the nine and a half tribes are the only tribes that took control of the land and drove out the enemies—and the two and a half tribes had no part in it. If they believe that story, then they will be susceptible to idolatry.
>
> We know how forgetful we are. We remember the time we came out of Egypt, when Moses went to a summit meeting on Mount Sinai, and we became impatient. We had our assistant pastor Aaron, the brother of Moses, make a golden calf. We marched around it and proclaimed, "These are the gods that brought us out of Egypt" (Exod. 32:4).
>
> We know how forgetful we are. In fact, we are so forgetful that one of us from each of the twelve tribes of Israel took a stone out of the Jordan River and piled them for a memorial on the eastern side in the city of Gilgal, the headquarters of Israel. We did that because we wanted our children to know what the stones mean and to have a story for us to tell when our children ask. So the stones could say in essence, "This is where God brought us through the Jordan River and made a superhighway in it and let us walk across it without even getting our feet wet."
>
> We want them to know that our God is powerful. We know we get amnesia. We built this memorial altar to remind the other tribes that the children of our two and a half tribes are written in the history books. Our children will look at this altar and be reminded of their ancestors' participation and faithfulness to the covenant.

> So we're not building this altar for sacrifice or worship. We're building this altar for remembrance. And we are not insensitive. We know what happened at Peor. We know what happened at Ai. We have kept our covenant of brotherhood even until this very moment.
>
> And we are not ungrateful. We know it's been the Lord who's brought us all the way through.

The delegation from the nine and a half tribes listened to those who represented the two and a half tribes, and heard what they said. Earlier they had heard rumors (Josh. 22:11). Then they heard perceptions. But finally they heard from the mouths of the people who knew the facts, and they were pleased (22:31). They concluded, "The Lord is with us because he kept us from slaughtering ourselves and committing mutual homicide." They heard. They were pleased. And they said, "The Lord is with us."

When they returned home to Joshua and the nine and a half tribes, they reported what they had heard. Then they named the altar a witness between them and God: "Here it is that the Lord *is* God" (Josh. 22:34).

* * *

Now what is God saying to us? Is he saying something to us about what he is able to do when we're on the verge of theological mutual homicide? Perhaps God is saying that we need to participate in a collaboration. Too many believers give too many monologues and not enough dialogues. Too many believers give many diagnoses but not enough prescriptions. We need to come to the place where we can begin to talk about racism in light of the gospel of Christ—not socializing the gospel, but gospelizing the social and letting the gospel address the problem.

I am appalled at evangelicals who say there is no such thing as racism in America. They say it's a minority philosophy and it's not really real. Perhaps they need to have an ophthalmological checkup and look around and see the racism. Even parts of the church are stricken with this blindness. Much of the church needs to be admitted into God's General Hospital where it can undergo a period of redemptive observation and have a redemptive blood transfusion because a sick church cannot minister to a critically ill world.

We have a theology of avoidance. We want to avoid racism as a topic, hoping it will go away. Some say that every time we talk about racism, we just keep ourselves in a militaristic mindset. This is not true. We need to collaborate and discuss what the blood of Jesus truly does in terms of changing our lives, our attitudes toward and love for one another.

We have a kind of patio mentality when it comes to addressing racism. When I grew up we didn't have a patio. We had a porch. We knew everyone who came down the street. We talked with them. We waved at them. They came up on the porch and had lemonade. If they needed six eggs, my mama gave them six eggs. If mama needed some milk, they gave my mama milk. It was a porch mentality. We knew each other.

But now we have a patio mentality that's closed in, and we just have our holy huddle together. As long as we are fine economically, educationally, socially, and psychologically, we are alright. We need to leave the patio and go to the porch sometimes. I'm not upset about a gated community. My problem is not a gated community but a gated heart where we have bars and won't allow anyone to get to us and we don't want to get to anyone else.

I think we need to understand that what we really need is an incarnational approach. Jesus is the Word who became flesh and dwelt among us, and we beheld his glory, the glory of the only begotten of the Father, full of grace and truth (John 1:14). Eugene Peterson's paraphrase of what Jesus did in John 1:14 is "He became flesh and blood and moved into the neighborhood."[5] Clarence Jordan in his *Cotton Patch* version of 2 Corinthians 5:19 says, "God was in Christ hugging the world back to himself."[6]

We call shaking hands reconciliation. There's too much space in a handshake. Many of us shake hands on Sunday, and when we see one another on Monday, we refuse to speak. But when we hug the

---

5. Eugene Peterson, *The Message Bible* (Carol Stream: NavPress, 2014).
6. Clarence Jordan, *Cotton Patch Gospel* (Macon: Smyth & Helwys, 2014).

world back to ourselves, we get some of ourselves on one other and experience reconciliation no matter where we are.

These guard gates must come down. We must participate in a collaboration. We have to talk about racism in light of the gospel. This is not about being a social activist. This is about being a gospel Christian who deals with social inequities in the context of the gospel. Only the power of the gospel can change the stigma of racism because of the stigmata in Jesus Christ.

I am not advocating compromising our convictions. We should not compromise our convictions. The nine-and-a-half-tribe delegation and the representatives of the two and a half tribes talked together. The nine-and-a-half-tribe delegation did not compromise its convictions. They believed an altar should not be built in an undesignated place. When they learned this was not an altar for sacrifice, but one for a memorial, they changed their approach. They didn't compromise the truth of the Word. The Bible does not need to be adjusted. The Bible needs to be trusted. Therefore, we need not compromise convictions about Scripture. When the Bill of Rights and the Bible collide, we must be directed by the Bible. When Capitol Hill and the hill far away collide, we must be directed by Calvary. When the flag and the cross collide, we must choose the cross. When government and God collide, we must choose God because the kingdom of this world will become the kingdom of our Lord and of his Christ and he shall reign forever (Rev. 11:15). When the White House and the right house of John 14:2 collide, we must choose the right house—"In my Father's house are many mansions." We don't compromise our convictions. We choose them.

We all need to admit our culpability. It's time to stop playing the blame game. If these two and a half tribes of Reuben, Gad, and Manasseh would have said to Joshua upon leaving the celebration on their way home, "Look we're going to build an imposing and large altar at the river. It's not for sacrifice but for a memorial," there would not have been a problem. But they didn't say that in advance. And if the nine-and-a-half-tribe delegation under Joshua would have consulted the Lord, the Lord would have informed them of the facts, so they would not have to go and confront their brothers. That was the problem in Joshua 9:14. That's why the ruse of the Gibeonites worked. They came dressed as if they were from far away. Their bread was brittle, and the wine sacks were broken. They really were from the next neighborhood. But because the children of Israel did not consult the Lord, they were tricked.

So both were culpable. The nine and a half tribes and the two and a half tribes were both to blame. Oh brothers and sisters, when will we come to the place when we stop blaming each other? When will we come to the place where we will say that all of us are culpable? All of us need to repent because racism is not a just skin problem—ultimately it's a sin problem. "It's me. It's me. It's me, oh Lord, standing in the need of prayer."[7]

It is not difficult to see the national covenant at work in this story from ancient Israel. These tribes knew that it was not only those directly involved in the conflict who would suffer if they violated the covenant, but that all of Israel would suffer. They knew that God judges not only individuals but all of Israel as a nation. They knew that the sins of individuals—poor communication, factionalism, mistrust, familial or racial pride, and unbridled rumors—gossip—would wreak havoc on the nation. They also knew what united them as a nation. Each side in this conflict of tribes wanted to reverence God; they had the same allegiance. Each side held the same foundational beliefs. Each side bore the burden of unity. This mandate to be one was confirmed each time the children of Israel recited the Shema (Deut. 6:4).

Centuries later, Jesus alluded to this need for unity in the nation of his disciples when he prayed that his followers would be one just as he and the Father are one (John 17:21). Brothers and sisters, God has redeemed for himself a people—a body—not merely individual members who are free to act alone, without regard for the whole body. The nine and a half tribes feared the retribution the whole nation would face from God if his covenant was violated. Their understanding of a national covenant is one the modern church desperately needs to learn. It is possible to be unified under the banner of the cross without being divided by the color of our skin.

There was a great baseball player named Rod Carew who wore number 29. He played eighteen combined seasons for the Minnesota Twins and the California Angels in the American League. He was an

---

7. African American spiritual, "Standing in the Need of Prayer," public domain.

All-Star for eighteen years. He was the Rookie of the Year his first year in the American League, won the Most Valuable Player Award, and won seven batting championships. He was voted into the Hall of Fame. In July 2016, Number 29 had a major heart attack while on the golf course. He was rushed to the hospital. He survived, but his heart was gravely damaged. Doctors said he would not live much longer unless he received a new heart.

In December of that year there was an NFL football player named Konrad Reuland. He was twenty-nine years of age when he had an aneurysm. They took him to the hospital where he remained in a coma, never to come out. After he was in the hospital bed for several days, his mother, Mary Reuland, got in bed with him and laid on his chest. She put her ear on his chest and stayed there all day because she wanted to memorize his heartbeat. She wanted to know her son's heartbeat if she ever heard it again.

Konrad died, but he was an organ donor, and his heart went to Number 29, Rod Carew. It took thirteen hours for Carew to go through heart surgery. The transplant was successful. Rehabilitation took over six months, but when he was able to leave the hospital, Number 29 Rob Carew made his way to Konrad Reuland's house where his mother and father, Mary and Ralph Reuland, lived.

The Reulands are white, and Carew is black. Rod took his wife, Rhonda, with him. She is white. Konrad's parents greeted them. Number 29 came in and gave a stethoscope to Mary Reuland. She took the stethoscope and put it on Rod Carew's chest. When she heard the heartbeat, she began to cry because she recognized the rhythm of her son's heartbeat.

A black man was living because a white man gave his life. Two families were brought together over the death of a man.

Brothers and sisters, there was a greater story than this. All of us were dead in trespasses and sin. We were not just anemic and weak; we were dead. One Friday on a dead man's hill, Jesus took on stigmata and died on the cross. But through the power of the Spirit of God, he has enabled us to overcome the curse of racism. He got up on Sunday morning with all power in his hand, and promised us we could use it if we want. One day we are going to stand at the river of Jordan. William Williams wrote in the hymn "Guide Me, O Thou Great Jehovah,"

> *When I tread the verge of Jordan, Bid my anxious fears subside;*
> *Bear me thro' the swelling current, Land me safe on Canaan's side.*
> *Songs of praises I will ever give to thee; Songs of praises I will ever give to thee.*[8]

One of these days beyond the river, the wicked shall cease from troubling. Beyond the river the weary shall be at rest. Beyond the river we shall beat our swords into plowshares and our spears into pruning hooks. Beyond the river we shall bow down and give God praise because the stigmata of Jesus Christ, empowered by the Spirit of God, enable us to overcome the stigma of racism.

On that day people from every nation, tribe, kindred and tongue (Rev. 7:9) shall bow down together to praise our God in the power of the Spirit ... and there will be no trouble at the river.

---

8. William Williams, "Guide Me, O Thou Great Jehovah," *The New National Baptist Hymnal* (Nashville: National Baptist Publishing Board, 2013), 234.

Subject and Author Index

1619 Project, xxxn45, 110
abortion, xxxi, 153, 161–73, 180, 256
Abraham, 4, 5, 14, 15, 22, 25–26, 27, 30, 39, 50, 143, 199
Aeneid, 31
Allen, William B., ix, xxx–xxxi, 99–120
Anti-Semitism, 36–37
Aristotle, xxxii
Asian Americans, xxviii, xxxii, 92n38
Augustine, xviii, xxv, 183, 256

Barth, Karl, xxxiii, 227, 228
Bavinck, Herman, 227, 230
Begin, Menachem, 23–24, 33
Bellah, Robert, xxv
Berman, Joshua, ix, xxx, 3–17
Biden, Joe, 177
Black, Hugo, 252
  and the Ku Klux Klan, 252
Black Lives Matter, 161, 169, 188, 213, 214n45
Black Power, 70, 70n60, 203, 209, 216, 220n59
Blight, David, xvi

Boaz, 4–5
Book of, 9–17
Boyd, Greg, 40
Brooks, David, xxvii
Brown v. Board of Education (1954), 65, 180
Bush, George W., 49
busing, 236–37

Calvin, John, 226–27, 259
  Calvinism, 39, 44–45
Carew, Rod, 269–70
Carmichael, Stokely, 70, 203n5
Carson, Ben, 178
civil religion, 41–42
Civil Rights Act of 1964, xxviii, xxxi, 67, 68, 69
civil rights movement (1960s), xxvi, xxxi, xxxiii, 37, 42, 57, 61, 66, 68, 70, 73, 74, 107, 113, 124, 129, 199, 202–3, 209, 236, 250
Civil War, xv–xvi, xx, xxiv–xxv, 37, 42, 48, 64, 182, 250, 254, 260
Cone, James, 203n6, 215
Constantine, xviii, xix
Constitution, U.S., 172, 173, 200, 201

SUBJECT AND AUTHOR IndIndex

covenant of grace, xxiii
covenant of marriage, 142–45
covenant, national, xvi–xxvi, xxx,
    xxxv, 22–27, 32, 34, 36–37
  Old Testament roots, 3–17,
    22–24, 27–34
  in American churches, 39–50
  in M. L. King, Jr., 51–75
  powerful religious concept, 122
  belongs to all of us, 132–33
  and abortion, 161–73
  broken by slavery, 183–86
  and black churches, 199–220
  and the Hispanic church,
    221–34
  illustration from ancient Israel,
    259–71

David, King, 16, 28, 73
Declaration of Independence, xxvi,
    46, 59, 74, 170, 172, 173, 200,
    201, 232, 235
Dostoyevsky, Fyodor, 34
Douglass, Frederick
  and national covenant, xv–xvi,
    xxiv, xxv, xxvi, xxx
  on God ignoring race, 89n20
  on blacks prospering in Jim Crow,
    114–16
  on the Constitution as a liberty
    document, 172
Du Bois, W. E. B., 91, 118, 135, 251

Edwards, Jonathan, xxii, xxiin20–
    21, xxv, xxxii–xxxiii
  slaveowner, xxxii–xxxiii, 253
Edwards, Jonathan Jr., xxxiii
Edwards, Sarah, xxxii
Emancipation Proclamation, 58, 67,
    182, 261
equality, xxxii, 12, 23, 35
  for M. L. King, Jr., 46–47
  for Tocqueville, 81, 123–24
  and scapegoating, 89–90
  and economics, 109
  persistence of inequality, 125

  understanding racial inequality,
    127–29
  no feasible racially based
    answers, 132–33
  of opportunity, 134–35
  rejection by Margaret Sanger, 166
  cannot be engineered, 188
  denial by early States, 200
  different interpretations, 203–06,
    209, 213, 217–18
  radical Christian vision, 232
  President Harding on, 251
eugenics, 161–73
Eusebius, xix
exile, 27–34, 121–40, 221, 233

Falwell, Jerry Sr., 49
forgiveness, xxxv, 21, 23–24, 33, 35,
    36, 49, 50, 144, 178, 188, 197,
    212, 218–19
Founders, American, see Founding,
    American
Founding, American, xxvi, 41,
    47n14, 69, 79, 80, 123, 162, 170,
    172, 200, 201, 232, 245

Genovese, Eugene, 148
George, Timothy, ix, xxxi, 249–58
God
  and nations, xv–xxvi, 39–50
  of Israel, xxxv, 4–17
  his love for all nations, 22–23
  his sacrifice for us, 25
  faithful to his covenant, 30
  and his Beloved Community,
    51–61
  and marriage, 143–45
  his love for Israel, 143
  creation, judgment, and race, 183,
    189–91
  his covenant with this nation,
    199–202
  in Christ, 224
  on the margins, 223–24
  acts in providence, 226–34
  enables us to overcome the stigma
    of racism, 259–71

Great Society, 43, 132
Green, Derryck, ix, xxxi, 199–220

Harding, Warren, 250–51
Hart, Drew, 215–16
Hauerwas, Stanley, 40
Herzl, Theodore, 32
Hispanics, xxxi
    the Hispanic church can show a way, 221–34
Holocaust, xxx, 19–20, 34
Hopkins, Samuel, xxxiii
Hosea, 30

Iceland, John, xxix
identity politics, 34–37, 79–97, 133, 188, 191, 205–07, 216
imago Dei, 202, 209, 217
incarceration, 141, 151–152, 157
Indians, *see* Native Americans
Isaac
    his sacrifice for his descendants, 25–26
Islam, Nation of, 61, 70n60, 192
Israel, ancient, xvi, xviii, xx, xxii, xxiii, xxiv, xxxv, 3–17, 39, 40
    never defined physiologically, 4
    Hebrew prophets, xvi, xxiii, 57
    cured by exile, 122
Israel, the land, 27, 28
Israel, modern, xxvii, 19–37
    diverse in race, 4

Jefferson, Thomas, xxxii, 47–48, 58–59, 81, 133, 180
    and slavery, 58–59
Jeremiah, 24, 29, 30–31
Jews, xxv, xxviii, xxxiii, 3–17, 19–37, 136–37, 192
Jim Crow, 64, 65, 70n59, 74, 79, 102, 114, 142, 173, 186, 201, 202
John Paul II, Pope, 253
Johnson, Lyndon Baines, xxxi, 43, 68, 69, 71, 72, 73, 100, 101
Jonah, xxiii, 22–23, 32, 50, 199

Justice, xxvi
    general principles, xvii–xviii
    not the chief problem, xxxi, 121–40
    impossible without national covenant idea, 41
    church needs to seek it, 44, 46, 50
    Jefferson on God's justice, 47
    nonviolent methods, 62–63
    M. L. King, Jr. on the bank of justice, 67
    not definitive for liberals, 81
    about innocent victims for identity politics, 88–89
    scales incapable of balancing, 95
    necessary to get the requirements of justice right, 113
    racial inequality not mainly a justice problem, 121–22, 129
    injustice undermines the black family, 141–60
    abortion as injustice, 162, 169, 256
    social justice warriors, 177
    and the new racism, 195
    long history of black churches' search for, 199–200
    beginning of end of systemic injustice, 202
    white atonement necessary for, 209
    should not be segmented, 212n42
    the shut up and listen approach, 213–14
    Tisby's approach, 218nn56–57
    Rosenwald a model, 246–48

Kant, Immanuel, 80–81
Kennedy, John F., 66–68, 71nn62–63
King, Alveda, x, xxxi, 161–173
King, Martin Luther Jr., xxx, xxxi, xxxiv, 36, 39, 42, 46–47, 50
    and national covenant, 51–75
    Beloved Community, 52, 54–55, 61–68

love, church, and covenant, 56–61
  falling short, 69–74
  betrayal of, 91n26
  his dilemma, 102–08
  his failure, 108–14
  call to dignity and respect, 172–73
Knox, John, 44
Ku Klux Klan, 66, 166, 189, 252

"Letter from Birmingham City Jail," 61n38, 61n39, 65n45, 65n46, 66
Lewis, C. S., xviin6
Lewis, Donald M., xix
liberal politics of competence, 80–84
liberation theology, 203, 204n8
Lincoln, Abraham, xx, xxiv–xxv, xxvi, xxxii, 39, 41, 44, 45, 48, 50, 58–59, 79, 116–17, 123, 182, 261
  and national covenant, 41, 44, 45, 48, 50
Locke, John, 80, 83, 84, 90
Loury, Glenn, x, xxxi, 121–40, 185
love, 21, 32, 50, 63–64
  God's, 25, 30n21, 31n22, 182, 228
  for enemies, 52, 57, 218
  its power, 55
  three Greek words for, 56
  in marriage, 144–45
  in the church, 232
Luther, Martin, xxxiii

Marshall, Thurgood, 252
Massey, James Earl, 249–50
McDermott, Gerald R., x, xv–xxxv, 47n14
Methodists, 45–46
Miller, Perry, xxii
Mitchell, Joshua, x, xxx, 79–97
Moses, xxi, 27, 75, 92n29, 261, 262, 263, 265
Moynihan Report (1967), 112, 141, 150
Murray, Charles, 197
Musgraves, Evan, x, 161–73

nationalism, 39–41, 70, 177–78, 190, 193
Nation of Islam, *see* Islam
Native Americans, xxiii, xxxiii, 37
natural law, xvii, xxvi
Niebuhr, Reinhold, 54–57, 60
Nixon, Richard, 43, 71n62
Noahic commandments, xxi, 22
Northam, Ralph, 180–81
Nostra Aetate, 3

Padilla, Osvaldo, x, xxxi, 221–34
Palestinians, xxvii
Pannenberg, Wolfhart, xx, xxvi
Parks, Rosa, 61
Passover, 26–27
Patterson, James, xi, xxx, 51–75
Patterson, Orlando, 135, 145–47
Planned Parenthood, 161, 163, 165, 184
Plessy v. Ferguson (1896), 64
Prohibition, 46, 54
Princeton, 253–54
Providence, xv, xviii, xxv, 46, 47, 178, 226–28, 230, 234
Puritans, xxi–xxiii, 41, 44

race
  a social (not biological) phenomenon, 126–28, 167, 184–85
  feeds on social tendencies, 185–86
  and fear, 191–95
  the idolatry of, 208–09
racism, white, xxix–xxx, xxxiii–xxxiv
  ethnic prejudice, 14–17
  racial stigma, 130–32
  racial supremacy, 187
  and the Bible, 189–91
  the new racism, 195–98
  racism is real, 266
racism, systemic, xxviii, xxixn44, 79, 92, 101, 149, 169, 202, 206, 213n44, 218n56

Rahab, 4, 5–9
Rashi, 33
Rauschenbusch, Walter, 54, 55
Reagan, Ronald, 48
reconciliation, xvi
    not only racism prevents it, xxx
    after the Holocaust, 21, 23–24, 30
    possible without forgiveness, 33–37
    impossible without national covenant concept, 41, 50
    and the Beloved Community, 59–61, 63
    possible only when all are embraced, 124, 132
    possible from forgiveness and New Testament principles, 177–98, 202, 204–05, 208, 210, 213–20
    some of it possible only in Christ, 231–33
    lessons in Birmingham, 249–50, 253, 255
    only through the gospel, 260, 267–68
Reconstruction, 64
Reconstructionism, 39–40
redeemer nation, xxi, xxii
reparations, 23–24, 35, 53, 96, 209, 218
Riley, Jason, xxviii, xxix
Rivers, Jacqueline, xi, xxxi, 141–60
Robertson, Pat, 49
Rocklin, Mitch, xi, xxx, 19–37
Roosevelt, Franklin Delano, xxxi, 100–01
Roosevelt, Theodore, 101
Rosenwald Schools, 246–48
Rustin, Bayard, 63, 67, 74n69
Ruth, 4, 9–17

sacrifice,
    paschal in Exodus, 9
    outsiders' sacrifices, 13, 15
    God's for us, 25
    ours for God, 25, 26
    being chosen by God, 26
    Jewish, 26
    of King's activists, 57, 59, 63
Samaritans, xxxiv
Sanger, Margaret, 161–68, 184–85
    and eugenics, 163–68
    and the Ku Klux Klan, 166
school violence, 238–40
Seib, Gerald, xxvi, xxvii
Shelton, Jason, and Michael Emerson, *Blacks and Whites in Christian America*, 205–8
slavery, xv, xvi, xxv, xxix–xxx, xxxii–xxxiii, 23, 24, 30, 34, 37
    slave trade, xxxii
    abolitionists, xxxiii
    in Israel, 24, 29–31
    in Jeremiah, 24, 29
    and Lincoln's Presbyterian pastor, 45–46
    in the early Republic, 79–80
    Frederick Douglass on, 89n20, 172
    R. Woodson on, 91
    Tocqueville on, 92n29
    its legacy, 95–96
    W. B. Allen on, 108–11
    return from, 121–39
    Eugene Genovese on, 148
    families in, 149, 152, 156
    and abortion, 173
    America's original sin, 121, 181–82
    and the Bible, 183–91
    sin against national covenant, 219
    at Princeton and Southern Baptist Seminary, 253–54
Smith, Robert, Jr., xi, xxxi, 259–71
Social Gospel, 42, 43, 46, 54, 55, 56, 57, 60, 74
Solzhenitsyn, Alexander, xxxiv–xxxv
Steele, Shelby, 208–09
suffering, ontological, 34–37
Swain, Carol, xi, xxxi, 177–98

Ten Commandments, xviii, 29
Thomas, Justice Clarence, 169–70
Till, Emmett, 261
Tisby, Jemar, 213n44, 215–16, 218nn56–57
Tocqueville, Alexis de, 80–81, 85, 92nn27, 29, 123
Tooley, Mark, xi, xxx, 39–50
Trump, Donald, 41, 177, 178, 187

Vatican II, 3
Vietnam War, xx, xxii, 43, 48, 72, 105
Vindiciae Contra Tyrannos, xix, xx
vouchers and school choice, 237–38

Wallis, Jim, 214–15
Washington, Booker T., xxxi, 114, 116, 118, 135, 136, 246
Washington, George, 108, 113, 118
Wesley, John, 45
white supremacists, 66, 70, 71, 177, 191, 192
Whitfield, Ed, xxviii
Wilcox, Brad, 159
Wilsey, John, 40
Wilson, Woodrow, 42, 101–02, 180
Woodson Center, xxxi, 238, 239, 241, 242, 244
Woodson, Robert, Sr., xi, xxxi, 82n7, 91n26, 96n34, 235–48

Yoder, John Howard, 39–40

Zionism, modern, 33